LOGOS

Logos

CONNECTING WITH UNIVERSAL PRINCIPLES OF INTEGRITY

Don Pierce

Heartwood Path

Contact:
Heartwood Path
info@heartwoodpath.com
805-689-7042
www.heartwoodpath.com

ISBN/SKU: 979-8-9857352-6-0
EISBN: 979-8-9857352-7-7

To my mentor, David Brower.

Contents

Read This First

Although anyone may find the practices, challenges, and under-standings in this book to be useful it is made available with the understanding that neither the author nor the publisher are engaged in presenting specific medical, psychological, emotional, sexual, or spiritual advice. Nor is anything in this book intended to be a diagnosis, prescription, recommendation, or cure for any specific kind of medical, psychological, emotional, sexual, or spiritual problem. Each person has unique needs and this book cannot take these individual differences into account. Each reader is encouraged to engage in a program of treatment, prevention, and cure only in consultation with a licensed, qualified physician, therapist, or other competent professional.

Introduction

REMEMBER EACH SECONDARY POSTULATE

Emerging from our primary postulate—that the greatest trustable truths of one's life arise during one's sensing of the Now in nature—are numerous secondary postulates, each serving as the main topic for each Heartwood Book. The guiding postulate for this book is:

Communing with nature,

as prescribed in our protocols,

reveals an inherent intelligence

in the form of universal principles of integrity.

These principles will guide you throughout your life, and particularly as you progress through the various Heartwood Path books. To benefit fully from nature's intelligence, do the activities that follow. Be sure to get up from your chair, get out of your head, go outside, and enjoy yourself as you make your way to happiness in life and a beautifully regenerated natural environment.

1

Universal Principles

UNDERSTAND UNIVERSAL PRINCIPLES AND THE ORIGIN AND STRUCTURE OF INTEGRITY

EartHearts are the pilgrims that follow the Heartwood Path and use it as a guide in their efforts to save the Earth one person at a time (beginning with themselves). They see the instructions that follow as the basis of their work.

Background information needed to best understand the information presented in subsequent Heartwood Path books is presented here. This background information is not superfluous. It is your ticket to a forgotten beatitude (a state of supreme blessedness).

As before, I will present activities to accompany this text. I will continue with activities that foster happiness, a rich form of contentment evident in those who devote a great amount of time with their family, give to others, have ample energy, are cooperative, are comfortable expressing gratitude, are liked by others, practice optimism, savor life's pleasures, exercise regularly, are deeply committed to the attainment of goals, and cope well in the face of challenge.

Below you will find more about the overarching strategy for achieving happiness. This over-arching strategy has to do with expressing gratitude by which I mean experiencing wonder, appreciating aspects of life, looking on the bright side of setbacks, fathoming abundance, thanking others in your in your life including the Absolute, counting blessings, savoring, not taking things for granted, coping, and living in the present. Expressing gratitude leads to happiness because it promotes savoring life experiences; bolsters self-esteem; helps people cope with stress; helps people move on and begin again; fosters moral behavior; builds social bonds; inhibits detestable comparisons with others; diminishes anger, bitterness and greed; and helps us "adjust rapidly to any new circumstance or event" (Lyubomrisky, 2007, p. 92-95). With all of these benefits, expect a considerable payback from doing the next activity. It is one more return to the topic of gratitude, presented to help get you in the habit of making its expression perpetual.

To Revealing Your Outstanding Acknowledgements…

HumaNatureConnect Activity

Start-up Protocol

If this is not a day when you prefer to spend time in nature without an agenda, do the Heartwood Path Start-up Protocol found in the Appendix. Then return here to do the remaining portion of this activity:

Identifying Debts Of Gratitude

For this activity, use the optimal functioning you will receive from being with your chosen natural being, assume its essence, and, as it, tell yourself what you need to do concerning gratitude. Make an affirmation that expresses your gratitude about something you have received in your life. Commit to regularly actively expressing gratitude. After doing so, write down in your journal what you did to express or meet your obligation and how expressing gratitude makes you feel.

Follow-up Protocol

For best results, write down your impressions of this activity in your journal using the Heartwood Path Follow-up Protocol found in the Appendix. Afterwards, consider sharing your interpretations with others.

Heartwood Path Axioms

Key Assertions From Waypoint 2.1

2.1.1.

Background information is not superfluous. It is your ticket to a forgotten beatitude (a state of supreme blessedness).

2.1.2.

Expressing gratitude leads to happiness because it promotes savoring life experiences; bolsters self-esteem; helps people cope with stress; helps people move on and begin again; fosters moral behavior; builds social bonds; inhibits detestable comparisons with others; diminishes anger, bitterness and greed; and helps people adjust to new circumstances.

Nocturnal Pilgrimage 2.1

For best results, write down your impressions of each night's dreams in your journal using the Heartwood Path Dreaming Time Protocols found in the Appendix. Afterwards, consider sharing your Dream Tending with others.

The field is Eco-psychology, which is a big part of the basis of the Heartwood Path, exists because...

the mind exteriorizes itself.

One's mind recognizes itself in the patterns of nature. One's mind reflects back to itself those patterns that best reflect its being. One's mind pauses, and in that opening, chooses what is best by the attractions it forms between itself and natural beings. This exteriorization is of utmost importance.

One creates the world by perceiving it.

One sees the world according to one's attractions to it. One gravitates towards preferred configurations. One ignores what one finds unappealing. One forms one's worldview by the parameters of one's attractions. These attractions and one's inner world experience of freedom and lightness open up possibilities and ground one to one's bodily experiences. It takes a delicate balance of inner and outer world influences to properly generate and limit new potentialities. How this is done will be revealed in the Nocturnal Pilgrimage Sections that follow. As you progress through this series of books you will learn a fantastic way to help you unfold a magnificent future. This way comes from a certain set of magnetic allies, as revealed in the next important point.

One makes the world according to one's attractions.

For this reason, I will ask you now to consider what you are drawn to, what pulls on you like a magnet. What patterns and images are foremost in you mind. Do they all come from work, from television, or from Modern Culture? Have you yet found enough of them from the two great sources of intelligence—Nature and Dreams? I suspect not; and I will, therefore, continue to send you forth in search of Attractive

Natural Beings and their reflective partners (or versions)—Attractive Natural Dream Characters.

As we will see, we need both of these types of allies in our efforts to bring forth happiness in a sustainable world. We need the outer world Natural Beings to help our minds, body, and spirit to function optimally and to ground to us in reality. This grounding is good because it is wise, appealing, and true. But it is sometimes hard to fathom. And our perceptions of it often become stagnant, which leaves us stultified unless we also turn to Natural Dream Characters who, at once, add clarity to the lessons from outer world Natural Beings and show us our memories, expectations, desires, progressions, answers to our queries, and Imagination.

You will know that you have unveiled your wholeness when the two-way door of inner world and outer world inputs is swinging in both directions equally. Getting to this point is a hero's journey, one that causes each world to be illuminated.

Along this journey, and along the Heartwood Path, one will be taught how to awaken as a visionary secular saint. This revered status is achieved by visiting all the waypoints of the Heartwood Path, which collectively will teach you, among other things, how to 1) perceive patterns in your attractions, 2) replace bad habits with better habits, 3) perceive and eliminate blocks in your imagination, 4) interacting with dreams in your waking state, 5) adjust the two-way door of inputs to achieve a balance of inner world and outer world benefits, 6) get back to your senses, and 7) awaken to Oneness.

Have a good night's sleep and record your dreams in your journal before you move to the next waypoint: "The Sojourn Continues." Congratulations!

Have a good night's sleep and record your dreams in your journal before you move to the next waypoint: "The Sojourn Continues." Congratulations! You have only a few more prerequisites—all rewarding, and presented in the next four waypoints of this book. With your continued involvement and the recruitment of additional participants, happiness and a sustainable environment lie ahead.

2

The Sojourn Continues

BE SURE YOU ARE ORIENTED PROPERLY

The Overture to the Heartwood Path is where you the reader had a chance to determine if the suggested route was suitable before leaving the comforts of home. Having read this far you likely have decided to begin making the Heartwood Path pilgrimage. Imagine now that you have left the old ways of home and that you are at a fork along the trail. The route to the left is uncharted. You do. It know where it leads. On the sign before you is an explanation for how the Heartwood Path proceeds to the right and how it leads you to the integrity needed for you to create a magnificent future for yourself and others.

Above this sign is a cloud with a silver lining, a symbol in nature that reminds sojourners on the Heartwood Path that noticing what is positive, feeling good about the world and your future, and trusting that you will make it through, leads to happiness and, by extension, environmental sustainability. Happiness and environmental sustainability are related, in part, because people who are happy have less of a need to overcome their misery by placating themselves in environmentally taxing ways.

We will all, on occasion, need to own up to situations, see clearly, remain on-guard to self deception, and pick the proper road ahead. While it is important to face the facts, it is also important to decide to be optimistic. Optimists are more, not less, vigilant of risks and threats. For these reasons, doing the following activity offers ample rewards.

To Exposing Your Best Shot For The Coming Times...

HumaNatureConnect Activity

Start-up Protocol

If this is not a day when you prefer to spend time in nature without an agenda, do the Heartwood Path Start-up Protocol found in the Appendix. Then return here to do the remaining portion of this activity:

Visualizing Your Most Optimistic Future

For this activity, use the optimal functioning you will receive from being with your chosen natural being, assume its essence, and, as it, describe to yourself your ideal life after five or ten years of successful toil. Write down your description of your ideal life. Make an affirmation that you feel optimistic about your future. Commit to actively expressing optimism.

Follow-up Protocol

For best results, write down your impressions of this activity in your journal using the Heartwood Path Follow-up Protocol found in the Appendix. Afterwards, consider sharing your interpretations with others.

Heartwood Path Axioms

Key Assertions From Waypoint 2.2

2.2.1.

Happiness and environmental sustainability are related, in part, because people who are happy have less of a need to overcome their misery by placating themselves in environmentally taxing ways.

2.2.2.

While it is important to face the facts, it is also important to decide to be optimistic. Optimists are more, not less, vigilant of risks and threats.

2.2.3.

We will all, on occasion, need to own up to situations, see clearly, and remain on-guard to self deception.

2.2.4.

To have a cluttered mind while tending to your dreams is to make them dull and stale.

Nocturnal Pilgrimage 2.2

For best results, write down your impressions of each night's dreams in your journal using the Heartwood Path Dreaming Time Protocols found in the Appendix. Afterwards, consider sharing your Dream Tending with others.

Declutter your mind before sleeping. Do not be preoccupied by the demands of your upcoming day when you record your dreams upon waking. To have a cluttered mind while tending to your dreams is to make them dull and stale. Be receptive, fluid, interactive, and grounded as you remember and record your dreams. Be centered in the "luxuriant beautiful Now" (Aizenstat, 2009, p. 27). Writes Aizenstat: "When we let go of our past and future concerns and simply meet the image in the eternal Now, we create an appropriate environment for good Dream Tending" (Aizenstat, 2009, p. 27).

After sleeping and recording your dreams, move to the next waypoint: "Map Symbols." There, you will reach an understanding of the symbols used in the map of the Heartwood Path. You will also learn a way to foster happiness.

3

Map Symbols

READ THE MAP PRESENTED HERE BEFORE EMBARKING DOWN THE HEARTWOOD PATH

To read any map it is necessary to understand its symbols. Some maps are diagrammatic representations of terrain usually found in books or on walls. Others are charts or guides and, if they are very lucid, they are referred to as maps—as in the Freudian Map of the Mind. The Heartwood Path can only become clear enough to be considered map-like if its symbols—it's signs of written communication—are prominently displayed and made to be understandable. That is the purpose of this waypoint. After this brief summary of some words that have been proven to be problematic to Heartwood Path wayfarers that did not bother with definitions, the Activity will further the goal of making sure the Heartwood Path is map-like in its clarity by presenting questions and offering prescriptions to help path-goers be in a suitable frame of mind. Going down the Heartwood Path, which is aimed towards increasing both your happiness and the sustainability of the natural environment upon which you depend, will be very difficult and unpleasant if you are pessimistic.

The symbols that are pulled out here for greater clarity are ones that will be more understandable and useful to you if you are optimistic. For this reason, be sure to do the activity at the end of this waypoint. Doing so will make you better prepared for what follows.

In reading the map that is the Heartwood Path you are reading the chart for the terrain. You are not reading the territory itself—which is you and your environment. Understanding the following oft-misunderstood symbols—four words, actually—will help you better understand and appreciate the text that follows. You will also better perform the activities that follow.

The first impediment we are hereby removing from the Heartwood Path is the sometimes careless definition of the word "states." We shall use this word (symbol) to mean "the circumstances, attributes, structure, form, phase, or condition of a person or thing." We will speak of states of flow, states of well-being, the state of separation, the state of being aware, the transient state, the state of harmony, and the state of the earth.

The second stumbling block is the poor understanding of the symbol (word) "stages." As we use this word, it means a single degree, step, phase, period, or position in a process. We shall speak of stages of self-transcendence, life stages, the integral stage of spiritual development, and the transpersonal stage of development. We shall also use the word "stage" as an elevated platform, as in the stage of your thoughts.

We shall use the sometimes problematic word "streams" most often to mean a continuous flow of anything. We shall speak of an enduring stream of energy, streams of email, the endless stream of television, streams of air, and streams of water.

Our use of the stumbling block word "varieties," which means being varied or diversified, has to do with gender differences, the variety of your feelings, the variety of your spiritual preferences, and the variety of experience.

Having such specific definitions for the words "states," "stages," "streams," and "varieties" will lower the chances of you having difficulty in perceiving the Heartwood Path Map Of Integrity and the wholeness of your life it represents. Another way to lower the likelihood of misunderstanding is to work on removing your inevitable, automatic, pessimistic blocking thoughts. As you will see in the following activity, there are a number of questions you can ask yourself that have answers which will help you to overcome thoughts that are barriers to your happiness, to overcome pessimism, and to remove some hindrances to your efforts to live in a sustainable environment.

To Hopefulness-producing Queries...

HumaNatureConnect Activity

Start-up Protocol

If this is not a day when you prefer to spend time in nature without an agenda, do the Heartwood Path Start-up Protocol found in the Appendix. Then return here to do the remaining portion of this activity:

Asking Questions That Help Create Optimism

For this activity, imagine that you are the natural being, and, as it, ask yourself the following questions: What is the most pressing bad situation in my life right now? What else could the bad situation in my life mean? Can anything good come from the bad situation in my life? What are the opportunities hidden in the bad situation? What life lessons can be learned from the bad situation? What strengths am I gaining by living through this bad situation? Write down your answers in your journal. Make an affirmation that, metaphorically speaking, you open doors when doors are shut before you. Commit to actively using challenges as opportunities for creativity, growth, and optimism.

Follow-up Protocol

For best results, write down your impressions of this activity in your journal using the Heartwood Path Follow-up Protocol found in

the Appendix. Afterwards, consider sharing your interpretations with others.

Heartwood Path Axioms

Key Assertions From Waypoint 2.3

2.3.1.

The map for the Heartwood Path, which is a map for your own More-Than-Individual happiness and development, has four main categories of symbols—states, stages, streams, and varieties. Each of these symbols represents things that are available in your own awareness (so they can be easily verified by yourself).

2.3.2.

In reading about the four symbols for the map to the Heartwood Path you are reading about the chart for the terrain and not about the territory itself—which is you and your environment.

2.3.3.

You will have difficulty perceiving the Heartwood Path Map of Integrity, and the wholeness of your life it represents, if you have automatic, pessimistic blocking thoughts.

2.3.4.

There are a number of questions you can ask that have answers which help you overcome thoughts that are barriers to your happiness.

2.3.5.

After your night time reveries, avoid dissecting your dreams by simply being curious about what the Dream Characters are doing rather than concerning yourself at this point about what these Dream Characters signify about your own ego.

Nocturnal Pilgrimage 2.3

For best results, write down your impressions of each night's dreams in your journal using the Heartwood Path Dreaming Time Protocols found in the Appendix. Afterwards, consider sharing your Dream Tending with others.

Throughout this series of books, we will often use the words "Dream Character." A Dream Character is the image of a person, place, or thing that appears in your dreams. We will generally use the words "Dream Figures" for the physical representations you will be making of the Dream Character in your dreams. I make my Dream Figures out of flat rounded sandstone rocks. I stack them up like little cairns and take pictures of them for the purpose of identification. You are free to make your own Dream Figures any way you like. This making of Dream Figures will occur in later Heartwood Path activities that ask you to attempt to glean guidance from your nocturnal reveries.

There is a natural tendency to try to interrupt one's dream, to ask "What does it mean?" and "Why did this happen?" Such questions are counterproductive because they create an orientation that kills surprise. "There are two questions," writes Aizenstat, "that are the fundamental pillars of the Dream Tending system . . . These questions are 'Who is visiting now?' and 'What is happening here?" (2009, p.33). Remember that dreams are living beings in the psyche. You would not ask a new person entering your door "what do you mean?" Doing so would create defensiveness and stops friendly interaction. You would ask "Who are you?" and doing so encourages open expression. With "Who is visiting now?" the Dream Character "senses our interest and begins to open up more completely about what he is doing. We learn from his talent, commitment, and intelligence" (Aizenstat, 2009, p. 35). Tomorrow, after dreaming, tend to your dreams rather than dissect your dreams by being curious about the Dream Character and what he is doing, not about "what he signifies about our own ego" (Aizenstat, 2009, p. 35). After engaging with our dream in this way, you are ready to move on to the next waypoint: "Denotation."

4

Denotation

KNOW SOME KEY DEFINITIONS AT THE OUTSET

Note how the following definitions of states of consciousness, stages of consciousness, lines of development, and varieties, useful for the text that follows, seem to also be like a guided tour of your own experience:

First. States of Consciousness include: waking, dreaming, and deep sleep, meditative states, altered states (induced by drugs, for example), and peak experiences (which occur during lovemaking, experiencing Nature, and listening to fine music).

Second. Stages of Consciousness are more permanent than states of consciousness. For our purposes, there are four main stages:

1. pre-conventional (ego-centric) wherein the person's awareness is self-absorbed (the key word in this stage is "me");
2. conventional (ethno-centric) wherein the person's awareness is focused on that person's particular group, clan, family or nation (the key word is "us");
3. post-conventional (world-centric) wherein the person's awareness and identity expands to include all people, regardless of

race, color, nationality, gender, or creed (the main words are "us all"), and

4. the integral stage wherein the person's awareness and identity expands to include everything while not erasing any of the aspects from the other stages (the main word is "all").

These stages build upon themselves (beginning with ego-centric and followed by ethno-centric, then world-centric, and then integral). Each stage cannot be skipped. One cannot have the psychological states from a higher stage of development until one has achieved, through practice and time, the correlating higher stage of consciousness. Those intermittent higher states that prematurely attempt to arise tend to slip rapidly away if they are not matched to the corresponding stage of consciousness. States are temporary and free. Stages are lasting and earned.

Third. Lines of Development are ways to chart your multiple intelligences, such as cognitive intelligence, emotional intelligence, musical intelligences, bodily intelligences, and so forth. Nobody, despite their claims, is excellent equally in all lines of development.

Fourth. Varieties can occur at any stage of consciousness. Some of the most interesting varieties have to do with the logic of the genders. In the subsequent Heartwood Path for Couples book (**Eros: Connecting Intimately For Transformation**) we will discuss how a more advanced stage of development—the Integral Stage—includes both masculine and feminine varieties. The inclusion of attention to varieties is a way to make sure one is being as comprehensive and inclusive as possible.

Men, for example, tend to voice matters of autonomy, justice, and rights; women, conversely, tend to voice matters of relationship, care, and responsibility. To be more accurate, what I am really referring to is not maleness and femaleness, but rather masculinity and femininity. Obviously, men tend to be more masculine than feminine, for example; but, in reality, each gender can exhibit both masculine and feminine varieties.

These and the other principles found in this book are significant and helpful but are also somewhat ponderous. It is, and will be, important to think about such heady issues, but it is not good to get bogged down in incessant mental rumination, especially when such mental toil leads to excessive thinking about causes, consequences, problems, personal significance, and judgmental comparisons. As I continue to give you a lot to think about, here is an activity to help you avoid overdoing it.

To Chill Out...

HumaNatureConnect Activity

Start-up Protocol

If this is not a day when you prefer to spend time in nature without an agenda, do the Heartwood Path Start-up Protocol found in the Appendix. Then return here to do the remaining portion of this activity:

Testing Ways To Stop Over-thinking About The Magnitude And Significance Of Your Problems

For this activity, use the optimal functioning you will receive from being with your chosen natural being to assume its essence (psychologically put yourself in the natural being's place) and, as it, visualize your life as a tiny dot on the earth, visualize how everyone you know will be gone one hundred fifty years from now, and the magnitude of your tiny problem when compared to all of the other problems on earth at this time. Write down three things you learned from this activity and what about you has changed as a result of this activity. Make an affirmation that you think about universal principles but do not over-dwell on them. Commit to actively holding judgmental and repetitive thoughts in perspective. After doing so, write down whether, and if at all, this activity helped you avoid replaying thoughts, especially repetitive thoughts that give undo significance to events and recurring thoughts about comparing yourself to others.

Follow-up Protocol

For best results, write down your impressions of this activity in your journal using the Heartwood Path Follow-up Protocol found in the Appendix. Afterwards, consider sharing your interpretations with others.

Heartwood Path Axioms

Key Assertions From Waypoint 2.4

2.4.1.

Go on a guided tour of your own experiences: waking states, dreaming states, meditative states, altered states and peak experience states, knowing that the experience of these so-called states are less permanent than the experience of the four main stages: ego-centric, ethno-centric, world-centric, and, integral.

2.4.2.

Lines of Development are ways to chart your multiple intelligences, such as cognitive intelligence, emotional intelligence, musical intelligences, bodily intelligences, and so forth.

2.4.3.

Some of the most interesting varieties have to do with the logic of the genders. With the integral stage of development one includes both masculine and feminine varieties.

2.4.4.

It is important to think about heady issues, but not good to get bogged down in incessant mental rumination, especially when such mental toil leads to excessive thinking about causes, consequences, problems, personal significance, and judgmental comparisons.

2.4.5.

Visualize your life as a tiny dot on the earth. Visualize how everyone you know will be gone one hundred fifty years from now. Visualize the magnitude of your tiny problem when compared to all of the other problems on earth at this time.

Nocturnal Pilgrimage 2.4

For best results, write down your impressions of each night's dreams in your journal using the Heartwood Path Dreaming Time Protocols found in the Appendix. Afterwards, consider sharing your Dream Tending with others.

After your next night of dreaming, when you are recording your impressions of your dreams in your journal, do not be play detective or cross-examine. Rather, gather information by allowing the Dream Character itself to unfold in your memory of it. Your work is to observe like a naturalist would, noticing the activity and particularity of the Character itself.

After recording your dream in this way in your journal, move to the next waypoint: "Spiritual Maturity."

5

Spiritual Maturity

MOVE TO THE INTEGRAL STAGE
OF SPIRITUAL DEVELOPMENT

Along the Heartwood Path, participants are encouraged to move beyond the first three Stages discussed above to the fourth level, the Integral Stage. Part of the challenge at this stage is to make sure healthy masculine principles of autonomy, strength, and independence do not become, respectively, alienation, a morbid fear of relationships and commitment, and a drive to destroy. Another part of the challenge of adding depth to one's character is making sure that the feminine aspect of flowing does not turn into panic, making sure relationships do not make one lose one's individuality, making sure connection does not turn into a meltdown, and making sure compassion does not turn into burn-out. These are some of the challenges that lie ahead for you as you develop into the Integral Stage of Consciousness.

As you will see, the Heartwood Path does not present a random heap of ideas and practices. Instead, there is a pattern that connects both the theory (reading the text) and the practices (doing the activities). That pattern cultivates body, mind, and Spirit, in Self, culture, and Nature.

That cultivation is the simplest way to state what is done along the Heartwood Path. Body, mind and spirit are the layers of depth; and self, culture and nature are the aspects of breadth. By working to add both depth and breadth to one's character, one grows fully. The growth occurs along a long route that requires a good map (described in the next section) and loving kindness (which will begin to be enhanced in you by the next activity).

To Benevolence…

HumaNatureConnect Activity

Start-up Protocol

If this is not a day when you prefer to spend time in nature without an agenda, do the Heartwood Path Start-up Protocol found in the Appendix. Then return here to do the remaining portion of this activity:

Developing Loving Kindness

Assuming the essence of your chosen natural object, tell yourself which acts of kindness you intend to do, how much, and how often. Make an affirmation that you offer loving kindness to others. Commit to actively varying your acts of kindness to keep them fresh and to provide for a good distribution of the benefits. Make sure that you do not over do it, as this will likely lead to bitterness or burnout. Sleep is perhaps the best way to not over-extend yourself.

How I sleep, for example, prepares me for my acts of loving kindness. I do not sleep under a roof, entombed in walls. Instead of lying in bed perusing the Internet on my iPad, I have the Outernet of stars, plants, comets, and other celestial bodies. My nocturnal ceiling, as if bedazzled by some mysterious cosmic disco ball, changes both with the seasons and with the daily turning of the earth. Sleeping as I do under the moon and the constellations shows me the benefits of breaking free of the walls of dogma, of breaking free of dry indoor mornings without a misting of dew, and of breaking free of indoor air devoid of the scented breezes and the negative ions that make me feel so positive. Sleeping each night outdoors under these conditions, and following whatever attractions I find in nature from just before sundown to just after sunrise, fuels my acts of kindness.

No jolting alarm clock can match the gently arousing and warming glow of daybreak as witnessed from a bed outdoors. Each sunrise shines like a universal smile of kindness.

After such a sunrise, the Sun and dew kindly sanitize my bed each day. After such a gift, I somehow find it easy to see the good of others in beautiful eyes and to more acutely hear the kind words of others from beautiful lips.

There is another Sun that brightens moods and spirits: the light of kindness. This Sun may not foster photosynthesis, but it does bring warmth and benevolence. Pay attention to both Suns. There is simply something transformative about waking up outdoors. Both bathing in natural sunlight and feeling the affection that shines in the light of nature's selflessness quickens the senses, heightens the intuition, broadens the perspective, and triggers the acts of kindness.

With benefits such as these, I, for one, do not need a walled-in bedroom any more than I need an enclosed temple. My philosophy comes from behind my own temples and from my own religion, learned mostly by communing with nature both day and night. My own cardinal direction can be summarized in two words: be kind. It is a philosophy the deaf can hear, the blind can see, and the not-so-smart can appreciate.

Worth more than money, the lessons from my roofless church come not from sermons or pulpits but mostly from natural beings, including the northern mockingbird that scolds me every morning if I lie back down after sunrise. The comparison of this vociferous but seemingly unproductive gadabout to the quietness of the string of hardworking parading ants under my bed demonstrates to me how often constant talkers teach the value of occasional taciturnity, just as the crows who are unkind to the hawk remind me not only of the value of kindness but also of the value of protecting one's own.

Down the hill from my outdoor sleeping place, about forty feet, are planted trees known by the fruits I can gather as my dog does his morning business: lemons, oranges, peaches, and avocados. Not yet known for my seeds, I, in contrast, am known for my deeds. The most important of these is the kindness I plant, meagerly, here and there. In this way I harvest the best reward: love.

Follow-up Protocol

For best results, write down your impressions of this activity in your journal using the Heartwood Path Follow-up Protocol found in the Appendix. Afterwards, consider sharing your interpretations with others.

Heartwood Path Axioms

Key Assertions From Waypoint 2.5

2.5.1.

Move beyond the first three Stages to the fourth level, the Integral Stage. Part of the challenge at this stage is to make sure healthy masculine principles of autonomy, strength, and independence do not become, respectively, alienation, a morbid fear of relationships and commitment, and a drive to destroy.

2.5.2.

Make sure that the feminine aspect of flowing does not turn into panic, that relationships do not make one lose one's individuality, that connection does not turn into a meltdown, and that compassion does not turn into burnout.

2.5.3.

There is a pattern that connects both theory (reading the text) and practice (doing the activities), a pattern that cultivates body, mind, and Spirit, in Self, culture and Nature.

2.5.4.

While recording your dream immediately after waking, pay attention to odd or unique behavior, notice what or who comes forward to greet you, and stick with any frightening images the best you can. Often difficult Dream Figures prove to be most important for your growth.

Nocturnal Pilgrimage 2.5

For best results, write down your impressions of each night's dreams in your journal using the Heartwood Path Dreaming Time Protocols found in the Appendix. Afterwards, consider sharing your Dream Tending with others.

As you have been doing after each waypoint, get a good night's sleep before you continue. Tomorrow, while recording your dream immediately after waking, "pay particular attention to any odd or unique behavior . . . notice what or who comes forward to greet you. Even if this image is frightening, stick with it as best you can. Often difficult Dream Figures prove to be most important to get to know" (Aizenstat, 2009, p. p.36).

After recording your dream you are ready to continue to the next waypoint. Do so by moving to the next waypoint: "Coherence Chart."

Your prerequisites are complete.

You are now prepared for an enjoyable and challenging section
of the pathway to Gladandgreen Junction.

6

Coherence Chart

UNDERSTAND THE MAP OF ONE'S INTEGRITY

Later in the Heartwood Path we will describe the layers necessary to add depth to your character. Here, we are going to let you know how to grow without becoming lob-sided.

To make sure you have balanced growth, we will employ the Heartwood Path Four Leaf Model of Integrity, based on the collected works of philosopher and author Ken Wilber (specifically his Four Quadrants) (Wilber, 1995, pp. 121-126). This map is vital to your successful spiritual maturity because it reminds you that there are four quadrants in which you need to grow if you are to be balanced in your development.

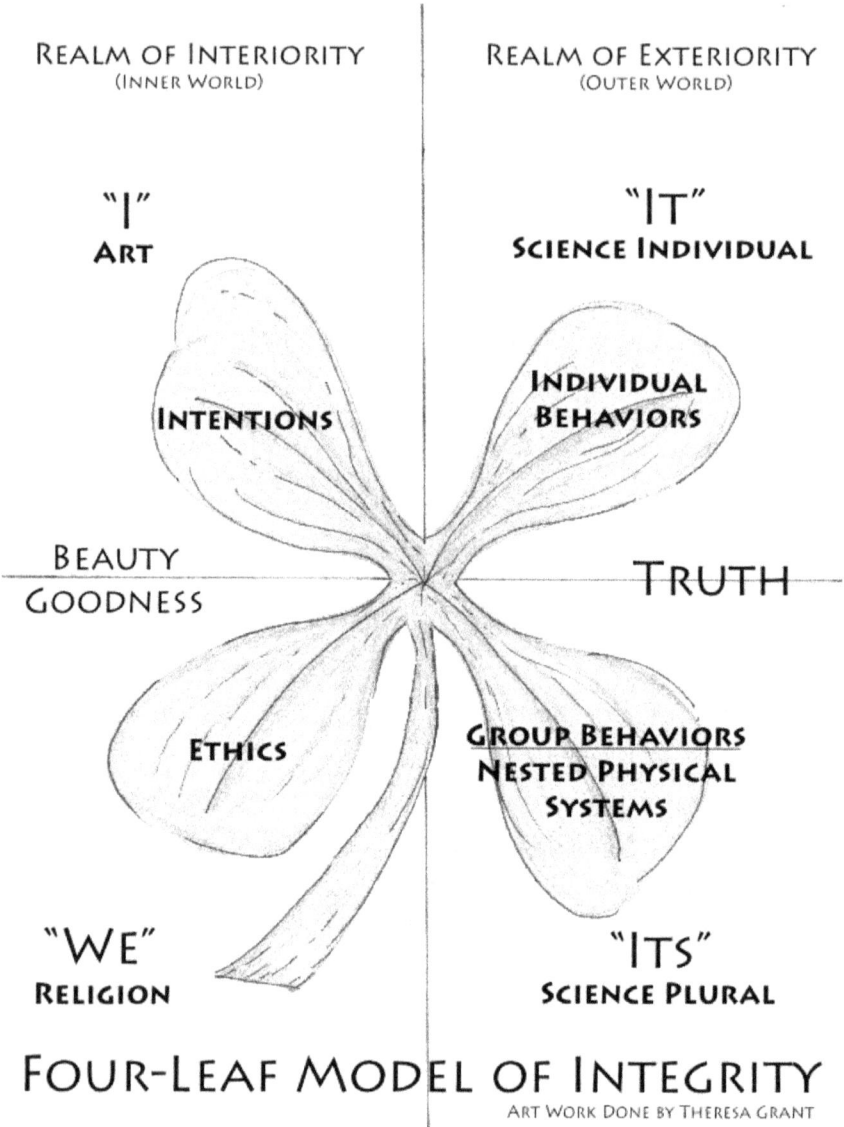

REALM OF INTERIORITY
(INNER WORLD)

REALM OF EXTERIORITY
(OUTER WORLD)

"I"
ART

"IT"
SCIENCE INDIVIDUAL

INTENTIONS

INDIVIDUAL
BEHAVIORS

BEAUTY
GOODNESS

TRUTH

ETHICS

GROUP BEHAVIORS
NESTED PHYSICAL
SYSTEMS

"WE"
RELIGION

"ITS"
SCIENCE PLURAL

FOUR-LEAF MODEL OF INTEGRITY
ART WORK DONE BY THERESA GRANT

Figure 1. The Heartwood Path Four Leaf Model of Integrity

The upper left leaf represents Beauty, expressed in reality often in language with the first person pronoun... "I."

The lower left leaf stands for Goodness, which in reality is expressed after discussion with or about two or more people who tend to use the second-person pronoun... "We."

The upper right leaf represents Truth, expressed in reality in its singular aspect with the word... "It."

Lastly, the lower right leaf represents Truth again in its plural social or environmental systems aspect (group behavior) and expressed with the word... "Its."

People grow, develop, and evolve in each of these four arenas simultaneously, but not necessarily uniformly. Trying to organize any personal growth program that does not reflect each of these four areas of development is doomed to failure. That is because it will not be in line with the way the universe works.

Again, the map in the form of a four-leaf clover will be useful to explain the terrain—the universe. The two leafs on the left are for discussing the inner world. The two on the right are for discussing the outer world. The two on the top are for discussing individual aspects of the universe—inner world individual aspects on the upper left (intensions) and outer world individual aspects on the upper right (individual behaviors). The lower two leafs are for discussing collective aspects of the universe—the lower left is for discussing the inner world of collective aspects (group ethics) and the lower right is for discussing outer world of collective aspects (group behavior). These "leaves"—these arenas of development—simply represent the "inside" and "outside" of the individual and collective aspects of the universe. Using this system, the upper left leaf is about intentions and lower left is about ethics. The upper right is about the "outside" of individuals, with individual behaviors being a dominant pertinent topic; and the lower right is about the "outside" of collectives, with nested physical systems and group behaviors being the dominant pertinent topics.

This symbolic model, with its four leafs, is a chart of one's Greater Self. It is also a map of integrity (both in terms of wholeness and in terms of moral soundness). Once one understands both its design and its symbols, it will be the single most helpful tool for those charting their way down the Heartwood Path. Use it repeatedly to make sure you are developing the poise that comes with developmental counterbalance.

The main point here is for you to be comprehensive in your efforts to be balanced and to grow in depth in all ways possible. An eartHeart's most comprehensive way to look at reality is to take into account all four arenas of development—intentions, ethics, things, and behaviors. In reality, these aspects of the universe occur only collectively—together, or not at all.

As an example of the usefulness of the Four Leaf Model of Integrity, I can think of no better application than how the model can foster better relationships. As you do the following activity, note where intentions, ethics, things and behaviors come into play. If you are confounded by this Model or seek special assistance I encourage you to reach a more comprehensive understanding by securing Heartwood Path Guidance.

To A Systematic Improvement Of Bonds...

HumaNatureConnect Activity

Start-up Protocol

If this is not a day when you prefer to spend time in nature without an agenda, do the Heartwood Path Start-up Protocol found in the Appendix. Then return here to do the remaining portion of this activity:

Applying The Model Of Integrity To Improving Relationships

For this activity, write down in your journal how you will:

1. identify or, if need be, develop at least three friends you can count on,
2. make time to be with someone you care about,
3. make at least five positive comments and engage in at least five positive actions for every one negative comment or action,

4. take delight in the good fortune of someone you care about,

5. disclose something about yourself to someone you feel close to, and

6. be supportive and loyal in your relationships and hug them often.

Review how each of the activities listed above are influenced by your intentions, ethics, physical things, and behaviors. Examine an action, compare any two outer world aspects of the Model of Integrity (behaviors and physical things) with any two of the Model's inner world aspects (ethics or intentions) and notice that deep meanings emerge in the juxtaposition (as when you compare an aspect of reality represented in one leaf with an aspect of reality in another). Here's an example of the kinds of juxtapositions you may want to do for yourself:

I have the intention to work to support myself and my family. That is an inner world goal that is represented by the upper left leaf on the Model of Integrity. My ethics, from the realm signified by the lower left leaf is to work in service to the disadvantaged. My behaviors, signified by the Upper right leaf, include driving to and from work, and helping client become more independent. The lower right leaf signifies the physical systems used in the action; which for me include the regulating agency, the easily washable clothes I wear, the plastic gloves, the computers, and the homes of the clients.

The point here is to make sure, when assessing how well you are doing, is to not just make adjustments in one or two realms, but in all of the realms. That's what is necessary for enduring, most-helpful compassion. Try such an assessment on something significant you are doing. Plan to make any adjustment, as needed.

Follow-up Protocol

For best results, write down your impressions of this activity in your journal using the Heartwood Path Follow-up Protocol found in the Appendix. Afterwards, consider sharing your interpretations with others.

Heartwood Path Axioms

Key Assertions From Waypoint 2.6

2.6.1.

The Heartwood Path Four Leaf Model of Integrity is vital to your successful spiritual maturity because it reminds you that there are four quadrant in which you need to grow if you are to be balanced in your development: Beauty; Goodness; Truth in its singular/individual aspect; and Truth again in its plural social or environmental systems aspect.

2.6.2.

Apply the Model of Integrity to Improving Relationships by identifying or, if need be, developing at least three friends you can count on; making time to be with someone you care about; making at least five positive comments and engage in at least five positive actions for every one negative comment or action; taking delight in the good fortune of someone you care about; disclosing something about yourself to someone you feel close to, and being supportive and loyal in your relationships.

2.6.3.

Strike a balance between Science, Morals, and Aesthetics by attuning your mind to Nature, by situating yourself conceptually and literally in Nature, and by giving blessings for the beauty of intentions—the ways that cause a fusing within you

as your Inner Witness becomes undifferentiated from that which you witness—and the rest of creation.

2.6.4.

Without building a personal growth program that takes Self, culture, and Nature into account, there is no integral, comprehensive, enduring positive change.

2.6.5.

Take into account all four arenas of development—intentions, ethics, things, and behaviors—plus the depth of body, mind, and spirit which occur only collectively—together, or not at all.

Nocturnal Pilgrimage 2.6

For best results, write down your impressions of each night's dreams in your journal using the Heartwood Path Dreaming Time Protocols found in the Appendix. Afterwards, consider sharing your Dream Tending with others.

Give yourself a chance to process today's waypoint by sleeping and dreaming. Remember, during Dream Tending, you are not asked to figure anything out. "You are not using your rational mind at all. Rather you are open to your sense of discovery. . . You are curious about who is visiting now?" . . . (and) . . . "what is happening here?" (Aizenstat, 2009, p. 36).

After Dream Tending, move to the next waypoint: "Conversion."

7

Conversion

TRANSFORM YOURSELF SO YOU CAN TRANSFORM THE WORLD

EartHearts cultivate body, mind, and spirit (a person's range of depth) in Self, culture, and Nature (a person's individual and collective breadth). Along with working on themselves, eartHearts work with others (across the width of the community) to take their Self, culture, and Nature to increasingly higher, wider, and deeper modes of being. In this way, eartHearts help others develop the wherewithal and perspective to improve themselves so they can then, in turn, improve their neighborhood (or bioregion, or planet).

One initial way to transform yourself is to increase your coping skills. Everyone eventually faces severe trauma. But these huge life event are not the only time to apply coping skills. Expected and normal daily challenges also produce low ebbs in your enthusiasm. Here are two ways to cope: 1) you can solve problems by breaking them down into steps, developing a plan of action, putting aside distractions, and obtaining trusted advice; and 2) you can overcome negative emotions by expressing how the negative situation caused you pain, by mentally compartmentalizing that which causes negative emotions from the rest of your life, by finding the meaning of events, by noting how much you have grown from the negative event, and by noting how much, if any, your relationships have grown as a result of the trauma.

One can also cope with stress, trauma, and hardship by disputing or challenging one's own pessimistic thoughts. A good technique for how to do so is included in the following activity, adapted from one of author Sonja Lyubomirsky's coping strategies (p. 167).

To Quell The Downers...

HumaNatureConnect Activity

Start-up Protocol

If this is not a day when you prefer to spend time in nature without an agenda, do the Heartwood Path Start-up Protocol found in the Appendix. Then return here to do the remaining portion of this activity:

Coping By Dispelling Pessimistic Thoughts

For this activity, follow the ABCDE's of pessimistic thought disputation: "A" is for Adversity. Write down something about the nature of your adversity. "B" is for Beliefs. Identify what negative beliefs are triggered by the adverse event. "C" is for Consequences. Write down the consequences of your adversity and beliefs on your feelings and actions). "D" is for Dispute. Challenge the negative belief, looking for other reasons for the adversity). And "E" is for Energy. Energetically boost your hopefulness by replacing anxiety-producing pessimistic thoughts with the identification of optimistic reasons for the adversity. Make an affirmation that you cope with pessimistic thoughts by following the ABCDE's of pessimistic thought disputation.

Follow-up Protocol

For best results, write down your impressions of this activity in your journal using the Heartwood Path Follow-up Protocol found in

the Appendix. Afterwards, consider sharing your interpretations with others.

Heartwood Path Axioms

Key Assertions From Waypoint 2.7

2.7.1.

Grow from having isolated identities of "me" (a person without a care for a neighborhood, for example); to collective identities of "we" (people caring for a particular neighborhood, for example) to "it" in its singular, individual aspect (your own behavior, for example); and to "its" or "us all" in its plural, communal aspect (people caring for everyone and every neighborhood or the enveloping environment).

2.7.2.

Here are two ways to cope with life's challenges: 1) you can solve problems by breaking them done into steps, developing a plan of action, putting aside distractions, and obtaining trusted advice; and 2) you can overcome negative emotions by expressing how the negative situation caused you pain, by mentally compartmentalizing that which causes negative emotions from the rest of your life, by finding the meaning of events, by noting how much you have grown from the negative event, and by noting how much, if any, your relationships have grown as a result of the trauma.

2.7.3.

Follow the ABCDE's of pessimistic thought disputation:

Adversity (write down something about the nature of your adversity);

Beliefs (identify what negative beliefs are triggered by the adverse event);

Consequences (write down the consequences of your adversity and beliefs on your feelings and actions);

Dispute (challenge the negative belief, looking for other reasons for the adversity); and

Energy (energetically boost your hopefulness by replacing anxiety-producing pessimistic thoughts with the identification of optimistic reasons for the adversity).

Nocturnal Pilgrimage 2.7

For best results, write down your impressions of each night's dreams in your journal using the Heartwood Path Dreaming Time Protocols found in the Appendix. Afterwards, consider sharing your Dream Tending with others.

Tomorrow, when you tend to tonight's dreams, "talk about a dream in the present tense. Say, for example, "an otter follows my canoe," not "an otter followed my canoe." Using the present tense helps to keep the Dream Characters alive in your mind.

After using such present-tense reporting in your dream journaling, move to the following waypoint: "Involvement."

8

Involvement

MOVE FROM THEORIES TO EXPERIENCES

As participants' capacities for Truth, Goodness, and Beauty expands and deepens with ever-greater consciousness, their embrace (that which they consider and act upon) becomes ever wider. This embrace is realized in the Self, is embodied in Nature, and is expressed in Culture. In this way, participants perfect themselves, neighborhoods become excellent, communities become better, and the world becomes a nicer place to live. These benefits will come to fruition more readily if participants move their awareness from high-sounding theories to programs such as the Great Work! of the Heartwood Path.

The next activity is the first of our many NatureConnect Dream Journal Activities. You have already begun using present tense reporting for your Dream Tending. In the following Activity, you will bring to use the other three recommended linguistic tools.

To Talk Up Dreams...

HumaNatureConnect Activity

Start-up Protocol

If this is not a day when you prefer to spend time in nature without an agenda, do the Heartwood Path Start-up Protocol found in the Appendix. Then return here to do the remaining portion of this activity:

Using Appropriate Dream Tending Tools

For this activity and for each time you tend to your dreams, use the following linguistic tools:

1. Talk about your dreams in the present tense (as previously instructed).
2. Use verbs ending in "ing." such as "the otter is following my canoe."
3. Remove all articles such as "a," "an," and "the" because such words "tend to reduce the image from a specific character with an independent identity to a generic class of beings such as "otter is following my canoe." And
4. Write the names of the Dream Characters using capital letters, such as "Otter is following my canoe."

Follow-up Protocol

For best results, write down your impressions of this activity in your journal using the Heartwood Path Follow-up Protocol found in the Appendix. Afterwards, consider sharing your interpretations with others.

Heartwood Path Axioms

Key Assertions From Waypoint 2.8

2.8.1.

As participants' capacities for Truth, Goodness, and Beauty expands and deepens with ever-greater consciousness, their embrace (that which they consider and act upon) becomes ever wider.

2.8.2.

The next time you tend to your dreams, vivify them by using the following linguistic tools:

talk about your dreams in the present tense;

use verbs ending in "ing." such as "the otter is following my canoe;"

remove all articles such as "a," "an," and "the" because such words "tend to reduce the image from a specific character with an independent identity to a generic class of beings; and

write the names of the Dream Characters using capital letters.

Nocturnal Pilgrimage 2.8

For best results, write down your impressions of each night's dreams in your journal using the Heartwood Path Dreaming Time Protocols found in the Appendix. Afterwards, consider sharing your Dream Tending with others.

You will be reminded to use the four tools for making Dream Journal entries—1) using the present tense; 2) using verbs ending in "ing;" 3) removing "a," "the," and other articles; and 4) capitalizing the names you use for the Dream Characters.

After a good night's sleep, tend to your dreams. Use the four linguistic tools to vivify your dreams in your journal. When you are ready, continue to the next waypoint: "Life's Work."

9

Life's Work

UNCOVER AND BEGIN YOUR OWN "MAGNUM OPUS"

Discovering the magnum opus—the great work of your life—can be a difficult task, but uncovering your mission in life can be exhilarating and life-altering in a positive way. Those who hold to the Vision of the Heartwood Path and who are taking steps to materialize that mental picture (as previously described) are working on the pivotal task called "The Great Work!" Each eartHeart works on his or her own magnum opus and/or adopts his or her own aspect of the Great Work!—the overarching magnum opus suggested for those who follow the Heartwood Path. Best taken in small steps, the Great Work! is a set of deliberate, conscious, intentional exercises that occur in Self, culture, and Nature. These exercises are practices—disciplined actions, repeated customs, and regular exercises—performed with the intension of perfecting (you could say "awakening," if you prefer) the Self to preserve one's environment (however that is defined).

Each practice will be aided if you increase your ability to savor. Ordinary experiences can be relished. You can transport yourself back in time with your memory. You can replay happy days, celebrate good news, and be open to beauty and excellence. You can be mindful by taking pleasure in your senses. Although you can pinpoint or frame your relishing by savoring with your camera, do not hide behind the lens or writing instrument. Become a participant and not just a recorder. Seek all experiences, even the bittersweet ones.

Before engaging in the kind of transformative cross training described in the next section, commit to your goals. They are the aims of your life, fortunes worth finding. They provide a feeling of control as one's sense of purpose narrows down distractions. Moving forward with goals helps you to manage your time, enables you to feel confident, and provides the impetus for social connections—all of which leads to happiness. Help with proper goal setting follows.

To Merry Aspirations...

HumaNatureConnect Activity

Start-up Protocol

If this is not a day when you prefer to spend time in nature without an agenda, do the Heartwood Path Start-up Protocol found in the Appendix. Then return here to do the remaining portion of this activity:

Engaging In Happiness-producing Goal Setting

For this activity, cast out extrinsic goals relating to money, beauty, or fame, especially if they are retarding your happiness. Replace them with intrinsic goals—those that are inherently satisfying, meaningful, growth-producing, and community-enhancing. Make sure your goals are your own, not those suggested or forcefully imposed in you by others. Make your sure goals are not about avoiding an undesirable outcome but rather involve approaching a desirable outcome. Make sure your goals complement each other. Keep them flexible and appropriate. Make sure they have something to do with activities such as hiking, volunteering, or learning. Choose goals that will influence how you are remembered. Be sure to log your five most important goals (or however many you are attracted to establish) in your journal.

Follow-up Protocol

For best results, write down your impressions of this activity in your journal using the Heartwood Path Follow-up Protocol found in the Appendix. Afterwards, consider sharing your interpretations with others.

Heartwood Path Axioms

Key Assertions From Waypoint 2.9

2.9.1.

Discovering the magnum opus—the great work of your life— can be a difficult task, but uncovering your mission in life can be exhilarating and life-altering in a positive way.

2.9.2.

Ordinary experiences can be relished: you can transport yourself back in time with your memory, replay happy days, celebrate good news, be open to beauty and excellence, be mindful by taking pleasure in your senses, and pinpoint or frame your relishing by savoring with your camera.

2.9.3.

Seek all experiences, even the bittersweet ones.

2.9.4.

Moving forward with goals helps you to manage your time, enables you to feel confident, and provides the impetus for social connections—all of which leading to happiness.

Nocturnal Pilgrimage 2.9

For best results, write down your impressions of each night's dreams in your journal using the Heartwood Path Dreaming Time Protocols found in the Appendix. Afterwards, consider sharing your Dream Tending with others.

People often endeavor to interpret dreams as a way to solve their problems. Many of these problems are caused because people have no goals or have goals that only pertain to fame, money, or physical beauty. Perhaps you are not as successful as you might like because you do not examine your situation with enough care. Perhaps you are not as skilled as you might like to be at recognizing the truth regarding the situations and circumstances of your life. By following the suggestion in the component of the After Dreaming Protocol entitled "Statement Of Problem" you will become better at identifying the complication, challenge or predicament displayed in your various dreams, a skill you can later use to identify the situations, plights, and quandaries of your life. Once your misadventures are identified, either in your dreams or in your life, you can apply yourself to the task of finding a better course or approach. Uncovering a problem may lead you to identifying previously unrecognized goal that has been previously hidden can now set you on a course of improvement.

Repetition is the sire of excellence. That is why we are here again turning our attention to the After Dreaming Protocol titled "Book Of Dreams." After your next tended dream, notice how using the four linguistic tools—1) talking in present tense, 2) using verbs ending in "ing," 3) removing articles such as "an" or "the," and 4) using capital letters when naming the Dream Characters) makes the Dream Image come alive, makes the Dream Character come into the room with you, and makes your own body open up "in new ways and with a new awareness" (Aizenstat, 2009, p. 39).

Observe your dreams. Get interested in them. Make a journal entry, using the four dream-vivifying linguistic tools mentioned in this nocturnal pilgrimage. After doing so, move to the next waypoint: "Whole Fitness."

10

Whole Fitness

ENGAGE IN TRANSFORMATIVE CROSS TRAINING

The practices relate to the diverse dimensions of human potential. The main dimensions are mental, emotional, physical, and spiritual. Experience demonstrates that working in one area—physical, for example—helps with the other dimensions. So cross training—doing something in each of the four main dimensions and, if time and commitment allows, doing practices in other subordinate dimensions of one's choosing (relationships, ethics, social action, for example)—will be most productive.

Before randomly starting any set of practices, put the wisdom found in this waypoint to work for you by doing the following five preliminary but crucial transformative practices. They will show you a sequence to use when constructing your own pathway that leads to the awareness (perfection) of the Greater (more than just individual) Self— an entity that includes, for example, both the individual and her enveloping neighborhood/environment. The five crucial transformative practices are:

1. scanning your current transformative practices,

2. identifying deficiencies in your current transformative practices,

3. evaluating your commitment to transformative practice,

4. determining what you are attempting to achieve in your transformative practices, and

5. choosing your transformative practices (Wilber, et. Al, 2008, pp. 317-325).

Frequently the "Magnum Opus"—great work—of one's life requires more than personal transformation. Usually the transmutation of one's Self and one's environment is necessary, and this is precisely the Great Work! of those who follow the Heartwood Path.

By following the path outlined in this book you are working to change your nature. You can be successful at this Great Work! if you follow certain parameters. Know, for example, the difference between "Nature" and "nature," "Cosmos" and "Kosmos," and "Spirit" and "Soul."

Often in this book I will begin the word "Nature" with a capital letter. I do this to remind the reader that embedded within Nature is Spirit. When I spell "nature" without the capital letter I am specifically referring to nature without Spirit (which is not how the universe usually works), usually as a synonym of the word "character."

The cosmos is the physical universe. Change the spelling of "cosmos" to "Kosmos" and the theological sphere of the universe is added to the meaning of the word. The whole Kosmos—both the inner realm of Spirit and the outer realm of form—is governed by universal principles.

The following activity will help you increase your happiness by helping you relate to the Kosmos and not just the cosmos. For some, relating to the Kosmos means going to church and, indeed, encountering like-minded and caring people is a source of security, a fountainhead of meaning, and, therefore, a source of happiness. With or without a church, searching for the sacred—by which I mean searching for meaning in life through something bigger than the individual—is likewise a source of happiness. Outside of church, this searching is accomplished through meditation; prayer; instilling a spiritual dimension to one's life through having goals, life schemes, and creative outlets; post-traumatic growth from anguish; strong emotions that accompany awe, wonder, and faith.

To Universal Delight...

HumaNatureConnect Activity

Start-up Protocol

If this is not a day when you prefer to spend time in nature without an agenda, do the Heartwood Path Start-up Protocol found in the Appendix. Then return here to do the remaining portion of this activity:

Training For Happiness

For this activity, consider your schedule and dedicate ample amounts of time to prayer. We will return to this topic later. For now, if you are not accustomed to prayer, focus on praying about sources of gratitude in your life. Next, look around you for examples of holiness in ordinary things. Do not get bogged down in hair-splitting here. How you define holy is up to you. It may mean, for example, "perfect," "awe-inspiring," "pure," "whole," "integrated," "pleasing to God," "the manifestation of the Absolute," or "supremely valued by you." By sanctifying everyday objects (or beings), you will naturally be more respectful of these objects (or beings) and receive, in return, a significant measure of happiness.

Follow-up Protocol

For best results, write down your impressions of this activity in your journal using the Heartwood Path Follow-up Protocol found in the Appendix. Afterwards, consider sharing your interpretations with others.

Heartwood Path Axioms

Key Assertions From Waypoint 2.10

2.10.1.

The five crucial transformative practices are:

1. scanning your current transformative practices,

2. identifying deficiencies in your current transformative practices,

3. evaluating your commitment to transformative practice,

4. determining what you are attempting to achieve in your transformative practices, and

5. choosing your transformative practices.

2.10.2.

With or without a church, searching for the sacred—by which I mean searching for meaning in life through something bigger than the individual—is a source of happiness.

2.10.3.

Outside of church, searching for the sacred is accomplished through meditation; prayer; instilling a spiritual dimension to one's life through having goals, life schemes, and creative outlet; post-traumatic growth from anguish; strong emotions that accompany awe, wonder; and faith.

2.10.4.

By sanctifying everyday objects (or beings), you will naturally be more respectful of these objects (or beings) and receive, in return, a significant measure of happiness.

Nocturnal Pilgrimage 2.10

For best results, write down your impressions of each night's dreams in your journal using the Heartwood Path Dreaming Time Protocols found in the Appendix. Afterwards, consider sharing your Dream Tending with others.

Tonight, before you fall asleep, set the intention that you desire to dream about sanctifying common objects/beings and to see what this action does, if anything, to your own level of happiness. Pay attention to a problem or difficulty that may be associated with these objects/beings, and how (if at all) these objects/beings change and affect outcomes, depending on whether they are recognized as being somehow holy—meaning bigger than themselves. Be sure to write down your impressions.

Expect to improve your dream tending by following the suggestion given in the After Dreaming Protocol titled "Culmination Or Response To The Problem." In doing so, you will get better at paying attention to and writing down how problems are resolved in your dreams. This skill will help you receive guidance from Dream Characters concerning how to solve the dilemmas of your own life.

Before examining the message at the next waypoint use the four dream-vivifying linguistic tools in your dream journaling. Then, when you are ready to make more progress, move to the next waypoint: "Up & Down."

11

Up & Down

ASCEND TO THE SPIRIT, DESCEND TO THE SOUL

Soul is the vital core of one's individual self. It is unique to each person, and deeper within than one's personality. Spirit permeates and animates everything in the universe and yet transcends all. The Spirit is the aspect that all things and all persons have in common. One's Soul is the agent for the Spirit. Both the Soul and the Spirit are sacred. Both add beauty, mystery, and meaning to our lives. Both transpersonal, the Spirit and the Soul are other than our selves and beyond our control. We are called to serve the Soul and to unite with the Spirit, the former being your own Cove in the Ocean of Spirit and the latter being the Source of all Creation. We will use the term "ascend" to describe how we draw closer to the Spirit and the term "descend" to describe how we draw closer to the Soul. These two directions mark the two realms of spirituality. Earthly mysteries and Nature are associated with the realm of the Soul, heavenly bliss with the realm of the Spirit. Remember these distinctions for they will come up often in the waypoints that follow.

To obtain a better understanding of the Spirit and the Soul, gain inner peace, explore higher reality, heal yourself, release your intuition or creativity, and attain insight by meditating. For help, do the following activity.

To The Parts Of Contemplation...

HumaNatureConnect Activity

Start-up Protocol

If this is not a day when you prefer to spend time in nature without an agenda, do the Heartwood Path Start-up Protocol found in the Appendix. Then return here to do the remaining portion of this activity:

Practicing The Elements Of Meditation

For this activity, practice the following elements of meditation: 1) recall or observe something and practice being nonjudgmental (having no evaluations); 2) consider how you can focus on progressing towards your goals but not be focused unduly on achieving your goals; 3) remember a time when you had to be patient and how that patience offered a reward; 4) think of an aspect of your life that requires trust and focus on having faith that something positive will occur; 5) practice paying attention to the little things around you in ways that keep you open to new experiences or aspects; and 6) free yourself of repetitive thinking about a topic of concern so that you can become "nonattached" to this worrisome topic.

Follow-up Protocol

For best results, write down your impressions of this activity in your journal using the Heartwood Path Follow-up Protocol found in the Appendix. Afterwards, consider sharing your interpretations with others.

Heartwood Path Axioms

Key Assertions From Waypoint 2.11

2.11.1.

Soul is the vital core of one's individual self.

2.11.2.

The Spirit is the aspect that all things and all persons have in common.

2.11.3.

We are called to serve the Soul and to unite with the Spirit, the latter being the Source of all creation.

2.11.4.

Earthly mysteries and Nature are associated with the realm of the Soul, heavenly bliss with the realm of the Spirit.

2.11.5.

Practice the following elements of meditation:

recall or observe something and practice being nonjudgmental (having no evaluations);

consider how you can focus on progressing towards your goals but not be focused unduly on achieving your goals; remember a time when you had to be patient and how that patience offered a reward;

think of an aspect of your life that requires trust and focus on
having faith that something positive will occur;

practice paying attention to the little things around you in
ways that keep you open to new experiences or aspects; and

free yourself of repetitive thinking about a topic of concern so
that you can become "nonattached" to this worrisome topic.

Nocturnal Pilgrimage 2.11

For best results, write down your impressions of each night's
dreams in your journal using the Heartwood Path Dreaming Time
Protocols found in the Appendix. Afterwards, consider sharing your
Dream Tending with others.

Continue practicing with the four dream-vivifying linguistic tools
for your dream journal. Make using such tools a habit.

After you have made your journal entry, move to the next waypoint:
"Transformers."

12

Transformers

GET TO KNOW YOUR CHAKRAS

The Soul, as previously mentioned, is your own personal cove in the ocean of the Spirit. One's own Soul has a structure in the "form" of a system of energy centers that provide one with both power and healing. These energy centers give structure to one's inner world. Called "chakras" these spinning transformers of energy enable one to become more refined and less animalistic. They enable one's personal power to become more transcendent, consummate, total, and exquisite. They are not physical objects, but vortexes of energy associated with various parts of the garage of the Soul—the body. They affect our moods and are affected by moods.

Chakras form a bridge between the body's energy field—our spiritual aspect—and the body's physical parts. They are the key way your body makes physiological responses to your thoughts.

Just as your circulatory system, respiratory system, and digestive system are primary components of your physical body, so too are the chakras one of the key systems of your energy body. This energetic portion of your being is the part that transmits and records your thoughts and interactions.

Chakras cause one's biology to be determined by one's biography. They are the links between one's good and bad experiences of events and one's physical body. In this way, the psychosomatic (mind/body) energy regulated by the chakras is the bridge between one's experience and one's body, between the visible and the sacred, between the microcosm and the macrocosm, and between sexuality and spirituality.

Here is a simple explanation of what the chakras do, from certified Reiki specialist and hypnotherapist Inessa Zeleski:

"Generally speaking . . . the three lower chakras (the root, belly and solar plexus chakras) correlate to basic primary needs - those of survival, procreation and will - and have a larger physiological component to their functioning. The four higher chakras are more related to our psychological makeup: the heart, throat and third eye chakras are more advanced and more mature, defining love, communication and knowledge; the crown chakra is purely spiritual, providing the connection to the universe beyond" (Zeleski).

When one arouses all the chakras through practices described in the Heartwood Path for Couples book (**Eros**), spirituality takes on a whole new meaning and importance in one's life. The particular brand of spirituality described in the Heartwood Path—Creation-based and largely in the Christian mysticism tradition—is, primarily, a way of passion that leads to compassion.

To The Pleasures Of The Beyond-the-brain Mind System...

HumaNatureConnect Activity

Start-up Protocol

If this is not a day when you prefer to spend time in nature without an agenda, do the Heartwood Path Start-up Protocol found in the Appendix. Then return here to do the remaining portion of this activity:

Getting To Know Your Chakras With The Help Of A Candle

For this activity, find a comfortable and private place to sit up-right on the ground. Clear a space for your lighted candle and place it on the ground in front of you. As you experience each of your chakras healing will occur because when the chakras are experienced the awareness sends energy to the chakras which, in turn, stimulate the important endocrine gland associated with each chakra, thus bringing forth increased flow of nutrients needed for the various functions of the body (as described subsequently). Look at the light and imagine a light growing inside of you, between your legs at the base of your spine. Close your eyes and focus your attention on the light in a relaxed and gentle way. Rub you hands together to create the heat necessary to bring warmth to the various parts of you body you will be touching. Whether you are a man or a woman, begin by spreading the warmth to your chest area and belly by moving your hands in a circular fashion. Then, rub your hands in the area of your genitals just enough to bring forth added arousal, heat, and tingling but not enough to induce an orgasm. Three to five minutes is usually sufficient (but never enough). As you increase your aliveness, imagine that the inner light is growing brighter. Once your sexual energy is aroused you will begin feeling your First Chakra. It will be a feeling of lust—hardness for men, wetness for women. Beyond these physical sensations notice any sensations of life and survival, including increased sex drive, the desire to go wild, and the need to be released or filled. With these sensations one's ovaries or testicles are being flooded with vital energy. Aware of such feelings, close your eyes again and breathe in through your nose, taking deeper and deeper breaths until you imagine that the air is filling you all the way down to your genitals. Regularly hold your breath and relax your body so as not to impede the inner flow of energy. In the moment between inhalation and exhalation (both through the nose), with a relaxed body, one is more likely to experience the feelings of ecstasy—

lightness and emptiness. As you hold your breath, repeatedly tighten and loosen the muscles around the anus and perineum. This is called the PC Pump. Continue this procedure three to six times, or until you feel energized in your belly and pelvic area, until you "see" the white light glowing brightly in the mind's eye, or until you feel warmth, a throbbing sensation, pulsing, or even mini-orgasmic sensations as you exhale slowly. You now have awareness of your First Chakra. Next, close your eyes again and, as you inhale, imagine that you are drawing up the white light to a spot about two inches below the navel. This is the location of your Second Chakra. It will be important throughout this activity to maintain the arousal of the First Chakra in the Sex Area. To do so, you can continuously and slowly rock your pelvis and, for greater effect, imagine that the light is descending with your exhalations so it can be recharged in the manner previously described. As you draw up the White Light and its associated lusty feelings to the Second Chakra, the associated feelings will change from lust alone to lust plus subtly enhanced emotions. These may include jealousy, competitiveness, dissatisfaction, criticality, or any of a number of feelings including the curious push-pull syndrome that makes one think "I want you, but go away." Along with these sensations is the flooding of the adrenals and kidneys with vital energy. Once you have drawn up the lusty feelings of the First Chakra and experienced any of the heightened emotions associated with the Second Chakra three to six times, it is time to move on to experiencing the Third Chakra. As before, close your eyes, exhale as you imagine the light moving down to be recharged by the First Chakra. After you are aroused again in the manner described above, imagine the charged light moving up with an extended inhalation through the First Chakra, through the emotions of the Second Chakra to that hollow and soft place just below the hard sternum of the rib cage. The sexual and emotional energy of the previous chakras moves up with the white light in your mind and will again change. Added to the sensations will be a sense of assuredness, personal power, charisma, and the ability to make things happen in the world the way you want. Along with these sensations is the flooding of the adrenals, pancreas, and kidneys with vital energy. Move the energy from the First to the Third Chakra three to six times. Recharge as before, but this time move the energy upward through the Second, and Third Chakras to the Heart area of the body, between the breasts. As you hold your breath you will feel warmth of love spreading throughout your chest. This warmth indicates that the thymus gland—which rejuvenates and guards the immune system—is being revitalized. Repeat the procedure three to six times or until you feel, along with the flowing and warming feeling of love, a sense of gratitude for the gift of life, expanded hope, and a sense of renewal. Having now experienced the Fourth chakra, the Heart Chakra, it is time to become aware of the Fifth Chakra, located in the throat. You will become aware of the Fifth Chakra as the imaginary white light—a representation of one's consciousness—energizes the thyroid in the throat (thus stimulating growth and aiding metabolism). As this occurs, "you know who you are and what you want, and you can express it" (Anand, 1989, p. 173.). Repeat pulling up the energy into Throat Chakra three to six times or until you feel a heightened sense of authenticity and expressiveness. When you move the energy up to the Sixth Chakra, between and behind the eyebrows the energy will activate the pituitary gland. This activations will make you feel crisp and you will have greater intuitive knowing. Once the energy moves to the Seventh Chakra, after inhaling and drawing up the light to the top of the head, the Crown chakra will activate the pineal gland—the center of dynamic thought and enlightenment. Once activated, it feels like a fountain gushing from your head and pleasurably—fantastically pleasurably—raining down over your body. Simultaneously, you will feel one with everything (Anand, 1989). When you write down your impressions of this activity in your journal include any physical or emotional sensations you feel as you draw up the light, chakra by chakra.

Follow-up Protocol

For best results, write down your impressions of this activity in your journal using the Heartwood Path Follow-up Protocol found in

the Appendix. Afterwards, consider sharing your interpretations with others.

Heartwood Path Axioms

Key Assertions From Waypoint 2.12

2.12.1.

The Soul is your own personal cove in the ocean of the Spirit.

2.12.2.

Power centers in the body, called chakras, enable one's personal power to become more transcendent, consummate, total, and exquisite.

2.12.3.

Chakras cause one's biology to be determined by one's biography.

2.12.4.

The psychosomatic (mind/body) energy regulated by the chakras is the bridge between one's experience and one's body, between the visible and the sacred, between the microcosm and the macrocosm, and between sexuality and spirituality.

2.12.5.

The particular brand of spirituality described in the Heartwood Path is a way of passion that leads to compassion.

Nocturnal Pilgrimage 2.12

For best results, write down your impressions of each night's dreams in your journal using the Heartwood Path Dreaming Time Protocols found in the Appendix. Afterwards, consider sharing your Dream Tending with others.

For tonight's dream practice, intend that you will follow the suggestion of the After Dreaming Protocol titled "Conclusion:" describe how your dream ended. Often, the main way your dream offers assistance occurs towards the end. Simply write down what happened at the end. It is counter-productive to reduce any part of your dreams to signs (like, for example, a dog means this; and a willow tree means that), which as too limiting. Let the full unlimited symbolism of your dreams unfold as they will, if left unencumbered by your limiting assignments of signs. For this reason, with tonight's dream, reinforce the habit of simply experiencing dreams, to their end, without narrowing them down to your own sign-giving.

With these suggestions in mind, note what happens at the end of your dream. And record notes that reflect or even add vividness to your dreams in your dream journal, as previously instructed. Then, move to the next waypoint: "Close & Key."

13

Close & Key

GROW THROUGH INTIMACY AND "ULTIMACY" BY FOLLOWING THE THREE CARDINAL DIRECTIONS TO INTEGRITY

During your journey down the Heartwood Path, especially if you enroll in the two subsequent courses, you will find a mixture of the microcosm of intimacy (with yourself and your partner) and the macrocosm of "ultimacy" (with others in efforts to effectively produce justice). This mixture will produce both enjoyment and justice for all if you follow the words on three prominent virtual signposts—the Three Cardinal Directions—along the Heartwood Path, which are:

1. Prepare Yourself for Love, a topic addressed the first four books;
2. Share Love With Another, a topic covered in the Heartwood Path for Couples book (**Eros**); and
3. Put Love to Good Use, a topic covered in Books Five, Six, Eight, and Nine.

Take the first step in following the First Heartwood Path Cardinal Direction (Prepare Yourself For Love) by engaging in this present book, entitled "**Logos**," which is about developing an understanding of the universal principles that lead to integrity. One needs to be both whole and appropriate to have integrity.

Think about how you can experience more of the joys of the Earth and spread them to other people. Pouring out your goodwill on others is a worthy process. It makes the world better and it builds integrity.

To do the best job for others one needs to make sure one sustains or even increases one's happiness by safeguarding one's positive emotions, by being curious, by being content, by varying your activities, and by having enthusiasm. Having already done some important activities to increase your happiness, now is a good time to work on another way to help you arrive at Gladandgreen Junction: arresting the chatter of Inner Dialogue.

To The Parts Cogitation...

HumaNatureConnect Activity

Start-up Protocol

If this is not a day when you prefer to spend time in nature without an agenda, do the Heartwood Path Start-up Protocol found in the Appendix. Then return here to do the remaining portion of this activity:

Meditating

For this activity you will need to find a pond, an ocean, or a stream. Imagine that this body of water is synonymous with your mind. Like the body of water, your mind is agitated on the surface but, deeper within, it is more serene. Thinking of the body of water as your mind, drop a pebble into the water. As the pebble sinks deeper, it passes from a surface world of disturbance to a deep world of silence and peace. Imagine the serenity deep within your mind. Concentrate on your breathing to control your thoughts. Practice becoming aware of the space or interval between thoughts. In your journal, write down the nature of the disturbance associated with the constant thinking at the surface of your mind and the lack of disturbance deep within your mind, at the space between your thoughts.

Follow-up Protocol

For best results, write down your impressions of this activity in your journal using the Heartwood Path Follow-up Protocol found in the Appendix. Afterwards, consider sharing your interpretations with others.

Heartwood Path Axioms

Key Assertions From Waypoint 2.13

2.13.1.

Follow the Heartwood Path's Three Cardinal Directions:

Prepare Yourself for Love,

Share Love With Another, and

Put Love To Good Use.

2.13.2.

Think about how you can experience more of the joys of the Earth and spread them to other people.

2.13.3.

Arrest the chatter of Inner Dialogue.

2.13.4.

Become a host for your imaginal Dream Characters by imagining that you are asking them into your home to join you in conversation.

Nocturnal Pilgrimage 2.13

For best results, write down your impressions of each night's dreams in your journal using the Heartwood Path Dreaming Time Protocols found in the Appendix. Afterwards, consider sharing your Dream Tending with others.

Now that you have Dream Tended for numerous inner world nocturnal episodes, it is time to become a host for one or more of your Dream Figures. "Relax, become receptive, and imagine that you are asking the (Dream Character, we have been using the words "Dream Image" for the same thing) into your home, to join you in conversation . . . Ask the Dream Character, "How are you?' Take the time to listen to the response" (Aizenstat, 2009, p. 41). Be patient. "Get curious about what the image is doing . . . Do not ask the (Dream Character or Dream Image) too many questions about yourself. . . Ask it questions about itself . . . Go back and forth in dialogue from a place of caring" (Aizenstat, 2009, pp. 42-43).

Once you initiate being a host to your Dream Character, continue by moving to the next waypoint: "The Merits Of Meditating."

14

The Merits Of Meditating

DETERMINE WHY YOU WAKE UP IN THE MORNING

Each person has tens of thousands of thoughts each day. The problem with having these thoughts is that they are usually the same as the day before and the same as those that will come each future day. Almost all that we think is mindless chatter—repetitive, judgmental, or otherwise unproductive. Meditation helps to slow down the chatter; finds the gaps between thoughts; and reveals in these gaps the illusion of one's separation from the Absolute, Nature, and each other. What remains after the meditation removes the thoughts, the concepts, the opinions, and the beliefs is the spaciousness of consciousness. In the space between thoughts you will find a sense of peace in a realm that is normally unknowable.

In that space of peace deep within the pond of your mind where the often-disturbing chatter of thoughts are not overbearing important knowings have a chance to emerge. One such important knowing—why you get up in the morning—can come to you by doing the next activity.

To The Deepness Of The Concentration...

HumaNatureConnect Activity

Start-up Protocol

If this is not a day when you prefer to spend time in nature without an agenda, do the Heartwood Path Start-up Protocol found in the Appendix. Then return here to do the remaining portion of this activity:

Entering Into The Depths Of Your Mind

For this activity, enter into the depth of your mind. Follow your breathing to control your thoughts. Once the chatter is minimized allow the following question to emerge into the deep, calmness of your awareness: "Why do I get up in the morning?" Answer this question and record your answer in your journal.

Follow-up Protocol

For best results, write down your impressions of this activity in your journal using the Heartwood Path Follow-up Protocol found in the Appendix. Afterwards, consider sharing your interpretations with others.

Heartwood Path Axioms

Key Assertions From Waypoint 2.14

2.14.1

Follow the Heartwood Path's pre-pilgrimage instructions.

2.14.2.

In that space of peace deep within the pond of your mind, where the often-disturbing chatter of thoughts are not over-bearing, important knowings have a chance to emerge.

2.14.3.

Ask yourself:

"Why do I get up in the morning?"

Nocturnal Pilgrimage 2.14

For best results, write down your impressions of each night's dreams in your journal using the Heartwood Path Dreaming Time Protocols found in the Appendix. Afterwards, consider sharing your Dream Tending with others.

Tonight, as you prepare for sleep, set the intention—by stating it over and over again—that you will look within your dreams for the presence of waking time attractive natural beings that are showing up as Dream Characters in your dreams. These may not be mirror images of the natural beings; but they are, to the best of your own ability, somehow linked in appearance, action, vibrations, empathy, or words to the beings from your waking time connection experience. Identifying such dreaming-time characters is better than finding gold. It means that the guidance, started with your chosen attractive natural beings, is being reinforced or clarified in your dreams. When this link occurs, you have found in your dreams a very good candidate to become physical representation of a Dream Character—a Dream Figure. Seriously consider adding the new Dream Figure to your Dream Council. With each new addition, hold a Dream Council session, always with the intention of finding important guidance.

Once you have experience being a host for one or more of your Dream Council sessions, ask one or all of the Dream Council members a very important question: "Why do you wake up in the morning?" Notice how you feel about the response. Take good notes. Share what is said with others, but only if it feels right to do so. Then, move to more of nature's better-than-gold gifts by continuing down the Heartwood Path to the next waypoint: "Encounter."

15

Encounter

FACE FAILURE, YOUR FEARS, AND REGRETS

Lester Levenson is reported to say: "Fear, and it will appear" (Dwoskin, 2009, p. 277). His disciple, Hale Dwoskin elaborates: "By placing a continual emphasis on avoiding what we fear, we call it to mind over and over again, like a perverse mantra, or a focal point for meditation, and it becomes a program limiting our happiness and freedom" (p. 277).

Concerning failures, to paraphrase Lord Tennyson: it's better to have acted and failed than never to have acted at all. Failure is just a judgment given to action. There are no failures, only produced results. These results contain valuable lessons. Each result judged to be negative shows you one way not to do things. You are not a failure because of your produced results.

Concerning your regrets, avoid them. You will most likely not regret what you do as much as what you did not do. If you do find yourself in regret, leave this wasteland. All you can do there is wallow in frustration. Learn from whatever you produce. Do things that you do not know how to do, if only to learn. Avoid concerning yourself about what others think.

While it is important for you, generally in your life, to minimize judgments that are evaluations, one way to help yourself do so is to make a self-assessment and then work on being done with the habit of constantly evaluating. The next activity will provide this outlet.

To An Assessment Of Your Life...

HumaNatureConnect Activity

Start-up Protocol

If this is not a day when you prefer to spend time in nature without an agenda, do the Heartwood Path Start-up Protocol found in the Appendix. Then return here to do the remaining portion of this activity:

Evaluating Aspects Of Your Life

For this activity, evaluate the aspects of your life on a scale of 1-10 (10 being very satisfied). Evaluate each of the following aspects of your life: time, purpose, values, vitality, careers, spirituality, talents, health, relationships, money, housing, and environment. What areas would you most like to improve, and how? Write your responses in your journal. Remember to make a reassessment when you finish this book and then periodically throughout your life.

Follow-up Protocol

For best results, write down your impressions of this activity in your journal using the Heartwood Path Follow-up Protocol found in the Appendix. Afterwards, consider sharing your interpretations with others.

Heartwood Path Axioms

Key Assertions From Waypoint 2.15

2.15.1.

Face failure, your fears and regrets.

2.15.2.

It is better to have acted and failed than never to have acted at all.

2.15.3.

Each result judged to be negative shows you one way not to do things.

Nocturnal Pilgrimage 2.15

For best results, write down your impressions of each night's dreams in your journal using the Heartwood Path Dreaming Time Protocols found in the Appendix. Afterwards, consider sharing your Dream Tending with others.

Tonight's before-sleep activity sets you up so that you can fulfill the suggestion found in the component of the After Dreaming Protocol titled "Freud's Approach." Begin by setting the intention that when you dream (and when you tend to your dream afterwards) you will write down how various images in your dreams are (or seem to be) associated with latent or hidden urges you may have in any of the follow life parameters: purpose, values, vitality, careers, spirituality, talents, health, relationships, money, housing, and environment. When working on talents, for example, you may have or remember a dream that you are delivering a riveting speech and associate that image with a previously unknown drive to become a talented public speaker. After making these associations by yourself, float them by your Dream Council to see if they can help you make sense about latent drives or hidden yearnings that impact the various life parameters: and, in so doing, possibly free yourself from emotional baggage associated with your recently uncovered urges. As another example, you may hear from River Otter, a revered member of your Dream Council. If, for example, River Otter says that you are sorely missed along Ozark Streams, you might want to associate this image with a latent desire to change your career and, more specifically, to return to conservation work in southern Missouri. Take note of similarities or differences in the associations you uncover from your chosen attractive beings, from random Dream Characters, and from your Dream Council members.

In addition to writing down journal entries about these revelations, notice how you feel about the association-related responses you receive. Then, by moving to the next waypoint, titled "Tug Of Peace," learn of the three opposing forces that shape everything, including your life.

16

Tug Of Peace

UNDERSTAND THE PULL OF THE THREE OPPOSING COSMIC FORCES

These forces include: 1) the pull to be singular against the pull to be plural; 2) the pull to be a formed physical thing (knowable through staring) against the pull to be formless (perceived in others through sharing); and 3) the pull to dissolve against the pull to add organizational depth (evolve). With these three forces working simultaneously, the Universe can be said to be differentiated into four realms, with each realm increasing in organizational depth over time (from the spirit-filled, formlessness of the Void, to the physical, to the living, to the mental, to the Soul, and to the Spirit again). The four realms of the universe are the same as those represented on the Four-leaf Model of Integrity: 1) the realm of the behaviors of formed individual entities understood best through science; 2) the realm of the physical fit of formed systems—organizations, businesses, bodies, ecosystems, galaxies, etc., also understood best through science, 3) the formless realm of the intentions of individual entities understood best through art; and 4) the formless realm of the morals and ethics of plural entities understood best through spirituality or religion. The third force—the pull to dissolve against the pull to add organizational depth—either adds depth or disintegration to each of the four realms.

The main point to carry away from this discussion is that as you work to facilitate your personal growth it is vitally important that you create both balance and depth. The balance comes into play as you make sure that the four realms—intentions, ethics, behaviors, and physical systems—are all considered and used. The depth comes into play when you add the layers of depth—physical, mental, and spiritual—to each of the realms. The spiritual level emerges from the physical level and mental levels and the mental level emerges from the physical level. Only when one transcends all layers—that is, as one becomes more integral (has more integrity) by including all layers of depth, can one properly show compassion for all sentient beings. The suggested goal for all eartHearts is to add more balance and more depth. In this way, life becomes good for yourself and others; but only as one overcomes the pulls to be singular (that is, individual only rather than both individual and integrated), the pull think of yourself only as a formed being with independent agency rather than also addressing the formless aspects of self such as being in relationship, and the pull to dissolve (to die unchanged) rather than to evolve (to grow in depth and to become balanced).

With all of these pulls working on you, you may have a sense that your own individual freedom is being modified and, in a sense, it is. You are an individual but you are not independent of the three opposing forces. You retain, however, the freedom of choosing your own, thoughts, perspectives, and behaviors. To increase this freedom, do the following activity.

To The Growth Of Expansive Views...

HumaNatureConnect Activity

Start-up Protocol

If this is not a day when you prefer to spend time in nature without an agenda, do the Heartwood Path Start-up Protocol found in the Appendix. Then return here to do the remaining portion of this activity:

Cultivating The Freedom Of Thought And The Expansion Of Perspective

For this activity, open the door to freedom by looking at things from a variety of unusual and extreme perspectives. Determine how you can best take time off for reflection, how you can take time for observation, and how you can read a lot. Determine how you can learn more from children. Pinpoint where in your life you need to remain more open-minded. Solicit feed back from others you admire. Make a list of one hundred questions that you deem significant. Start by listing ten such questions in your journal.

Follow-up Protocol

For best results, write down your impressions of this activity in your journal using the Heartwood Path Follow-up Protocol found in the Appendix. Afterwards, consider sharing your interpretations with others.

Heartwood Path Axioms

Key Assertions From Waypoint 2.16

2.16.1.

Understand the pull of the three opposing cosmic forces.

2.16.2.

The three opposing forces are: 1) the pull to be singular against the pull to be plural, 2) the pull to be a formed thing against the pull to be formless, and 3) the pull to dissolve against the pull to evolve.

2.16.3.

You are an individual but you are not independent of the three opposing cosmic forces.

Nocturnal Pilgrimage 2.16

For best results, write down your impressions of each night's dreams in your journal using the Heartwood Path Dreaming Time Protocols found in the Appendix. Afterwards, consider sharing your Dream Tending with others.

Being a host for your Council of Dream Figures once again, ask what perspective, if any, will be most useful for the members at this time? Perhaps the perspective will be that of the chosen natural being or perhaps that of another attractive natural being. Adopt this perspective and, turning the question towards yourself, ask "Why do I wake up in the morning?" Notice how you feel about the response as delivered from the suggested perspective, as compared to how you answered it yourself in a previous waypoint.

Having answered such an important question, notice the liveliness you have as you proceed down the Heartwood Path by moving to the next waypoint: "Newness." There, you will come to know the universe's creative advance into novelty. Moving forward towards new things tends to quicken the step and elevate the mood.

17

Newness

UNDERSTAND THE UNIVERSE'S CREATIVE ADVANCE INTO NOVELTY

Here, novelty is defined as the new forms and capabilities that somehow emerge in the universe. This advance into novelty refers to both consciousness in the interior realm of existence (from primitive sensations in plants or animals to advanced concepts in humans, for example) and form in the exterior realm (from atoms to molecules, to cells, to organisms, to ecosystems, for example).

Everything in the universe is "pulled" to transcend through a mysterious force called "telos"—the power that leads everything to its ultimate end or object. Through this telos-driven transcendence all higher levels contain the essentials of the lower levels plus something extra.

Darwin's theory of natural selection explains how the novelty is selected to endure (random positive changes create offspring with advantages and, therefore, the novelty is carried on to future generations) but Darwin's theory does not explain how novelty emerges in the first place. Somehow, where Spirit is favorable, matter emerges; where matter is favorable, life emerges; where life is favorable, mind emerges; where mind is favorable, the Soul can be contacted; where the Soul is contacted, the recognition of Spirit emerges. Each level transcends and includes its predecessors.

Applying the principle of "As above, so below" the main point here is that one needs to apply the way whole species have evolved to the way you need to grow in depth; that is, from your current level of spiritual development transcend to the next higher level by keeping all levels that are supporting you now, adding the new level of depth, integrating into your being all levels, and witnessing, not how you have changed, for that would mean that you threw out your multi-level foundation, but how you have added a new level to your existing levels. It is not important to know the nature of these levels of development at this time. These levels will be described in the next Heartwood Path book. For now, just understand that life is not static, that positive newness comes to life, and that the Heartwood Path and its guides will help you bring important new levels of spiritual development to your life.

To The Emergence Of Newness...

HumaNatureConnect Activity

Start-up Protocol

If this is not a day when you prefer to spend time in nature without an agenda, do the Heartwood Path Start-up Protocol found in the Appendix. Then return here to do the remaining portion of this activity:

Advancing Into Novelty

For this activity, consider the expansiveness of the limitless universe, how the earth--finite and small-- is a part of the universe, and how you--whose problems are trivial when compared to the totality of problems on earth--sprang from the earth. Despite your relative smallness, ponder how the same forces that guide and shape the universe and the earth also affect you. Ponder the novelty of the earth floating in space. Think about what makes you a unique gift to the world. Write down any related impressions, including the nature of your uniqueness, in your journal.

Follow-up Protocol

For best results, write down your impressions of this activity in your journal using the Heartwood Path Follow-up Protocol found in the Appendix. Afterwards, consider sharing your interpretations with others.

Heartwood Path Axioms

Key Assertions From Waypoint 2.17

2.17.1.

Understand the universe's creative advance into novelty.

2.17.2.

The universe advances newness in both the realms of consciousness and form.

2.17.3.

Somehow, where Spirit is favorable, matter emerges; where matter is favorable, life emerges; and where life is favorable, mind emerges.

Nocturnal Pilgrimage 2.17

For best results, write down your impressions of each night's dreams in your journal using the Heartwood Path Dreaming Time Protocols found in the Appendix. Afterwards, consider sharing your Dream Tending with others.

Talk to your your Dream Figures once again, asking them what newness needs to emerge in your thoughts and in the outer world. Notice how you feel about the response you receive.

Having learned what newness needs to come into your life, continue down the Heartwood Path by moving to the next waypoint: "Bonds." There, you will discover the bond that unifies everything and how you are both a being and a process of relating.

18

Bonds

UNDERSTAND THE MECHANISMS OF ONENESS: HOLARCHY AND THE GREAT CHAIN OF BEING

There is a oneness, a commonality, a seamless fabric that unites the smallest, least complex with the largest, most organized. We all recognize that we are a part of the universe; but most people still perceive themselves as a separate, albeit related, part. Most have more clarity about their individuality than they do about their universality. Every human is both an individual being and a process of relating. The whole universe works this way.

To Know Unification…

HumaNatureConnect Activity

Start-up Protocol

If this is not a day when you prefer to spend time in nature without an agenda, do the Heartwood Path Start-up Protocol found in the Appendix. Then return here to do the remaining portion of this activity:

Understanding Oneness

For this activity, ponder a few important aspects of oneness. In your journal write down good and bad outcomes of being one with the following: worrying, suffering, seeking refuge in things of this world (wealth, riches, fame, status, living in a governed state, pleasures), and seeking refuge in things beyond this world (spirits, ghosts, and divine beings).

Follow-up Protocol

For best results, write down your impressions of this activity in your journal using the Heartwood Path Follow-up Protocol found in the Appendix. Afterwards, consider sharing your interpretations with others.

Heartwood Path Axioms

Key Assertions From Waypoint 2.18

2.18.1.

Understand the mechanisms of oneness: holarchy and the Great Chain of Being.

2.18.2.

There is a oneness, a commonality, a seamless fabric that unites the smallest, least complex with the largest, most organized.

2.18.3.

Every human is both an individual being and a process of relating.

Nocturnal Pilgrimage 2.18

For best results, write down your impressions of each night's dreams in your journal using the Heartwood Path Dreaming Time Protocols found in the Appendix. Afterwards, consider sharing your Dream Tending with others.

For tonight's leg of your nocturnal pilgrimage, develop the intention to look in your dreams for images that seem to represent universal positive forces. These forces may appear as Archetypal Dream Characters such as Superman, the Nurturing Mother, or the Wise Owl. They will be Dream Characters that are recognized by all cultures to symbolize goodness and helpfulness. In making note of such Archetypes in your dreams, you are fulfilling the suggestion of the component of the After Dreaming Protocol titled "Jung's Approach." Given their benevolence, such Dream Characters will make particularly powerful additions to your Dream Council.

Having identified in your dreams some of the most powerful advisors imaginable, continue down the Heartwood Path by moving to the next waypoint: "All Is One." There, you will discover a way to balance your uniqueness with your oneness.

19

"All Is One"

MODERATE THE TRANSCENDENTAL WITH THE IMMANENT

According to the idea of the Great Chain of Being, reality is composed of the following interlocking (or nested) levels: matter; body, mind, Soul, and Spirit. Each of these levels is said to include but transcend the preceding level—Spirit is different from but contains Soul, mind, body and matter; Soul is differentiated from but contains mind, body and matter; mind is not the same thing as but contains body and matter; and body is different from but contains matter. The gentle, hidden drive that causes the universe to envelope, encompass, integrate and transcend each link in the Great Chain of Being is Eros.

This power causes a wider sense of Self, the development of a broader compound identity that is not Ego-centered but Eco-centered or perhaps even Spirit-centered. To keep the ascending Eros from causing us to lose our solid footing, we can rely on our immanence to give us roots. In this way, the transcendental is moderated by the immanent.

To A Balance Between Uniqueness And Oneness...

HumaNatureConnect Activity

Start-up Protocol

If this is not a day when you prefer to spend time in nature without an agenda, do the Heartwood Path Start-up Protocol found in the Appendix. Then return here to do the remaining portion of this activity:

Moderating The Transcendent With The Immanent

For this activity, ponder the following three questions: Do you have a Master that you respect and follow? If so, describe the pros and cons of this relationship? Do you adhere to Dharma—a set of universal truths that are excellent, cause no afflictions or defilements, and are permanent? Can you think of anything else beside universal principles that is permanent? Describe your relationship to Dharma. Lastly, are you in fellowship—by which I mean are you a member of a congregation or, using a Buddhist term, are you a member of the "Sangha"—those who follow a Master and Universal Principles? (By the way, there is and will be no Master for eartHearts). How, if at all, does your membership in the Congregation/Group/Sangha bring you joy, harmony, and purity? Describe your experience in the Sangha or, if this is more pertinent to you, how you feel living outside of the Sangha. Explain how, if at all, having a Master, adhering to Dharma, and being a member of a congregation or a Sangha helps you deal with the Immanent and the Transcendent.

Follow-up Protocol

For best results, write down your impressions of this activity in your journal using the Heartwood Path Follow-up Protocol found in the Appendix. Afterwards, consider sharing your interpretations with others.

Heartwood Path Axioms

Key Assertions From Waypoint 2.19

2.19.1.

Moderate the transcendental with the immanent.

2.19.2.

According to the idea of the Great Chain of Being, reality is composed of the following interlocking (or nested) levels: matter; body, mind, Soul and Spirit.

2.19.3.

The gentle, hidden drive that causes the universe to envelope, encompass, integrate and transcend each link in the Great Chain of Being is Eros.

Nocturnal Pilgrimage 2.19

For best results, write down your impressions of each night's dreams in your journal using the Heartwood Path Dreaming Time Protocols found in the Appendix. Afterwards, consider sharing your Dream Tending with others.

Talk to your Dream Figures again, asking them to comment on how well you are adhering to universal truths. Notice how you feel about the response you receive. Talking to Dream Figures is a way to animate your Dream Characters. Recognize Dream Characters as living beings that reside in your dreams. Such animation allows you to easily have revealing ongoing conversations with helpful and powerful advisors. Doing so fulfills the suggestion of the component of our After Dreaming Protocol, entitled "Hillman's Approach."

While not ignoring the approaches of Freud and Jung, Hillmans' suggestion to animate your Dream Characters is the main way eart-Hearts gain meaning from their Dream Characters, especially those who seem to represent the eartHearts' chosen natural beings.

Having done some dream animation, continue down the Heartwood Path by moving to the next waypoint: "Rich Interpretations." There, you will discover a way to interpret your More-Than-Individual, compound Self.

20

Rich Interpretations

MAKE RICH INTERPRETATIONS
OF YOUR SACRED COMPOUND SELF

The making of interpretations means to come to an understanding, an explanation, and a knowing. I shall define "rich interpretations" as something other than beliefs. Rich interpretations occur after careful observations and analysis. They agree with reason.

It is important to distinguish between believing and knowing. In this book, I shall present very few beliefs. All will be labeled as such. Even matters of faith need not here be followed out of conjecture, because they come from the words of old sages, or because the subject matter is handed down through the generations. Faith can have a basis in reason. Revered texts such as the Bible are used here because, being tested over time, they have proven to be useful to people.

Interpreting the world richly, as described above, is a way to add to one's sense of oneness. Conversely, being duped to accept false claims separates you from the truth and, therefore, diminishes your integrity. The next waypoint helps one guard against such false assertions.

Decipher Your More-Than-Individual Nature...

HumaNatureConnect Activity

Start-up Protocol

If this is not a day when you prefer to spend time in nature without an agenda, do the Heartwood Path Start-up Protocol found in the Appendix. Then return here to do the remaining portion of this activity:

Interpreting Your Compound Self

For this activity, write down in your journal how well you adhere to Buddhism's Ten Good Precepts:

— three that are physical: 1) not killing, 2) not stealing, and 3) not engaging in improper sexual conduct;

— four that are verbal: 4) not lying, 5) not backbiting (talking negatively about someone secretly), 6) not speaking evil words, 7) not speaking frivolously; and

— three that are mental: 8) not being greedy, 9) having no anger, and 10) not having deviant views (those that would mess up your karma)."

Write down your rich interpretations about your adherence to the Ten Good Precepts. Be sure to avoid expressing beliefs about yourself. Record only the results of careful observations and analysis.

Follow-up Protocol

For best results, write down your impressions of this activity in your journal using the Heartwood Path Follow-up Protocol found in the Appendix. Afterwards, consider sharing your interpretations with others.

Heartwood Path Axioms

Key Assertions From Waypoint 2.20

2.20.1.

Make rich interpretations of your sacred compound self.

2.20.2.

Rich interpretations, which agree with reason, occur after careful observation, analysis.

2.20.3.

Accepting false claims of separation diminishes one's integrity.

2.20.4.

A good life comes to those who follow Buddhism's Ten Good Precepts: do not kill, do not steal, do not engage in improper sexual conduct, do not lie, do not backbite, do not speak evil words, do not speak frivolously, do not be greedy, do not have anger, and do not have views that mess up your karma.

Nocturnal Pilgrimage 2.20

For best results, write down your impressions of each night's dreams in your journal using the Heartwood Path Dreaming Time Protocols found in the Appendix. Afterwards, consider sharing your Dream Tending with others.

Talk to your Dream Figures again, asking them to evaluate and discuss with you how you are doing with the previously-mentioned Ten Good Precepts. Notice how you feel about the response you receive.

After talking to your Council of Dream Characters about your adherence or lack of adherence to the Ten Good Precepts, continue down the Heartwood Path by moving to the next waypoint: "Bona Fide."

21

"Bona Fide"

TEST THE VALIDITY OF CLAIMS

We all need to know whether what we experience is sincere, true, and appropriate. Sometimes we fall off course in our lives because we seek claims of truth where claims of appropriateness are more fruitful, or because we seek claims of sincerity where claims of truth are what really matters. There is, for example, no point in testing the truth of my claims of intentions when it is my claims of sincerity that are telling. In the same way, there is less to gain by testing the validity claims of behaviors in terms of appropriateness when the truth of the behaviors is a more useful test. The test for ethical claims is not a matter of truth or sincerity, but of appropriateness.

Testing the validity of personal assumptions and the claims presented to us by others requires an understanding of the four major aspects of Oneness described previously. Each realm has its own criterion for testing the validity of claims (the expressed soundness of what is planned, said, done, or claimed): sincerity is the criterion for testing claims in the realm of intentions; truth for the realm of behaviors and for the realm of physical fit of systems and collective behaviors (in each of these exterior realms oral or visual "maps/models" need to match the territory, for example); and appropriateness is the criterion for testing claims for the realm of ethics and morals. Keep these criterion in mind whenever you test the validity of a claim, both in and outside of the Heartwood Path.

To Valid Assertions...

HumaNatureConnect Activity

Start-up Protocol

If this is not a day when you prefer to spend time in nature without an agenda, do the Heartwood Path Start-up Protocol found in the Appendix. Then return here to do the remaining portion of this activity:

Testing The Validity Of Claims

For this activity, consider the three ways to test validity: sincerity, truthfulness, and appropriateness.

For sincerity, consider whether you give for your own sake. To give for the sake of others is a way to develop (or display) an important ingredient of your compound, higher self. Do you give only to look virtuous? Do you give for the sake of your own liberation or to attain Nirvana? Does your giving display the virtues of your Higher Self? If so, write down how you give as a true bodhisattva (benevolent person) would, that is, for the sake of others. In this journal writing, here are some things to consider: explain how you do, or do not, deny your virtues in giving nor pay attention to them; explain how, if at all, your giving provides happiness or alleviates suffering; explain how, if at all, you give in person, in slowly increasing amounts, until it hurts (this requires some getting used to) but not to the extent that it will test your patience unduly nor cause you considerable hardship or aggravation and not if the request is harmful or embarrassing to the receiver in some way.

For truth, there is much for you to ponder and write down. Here are some key elements for you to consider: Explain how, that in this moment, you understand or do not understand what is meant in Buddhism that "all things are without an inherent nature" and "indescribableness" is the ultimate nature of all things" (Yin-shun, 1998, p. 307). If these statements are true then there is no distortion and they reflect what is real. Can you see how any thing that is considered deeply, that is inspected carefully, and that is faithfully described is both true and partial? Can a thing be true and described completely? Can it be untrue and described in part? Can it be untrue and described completely? What aspect of the true world do you find most important? Buddha suggests suffering, accumulation, extinction, and the Way as the Four Noble Truths (described subsequently). Using his model, consider now the truth of your own suffering. Describe how you do or do not have what you desire. Describe how you suffer over being with those you dislike. Describe how you suffer from being apart from those you love. Describe how you suffer from being born, being old, being sick, or being terminally ill. Is suffering the real truth of your life, is it the whole truth of your life, or is the suffering in your life both true and partial? How, if at all, is your suffering caused by the accumulation of greed, desires, ignorance, and anger. How, if at all, is your suffering dependent on the origination of such accumulations? Describe how past causes (pick any of the accumulations such as anger, or clinging to desires) have engendered a present effect. Next, look at what Buddha means by "extinction." He is referring to the end of ignorance about the importance of understanding the nonexistence of the self and the end of attachment to things, falsehoods, and greedy desires. Describe how, if at all, getting rid of greedy desires in your life could liberate your mind and result in the end or reduction of suffering. How, if at all, could detaching from the accumulations of desires and falsehoods eliminate or reduce suffering in your life? Write down specifics.

For appropriateness, the test for validity is not solely within yourself. It rests in your culture. Write the answers to the following questions in your journal: Does your culture develop language and interactive skills that promote mutual understanding? Does your culture promote justness? How well is your culture doing about the business of devoting and living by morals and ethics? Do you know and always follow the common law? In what ways would you support or engage in civil disobedience? In what ways, if any, do you see yourself in others? How does seeing yourself in others in your life promote concern and care—two hallmarks of appropriateness?

In this query about testing for claims in the realms of sincerity, truth, and appropriateness, we have stumbled into the use of three of Buddha's Four Noble Truth's. Given what it has taken to answer the questions for this activity, I am sure you will be happy to leave our discussion of Buddha's Fourth Noble Truth—"The Way"—to the next activity.

Follow-up Protocol

For best results, write down your impressions of this activity in your journal using the Heartwood Path Follow-up Protocol found in the Appendix. Afterwards, consider sharing your interpretations with others.

Heartwood Path Axioms

Key Assertions From Waypoint 2.21

2.21.1.

Test the validity of claims.

2.21.2.

Testing the validity of personal assumptions and the claims presented to us by others requires an understanding of the four major aspects of Oneness.

2.21.3.

Sincerity is the criterion for testing claims in the realm of intentions, *truth* for the realm of behaviors and the physical fit of systems, and *appropriateness* for the realm of ethics and morals.

Nocturnal Pilgrimage 2.21

For best results, write down your impressions of each night's dreams in your journal using the Heartwood Path Dreaming Time Protocols found in the Appendix. Afterwards, consider sharing your Dream Tending with others.

After such a long waypoint it may be necessary to sleep before continuing. Continue to amplify your dreams, use the dream-vivifying linguistic tools, and practice being a good host to your living Dream Characters. Enjoy your deepening relationship to these characters. Do not lead the image. Remain open to the spontaneity of the conversation. Watch for any surprises. If you see value in the relationship, construct a Dream Figure and ask it the two most important and helpful questions, as recommended in the component of the After Dreaming Protocol titled "Right Information:" "Who is visiting now?" and "What is happening here?" You will be reminded to ask these two critical questions over and over again.

After tending to your dreams, continue to the next waypoint: "All-embracing Principles." There, you will learn of the importance of being the change you seek for the world.

22

All-embracing Principles

KNOW THE HERMETIC PRINCIPLES

Hermeticism, also called **Hermetism,** is a religious, philosophical, and esoteric tradition based of the writings of Hermes Trismegistus. Meaning "Thrice Great," Trismegistus is variously said to be a syncretism (amalgramation) of various schools of thought, the son of the Greek god Hermes, the son of the Egyptian god Thoth, a man who lived at the time of Moses, and, in the Third Century A.D, the author of the seven Hermetic Principles. Considered the source of the "greatest natural laws," the Hermetic Principles are said to govern our material and spiritual life. While their exact origin is unclear, the Hermetic Principles have stood the test of time and are thought to have had a significant influence over the development of the tenets of all of the worlds major religions. Knowing these principles will give you profound insights into the deeper spiritual nature of reality. You can avoid being a victim of your own ignorance by memorizing the seven Hermetic Principles. Here, now, are the most significant influences over the Greater Self:

Universal Principle # 1:

107

"All is mind."

By including this first Hermetic Principle I am not saying that everything is just a figment of one's imagination. Matter exists. But the importance of the imagination cannot be discounted. As Henry David Thoreau says,

"The world

is but a canvas

of our imagination."

The two main points here are: 1) all matter has some level of consciousness and 2) the mind evokes order out of physical creation. Says Wallace Stevens: "Reality is not what it is. It consists of the many realities which it can be made into" (Sewall, 1999, p. 22).

The consciousness of ideas is the basic element of reality. As you will discover as you continue down the Heartwood Path, too much of what has to be understood to grow, evolve, energize, and help others as an eartHeart cannot be explained through materialism or idealism. Throughout the Heartwood Path a third tradition, that of panpsychism, will be employed.

Panpsychism—a theory that all nature has a psychic aspect—balances the problems left by materialism and idealism. Materialism, in part, means that physical matter is the only reality. But bodies without minds are too brutish. Idealism is a theory that regards reality as essentially spiritual or an embodiment of the mind. But minds without bodies are too ethereal. Panpsychism transcends this duality through the integration of mind and body. Such integration is a better way to understand the nature of all nature—a word used over and over again along the Heartwood Path and, therefore, ought to be carefully define. Nature, when it is spelled with the first letter in lower case, means essential character, prompting force, things exclusive of mental, opposite of state of grace; the unregenerate soul; a state preceding the foundation of organized society; a thing that is not made, perfected or ordered by humans; natural scenery; and the aspect found out-of doors. When I begin the spelling of "Nature" in upper case I am referring to Nature as a singular sentient being, which is scientifically debatable, but consistent with the felt experiences and perspectives of many people. The nature of any aspect of the world is manipulated by the way we look at the world, by what we see.

Here we shall explore a basic premise of this book, that we create a future by the way we think and that we evoke the material world through the way we think. If one wants to protect the environment or improve oneself, it is one's thinking that will begin to do the job.

"We are a landscape of all we have seen" writes Laura Sewall.

"In an immediate and active sense, we are integrators, mixing and matching the complexity of each past moment with new incoming signals. In do doing, by focusing our attention on this moment or the next, on this flower or that item, we are creators of self and world. In other words, we choose—and thus we become" (1999, p. 266).

The consciousness of ideas is the basic element of reality. Instead of positing that everything, including consciousness, is made of matter; everything, including matter, exists in and is manipulated from consciousness. Matter is real, but secondary to consciousness. It is, therefore, very important to recognize what enters into your awareness. It is not what you look at that matters. One can look at a lot of things without ever paying any significant attention to them. It is rather what you see that counts.

According to a fundamental tenet of quantum theory, the nature of reality—and probably "being-ness" itself—can be described as having the dual qualities of a particle (like individual billiard balls on a table) and a wave like (undulations on the surface of the sea). The greater hidden aspect behind all reality is not that matter is either a wave or a particle. To be is to be both. Observers evoke what is already there by the way their consciousness directs them to perceive it (although I'd like to, I can't turn wave packets of macaroni and cheese into snow cones, for example).

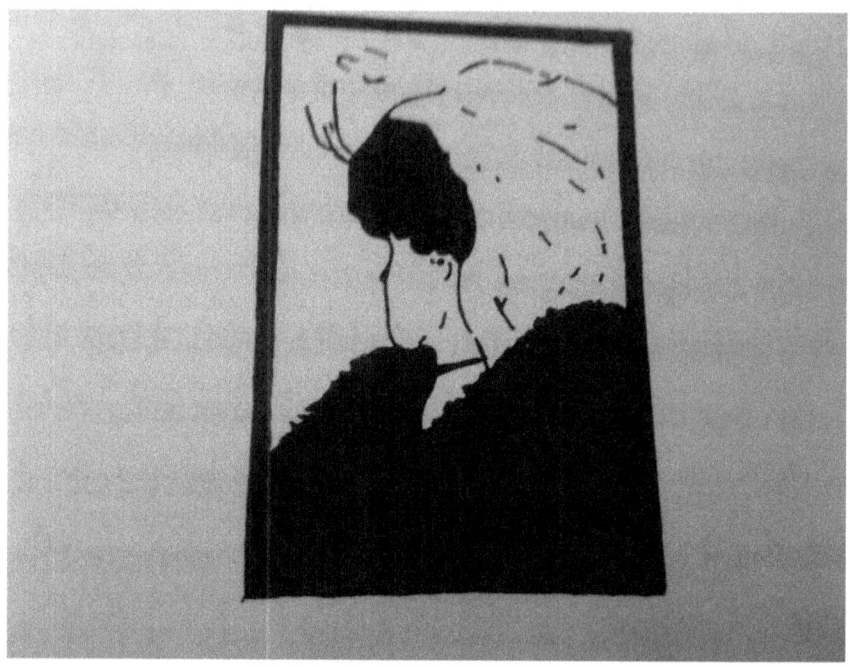

You may have seen the popular line drawing, shown above, of a woman who, depending on how you choose to view her, looks either like an ugly old woman or a beautiful young woman. Just as light has dual aspects (waves and particles) that collapse upon observation and choice, these pictures have simultaneous dual aspects that are revealed only after observation and choice. The process of evoking manifestation is something like this.

EartHearts seek to evoke a better picture, in part, by putting more attention into what and how they see, by truly seeing nature, for example, and by choosing to help others join them in conservation activities. EartHearts seek to change themselves and influence others so that more psycho-spiritually developed minds are evoking the best possible future. Right actions become prevalent and automatic when one achieves the higher levels of consciousness.

A good way to determine if the action is for good or bad (evil) is to assess whether it serves others. Evil things do not serve others. If it glorifies the Absolute, serves the greater good, and serves other individuals without harming anyone else, it is good.

When we view "doing good" as both a practice for the Self and as a service for others this action is "Karma yoga"—the path of service. This is one of three paths used to shift identity. The other two are the path of illuminating the intellect with intelligence and the pathway of mystical sexuality. The Heartwood Path overlies, includes, and connects all of these identity-shifting methods.

The way to become an exalted being from which appropriate actions flow—certainly a goal suitable for those who traverse the Heartwood Path—involves a three-step process:

Step One: practice action without coveting the particular result of the action. Such coveting programs one's brain-mind and creates a type of psychological conditioning that interferes with creativity because the mental sampling of all possibilities is limited.

Step Two: act in service to the Absolute. This means to love God or the Absolute through loving the Self, through service itself, through friends, through family, and through an intimate companion in ways too numerous to mention here but described in the Heartwood Path for Couples (**Eros**) book.

Step Three: become the agency of appropriate action and not a subject working on an object. This means one ought to focus on the appropriateness of the action more than on oneself or on the object of one's good deed.

There is no distance between the spiritual realm and Nature. Nature wears the hues of the Spirit. The Spirit is the sentience and creative activity of all matter and energy. Nature is both a "thing" of matter and energy and a "spirit" which is the animating force within physical existence that operates through feelings, processes, interactions, and relatedness. The Spirit also exists beyond the natural world of space and time. It is by tapping into the boundless and timeless realm of the Spirit that one can expand consciousness enough to make, ultimately, cosmic connections. Once one sees and feels the whole, sympathy for global ecological restoration naturally follows. Still, as we shall see, fear often blocks the way to sufficient action.

There are many reasons why people hold themselves captive in their limited individual consciousness and, therefore, inhibit their motivation for environmental (and other forms of) action. Most of these reasons are various forms of fear.

Overcoming these fears, both within themselves and amongst the population at large, is a crucial endeavor for eartHearts. Fear is a negative emotion that blocks the portal to the Soul. It also tends to limit or prevent one's ability to sustain actions that would restore the Earth's ecological integrity.

Fortunately, there are principles eartHearts can use to trade fear for empowerment:

1. feelings of pain for our world are natural and healthy and not to experience pain would be a sign of moral atrophy;
2. the pain of fear is morbid only if denied (once we allow ourselves to experience fear it floats away);
3. it is more about fear of involvement than it is about lack of information that prevents our own empowerment regarding working to solve ecological issues; and
4. catharsis—the figurative cleansing of the emotions—occurs when we repress our distress by experiencing it and letting it float away.

There is much to do to make modern culture a part of the solution rather than a part of the problem. Improvements are needed in the cultural arena because its "organs" do not have the prerequisite "boundless heart." The cultural arena is, therefore, presently inadequate for the task of securing human and global survival. To help correct this inadequacy, start by working on yourself and work outward from there. The following Hermetic Principle will explain how improving the person will affect the culture.

Universal Principle # 2:

"As within, so without; as above, so below."

The integration of the individual, the culture, and Nature is the big challenge for today and tomorrow. It is vitally important that there be an integration of the interiority of the subjective world of each individual with the exteriority of the objective world of Nature—an integration of the noosphere (Ego) with the biosphere (Eco).

This integration is a goal of those who follow the Heartwood Path. The journey on the Heartwood Path combines the Ego, the Eco, the Theo (the Spirit) and the Ero (sexuality). By "Ero" I mean the Great Life Force, the most fundamental way the Spirit is expressed in the biosphere.

This Great Life Force, also known as "prana" or "chi" is like a cosmic libido. Chi is our link to the universe; the glue between our body, mind and Spirit; the link between our perceptions of the inner and outer world.

The concept of "as within, so without; as above, so below" means that through the Great Life Force the whole universe is contained in both the inner and outer realms of the individual. The main point to be derived from this Hermetic principle is to be the change you seek for the world.

Universal Principle # 3:

"All is in vibration."

We live in a world that is pulsing. Each individual component rocks in time with everything else. Thus, the universe is a "rhythmscape." As we shall see, this vibration is musical and the universe is more like music than like matter. Chaos is brought to order by the three components of music: rhythm, which creates concordance out of divergence;

melody, which exacts continuity upon the disconnected; and harmony, which imposes unity upon the incompatible.

Rhythms create concordance out of divergence because Nature is efficient and takes the course that requires less energy. If two rhythms are nearly the same and their sources are in proximity the two similar and close-by rhythms will entrain—that is, fall into synchrony. The bobbing of heads and the urge to dance when people are exposed closely to rhythmic music are examples of bodily entrainment. Additionally, the cortex allows humans to use rhythm for work, communication, war, play and access to the world of the Spirit.

Those who seek to beat on the doors of the higher domains often "ride their drums" beyond the humdrum. The rhythms they create drive them to the margin of magic. Performing in this way is truly pounding on the rim of enchantment.

Music attains universal order through fundamental relationships of geometrical and mathematical proportion. Through these relationships music becomes the blueprint of life and the universe. Sound moves and changes what it contacts. This affect is caused by the influence of sonic vibrations, also known as sympathetic vibration or resonance— the ability of a vibration to reach out through waves to set off a similar vibration in another body.

When one listens to music one can transcend the chasm that seems to create pervasive separation. Music helps one shift out of a mental state of fragmentation into a state of wholeness.

It is very important that you understand "resonance" as it is defined here because this fact of nature will be applied often in the activities that follow. For our purposes here, "resonance" will be defined as a sympathetic vibration, one that elicits a greater sense of integration or oneness between one natural being and another. Later in this book series, you will be asked over and over to make a sound that allows you to feel a sense of oneness to one or more attractive natural beings. In doing so, you will become less reliant on words and rational cognition and more open to guidance conveyed—by a host of natural senses—

from natural beings. In our culture, skepticism about such invisible unity-producing waves is commonplace and cannot be dispelled very effectively through written words. Uncertainty about such matters can best be eliminated by sensing and interpreting the resonate vibrations perceived while doing the kind of activities that will begin midway through Heartwood Path Book Four.

For eartHearts, it simply will not be enough to allow the eyes to take them into the world; they need to learn to truly use the ears so that the world can come into them. On the elaborate journey from sounding to resonating—that is, from the making of a sonic vibration to the perceiving the auditory energy—sound provides a connection between the source of the sound and the perceiver of the sound. On this journey sound changes form, moves between the realms of Exteriority and Interiority, and begins as a vibration of matter and ends as a vibration with meaning. In this way, listening makes matter, well... matter (mean something).

Universal Principle # 4:

"Everything is dual."

Here we take the next crucial step down the Heartwood Path by discussing what at first seems to be topics that contradict the fourth Hermetic principle: positive and negative charges and the Taoist ideas of yin and yang. Substance without motivation is inert mass; motivation without substance has nothing tangible to motivate. You cannot, therefore, understand or do anything with yin without yang. Together, like front is to back, they are differing aspects of one.

Universal Principle # 5:

"Everything flows."

Those who traverse the Heartwood Path will discover that when a person achieves some depth to his or her psycho/spiritual development there is a substantial increased flow of energy, creativity, and purposefulness from the universe to the individual and vise versa. This flow helps the individual continue to develop psycho/spiritually and makes the individual more competent in fulfilling his or her cosmic assignment—which, for humans, is helping the universe become self-aware, unfold faster, develop more extensively, and evolve in a way that is beneficial for all. This assignment is accomplished by the pivotal role humans play in the cosmic scheme of things.

Called the "Participatory Anthropic Principle" by physicists and those who study the origins of the universe, this role is bestowed on humans because we are a species that is highly developed mentally, spiritually, physically, and culturally. According to this principle, the ability to observe consciously enables humans to evoke reality.

What humans think about comes about. Materialization, therefore, depends on human visualization. Made in God's image, humans have the capacity to create. Your ability to make conscious choices places a special responsibility on your shoulders: you help to manifest the future. With this responsibility, you need to be the best person you can be.

The collective evocation of reality depends on the particular talents and skills of each participating individual. Since we all participate in this assignment, it is very important to the future of the world that each individual be as effective, resourceful, and insightful as possible. The Heartwood Path helps people advance in their personal development, fulfill their cosmic assignment, and include a conservation ethic into the act of unfolding reality—both as a way to foster personal psycho/spiritual development and happiness and as a way to evoke a more tolerable planet.

Universal Principle # 6:

"Everything happens according to law."

The idea that everything is determined in advance and is, in principle, predictable has largely given way to the ideas of indeterminism. The Absolute may have determined the overall invisible plan but it takes humans to think that plan into reality. Through observation, meditation, and prayer humans can determine the Absolute's laws and, if it is the will of the Absolute, evoke reality according to the way humans consciously observe.

The cold atoms of Newtonian physics have in the minds of knowing people dissolved into warm structures of rhythmic activity. Even the laws of Nature may not be eternally fixed. They may be evolving along with Nature.

Universal Principle # 7:

"Everything has its masculine and feminine aspects."

The differences between masculinity and femininity are not dependent on men and women. Culture determines a person's gender, just as biology determines a person's sex. Women can exhibit masculine characteristics just as men can exhibit feminine characteristics. Along with the masculine aspects of virility, strength and aggression, revere and respect the feminine aspects of creation: value, for example, the Mother Earth, creativity, respecting unique differences, relaxing, rejoicing, intuiting, receiving, feeling, Eros, women, and a woman's point of view.

Unlike the seven previous topics, the following important notion is not a Hermetic Principle. It has been stated briefly and differently earlier in this book, but deserves elaboration. It is a defining principle of the Heartwood Path and a worthy, time-tested, universal truth:

Universal Principle # 8:

Be the change you seek for the world.

To seek changes in the world, change yourself. To make sure you make the best possible changes, establish the intention of being a success—both for yourself and for others.

As with the Universal Principles discussed above, the following success principles only work for you if you work on them: Determine what will drive your economic engine. Focus on what you can do better than anyone else. Do what brings you joy. Mind your English. Do your homework. Care. And, importantly, give thanks for everything you receive. Gratitude is one way to recognize that the Absolute is in your Greater Self.

Stop blaming external circumstances for your unhappiness. Circumstances do not make a person. Circumstances reveal a person.

Let go of all attachments to the past as excuses for how you live today. Blame is the result of looking ungratefully to the past. Remove blaming from your vocalizations.

To The Implementation Of Tenets That Lead To Favorable Outcomes…

HumaNatureConnect Activity

Start-up Protocol

If this is not a day when you prefer to spend time in nature without an agenda, do the Heartwood Path Start-up Protocol found in the Appendix. Then return here to do the remaining portion of this activity:

Applying Universal Principles And Success Principles To Your Life

In the previous activity we addressed the first three of the four components of Buddha's Fourfold Truths (suffering, accumulation, extinction,) that will bring happiness to your life. Here we will address the fourth Noble Truth. It is called "The Way"—Buddha's Eight-fold Path. "The Way" tells you what you need to do to alleviate suffering and, thereby, promote happiness in your world or in the world of those close to you. Now is your chance to assess what aspects of your life need more attention. For each of the "rights" listed below, write down in your journal your answer to the associated question:

1. right understanding—do you have the right concepts and ideas?
2. right thought—do you have the right differentiations, determinations, awareness, and intentions?
3. right speech—do you have the right words of truth, compassion, praise and altruism?
4. right action— do you have actions that protect life, display compassion, and offer charity?
5. right livelihood—do you have a moral occupation?
6. right effort—do your exertions display diligence, skill, courage, and care?
7. right mindfulness (sole attention to the present)—do you have a mind that is pure, aware, focuses on the present, and follows the right path? And
8. right concentration—do you have a concentrated mind that leads to peace and calmness?

Do not just answer "yes" or "no." Look over your answers and then describe how each of Buddha's aspects of "the Way" plays out in your world. Are you doing fairly well, or do you need to improve any of your endeavors? Write your answers in your journal.

Additionally, use the following format in your journal, over and over, until you feel ready to move on:

"Based on the universal principle of (list one from the discussion of Hermetic Principles in this waypoint) "_____." I will use an aspect of the Eightfold Path (circle one: right understanding, right thought, right speech, right action, right livelihood, right effort, right mindfulness (sole attention to the present), and right concentration in the following way (describe what you are going to do) _____ as a way to extinguish my unwanted accumulation of (enter a thing, a falsehood, a greedy desire, or an area of ignorance) and alleviate or eliminate my suffering over _____."

Follow-up Protocol

For best results, write down your impressions of this activity in your journal using the Heartwood Path Follow-up Protocol found in the Appendix. Afterwards, consider sharing your interpretations with others.

Heartwood Path Axioms

Key Assertions From Waypoint 2.22

2.22.1.

Know the Hermetic Principles: all is mind; as within, so without; as above, so below; all is in vibration; everything is dual; everything flows; everything happens according to law; and everything has its masculine and feminine principles.

2.22.2.

Reality consists of the many realities which it can be made into.

2.22.3.

Be the change you seek for the world.

2.22.4.

The ability to observe consciously enables humans to evoke reality.

2.22.5.

Follow the Eight-fold Path of right understanding, right thought, right speech, right action, right livelihood, right effort, right mindfulness (sole attention to the present), and right concentration as a way to extinguish any unwanted accumulation of things, falsehoods, greedy desires, and ignorance and to alleviate or eliminate suffering.

Nocturnal Pilgrimage 2.22

For best results, write down your impressions of each night's dreams in your journal using the Heartwood Path Dreaming Time Protocols found in the Appendix. Afterwards, consider sharing your Dream Tending with others.

Begin to use your senses more as you host your Dream Figure. If you are working with Otter, to use one of my Dream Figures as an example, imagine smelling its coat, hearing its call, seeing its pleasant face, and making contact with the living image in sensory ways. This will encourage Otter to become embodied and to begin to assert its autonomy. Sensually, pick out details. Allow it to become an individual, different from other otters. Notice everything you can.

Here's an important reminder before you move to the next waypoint: "Big View," where you will develop a vision worthy of the compound self. As stated in the component of the After Dreaming Protocol titled "The Richest Treasures": "Do not force narrow interpretations upon the natural being impressions that reappear in your dream by condensing them into limited signs when it is more fruitful to simply engage with them as living beings that reside in your dream, possibly with infinite symbolic value."

23

Big View

DEVELOP A VISION WORTHY OF YOUR COMPOUND SELF

It is possible to psychologically toss aside your body and feel as if you are everywhere. It is your Ego that makes you feel skeptical of such statements. Your Ego makes you feel limited by your body. It is your attachment to your body that is limiting you, not your body. Your body creates no barrier between you and the rest of reality. Even your skin is just a porous filter, and not a very good barrier. Your attachment to your body is a contrived blockade. The whole of existence is your body. It is not separate. Your body is really only the closest existence to you. It spreads out to all corners of the Earth—and beyond. When you get rid of your attachment to your individual body, you lose your psychological imprisonment and find that you are everywhere. This is a key task for those seeking to become happy.

When you psychologically surrender your individual self you find your Compound Self—your Sacred Self. This Compound Self is an Ecological Self or a self in relationship to other people, other beings, the Earth, and the universe. Human growth, happiness, healing, and fulfillment cannot be achieved without also healing all relations and the Earth. Humans have deep Earth-rooted-ness. We relate to each other and to the Earth as a whole. This profound connection is so pervasive the Earth can be seen as a lost dimension of the Self—a forgotten component of one's own complete, compound identity.

To heal—that is to make our selves whole, healthy, and holy—we as a species need to rediscover, befriend, and help save the earthy core of our own being. Spiritually speaking, to heal is to foster the return to a state of unity—that is, unity between not only one's mind, body, and Spirit but also between one's self, one's beloved, and one's environment.

There is an ecological base to one's personality. As an individual, one will never be whole if one does not pay attention to one's body, mind, Spirit, and relationship to the Earth. One needs to claim and enjoy one's energizing, life-enhancing, and nurturing connection to Nature—thus combine what is Human and what is Nature into what we call "humaNature." Dr. Cohen's methodologies are a good way to begin to foster such connectedness.

To further break down eco-alienation, a person needs to first identify the segment of the world in which she lives as a part of herself. By setting aside the "Ego-self," and replacing it with a more expansive and encompassing "Eco-Self"—that is, a sense of self connected deeply with all of life—one's understanding of what constitutes real self-interest will begin to include the protection, preservation, and restoration of the Earth. One of the best ways I have found to bring forth this Eco-self is to mentally paint a picture of yourself as being like a virtuous bodisvhissatva--an altruistic person capable of giving amply, wisely, and sustainably to others.

To See The Full Size Of Your Self...

HumaNatureConnect Activity

Start-up Protocol

If this is not a day when you prefer to spend time in nature without an agenda, do the Heartwood Path Start-up Protocol found in the Appendix. Then return here to do the remaining portion of this activity:

Visioning The Compound Self

For this activity, create a vision of yourself in your mind as if you were a person of great virtue. More specifically, you are in this vision of yourself a person who has taken a faith vow, a person of compassion, and a person of wisdom. Choose whatever vow suits you. The vow of a bodhisattva would be something like "I vow to save boundless sentient beings, to eliminate endless afflictions, and to learn innumerable doctrines." You may want to include as part of your vision of your Compound Self a picture of yourself in your mind giving in a way that is unattached--that is, being unattached to yourself as a giver, being unattached to the thing or service being given, and being unattached to the person receiving the gift. Concerning the aspect of your vision as a person of boundless compassion, picture yourself offering compassion without limits or boundaries. Write down ways you plan to become diligent in your giving. Concerning the attainment of wisdom, imagine yourself relying on the validity, soundness, and factualness of direct experience in nature. Consider using the direct experience of nature—as felt through your numerous natural senses—to gain wisdom. Additionally, meditate:

1. on human impurity as a way to counteract desire;
2. on compassion as a way to subdue anger;
3. on dependent origination (by which I mean "this causes that," such as birth causes aging, etc.);
4. on how to temper ignorance of the different realms (desire, form, and formlessness, for example);
5. on how to counteract arrogance; and

6. on how to be mindful to counteract excessive thinking or "scatteredness" of mind.

Look around you in nature. Contemplate how affects are originated by causes and how everything is impermanent. Write down how, if at all, such contemplations increased your wisdom.

Follow-up Protocol

For best results, write down your impressions of this activity in your journal using the Heartwood Path Follow-up Protocol found in the Appendix. Afterwards, consider sharing your interpretations with others.

Heartwood Path Axioms

Key Assertions From Waypoint 2.23

2.23.1.

One's body spreads out to all corners of the Earth—and beyond.

2.23.2.

The Earth can be seen as a lost dimension of the Self—a forgotten component of one's own complete, compound identity.

2.23.3.

Spiritually speaking, to heal is to foster the return to a state of unity—that is, unity between not only one's mind, body, and Spirit but also between one's self, one's beloved, and one's environment.

2.23.4.

Human growth, happiness, healing, and fulfillment cannot be achieved without also healing all relations and the Earth.

2.23.5.

One needs to claim and enjoy one's energizing, life-enhancing, and nurturing connection to Nature—thus combine what is Human and what is Nature into "humaNature."

Nocturnal Pilgrimage 2.23

For best results, write down your impressions of each night's dreams in your journal using the Heartwood Path Dreaming Time Protocols found in the Appendix. Afterwards, consider sharing your Dream Tending with others.

Your dreams are a richly expressive view of your private life. As such, it is best to keep them private. As stated in the component of our After Dreaming Protocol titled "Privacy:" "Store your dream journal in a safe place and, where appropriate, share your dream with others."

With this suggestion in mind, dream before visiting the next waypoint. Remember not to try to interrupt your dreams. Instead, bring them to life. After doing so, proceed to the next waypoint: "Rightness," where you will learn to be moral, not moralistic.

24

Rightness

BE MORAL, NOT MORALISTIC

Do not allow your vision or perspective to be too small and personal. Moralistic attitudes (which stem from moralism—undue emphasis on morality, the habit of moralizing) often occur in people who demonstrate signs of a constricted heart and who exploit morality as a way to repress desire, love, and longing. Moralism is a sign that Eros is being constrained. Moralism is a neurotic complex, a failed attempt to be moral, a set of attitudes and behaviors that leads to poor judgment and—ironically—an obsession for what is being denied. Yielding appropriately to temptation, therefore, is one way to get rid of unwanted enticements. Unlike moralism, morality leads to positive ethics and compassion, the latter being hard to give away because it always comes back.

To Tackle The Polarity Of Principles And Pontifications...

HumaNatureConnect Activity

Start-up Protocol

If this is not a day when you prefer to spend time in nature without an agenda, do the Heartwood Path Start-up Protocol found in the Appendix. Then return here to do the remaining portion of this activity:

Addressing The Difference Between Expressions Of Morality And Moralistic Expression

For this activity, look around to find examples, if any, of morality in animals or imagine an animal displaying morality—that is, chastity, virtue, or conformity to the rules of right conduct. Note that such examples of moral behavior do not require a belief in God unless you believe that animals have a belief in God or the Absolute. Morality, whether in animals or people, is shown by praise, condemnation, reward, and punishment. Moral actions, human or otherwise, are done to alter the dispositions of other members of the group. Examples in nature of condemnation include such things as the bearing one's teeth, making aggressive sounds, taking a threatening posture, displaying telltale facial expressions, or ignoring the perpetrator in a particular context. Punishments can sometimes inflict harm on the perpetrator. Lessons are not taught only to the perpetrator but also to all the other members of the community witnessing the corrective actions. In morality, actions can be like the metaphorical punishing "stick—a punishment—or they may be more like the metaphorical reward of the metaphorical "carrot—a reward." Rewards can take the form of grooming, sharing food, and allowing sex to those who exhibit behavior that the animal in question has an interest in promoting. Witness mammal's facial expressions or friendly gestures and you may be looking at a form of praise. It communicates to all witnesses that the behavior is welcomed and appreciated. Such antics of animals seem to portray an attempt to induce or enforce a type of morality, primitive and wordless. Without any apparent belief in God, wild animals seem to set up a moral system. These "carrots" and "sticks" seem to be purely natural facts that seem to promote or inhibit certain actions in others.

In your journal write down whether you think animals sometimes enforce natures' version of a code of morality. Is there, in your opinion, a code or codes of acceptable behavior in the wild? Do you think that such codes can exist without there being also a belief in God? Is your opinions about animal morality--pro or con--an example of you responding to animals' morality or lack of morality in a moralistic way? Does your opinions about animal morality have anything to do with your acceptance or rejection of using animals as models for your own behavior? Are humans so different from animals that nothing we see them do is instructive? What is the pertinence of such discussions?

Follow-up Protocol

For best results, write down your impressions of this activity in your journal using the Heartwood Path Follow-up Protocol found in the Appendix. Afterwards, consider sharing your interpretations with others.

Heartwood Path Axioms

Key Assertions From Waypoint 2.24

2.24.1.

Moralistic attitudes (which stem from moralism) often occur in people who demonstrate signs of a constricted heart and who exploit morality as a way to repress desire, love, and longing.

2.24.2.

A sign that Eros is being constrained, moralism is a neurotic complex, a failed attempt to be moral, a set of attitudes and behaviors that leads to poor judgment and—ironically—an obsession for what is being denied.

2.24.3.

Yielding appropriately to temptation, therefore, is one way to get rid of unwanted enticements.

2.24.4.

Unlike moralism, morality leads to positive ethics and compassion, the latter being hard to give away because it always comes back.

Nocturnal Pilgrimage 2.24

For best results, write down your impressions of each night's dreams in your journal using the Heartwood Path Dreaming Time Protocols found in the Appendix. Afterwards, consider sharing your Dream Tending with others.

Sleep before visiting the next waypoint. Dream and tend to your dreams. This time notice not only the details of the Dream Character but also what the imaginal character is doing to you. "What do you notice about your own body experience? Write down your findings in as much detail as possible, as well as your reflections about them," writes Aizenstat (2009, p. 46).

To take the next step down the Heartwood Path, move to the next waypoint: "Leniency." There, you will discover the value of mercy over judgmental condemnations. Prepare to raise your own standards of acceptance.

25

Leniency

SHOW MERCY TO OTHERS

Displaying mercy is one of the best ways to practice being moral. Mercy keeps you focused on what you are for rather than on what you are against. Rather than being against starvation, through mercy you feed the hungry, for example. Mercy encourages you to find loving solutions rather than angry reactions. It helps you rectify affronts rather than exacting retributions.

The next time you have the opportunity, seek justice but temper it by forgiving someone whom you could punish. Practice leniency by relieving the suffering of someone you dislike. As you do such things notice how mercy triumphs over judgement. Start with yourself. Give yourself compassion for past actions. When facing injustice, state how you feel and then let it go. When you speak of your wrath your wrath will end.

To Leniency...

HumaNatureConnect Activity

Start-up Protocol

If this is not a day when you prefer to spend time in nature without an agenda, do the Heartwood Path Start-up Protocol found in the Appendix. Then return here to do the remaining portion of this activity:

Showing Mercy To Others

Look around you to determine if you can see more acts of mercy than judgmental condemnations. In your experience, are animals in nature more merciful, judgmental, both, or neither? Write down your answer in your journal. Next, think about how someone has wronged you or did something that you find difficult to condone. Think of this wrongdoing not as the wickedness that comes from bad intentions (because there are none) but as an error-in-practice, a misstep as one attempts to do right but fails. If you are having difficulty allowing mercy to triumph over judgement then focus not so much on the wrongdoing but on your own inability to find forgiveness, or on relieving the suffering, or on understanding the root cause(s) of the poorly chosen act(s). There are always understandable antecedents that cause unfortunate behaviors. It is your job to find them. Do not merely punish someone for a wrongdoing. Focus instead on root causes rather than on the poor behaviors. Work hardest on finding the mercy within yourself. Work on raising your own standards of acceptance, never by condoning bad acts, but rather by focusing on putting mercy over judgement. After a bad act, love the offender anyway. Forgive. Seek to relieve the suffering that is likely to be behind the bad action(s). Never expect rapid changes in behavior. If necessary, remove yourself from harm's way. Be patient and allow your own suffering over the bad actions to, persistently, give way to service. It is an act of faith to assume that there will be unexpected positive surprises ahead. When they occur, acknowledge them and offer praise. I started such a process on 12/12/12 and by 12/21/12 it truly seemed like the dawning of a new world. I can now let bygones be bygones. See if repeating these steps opens up a new world for you. These are the ways to exercise your mercy muscle and to launch a new era. Write in your journal how you will show mercy to a difficult someone. Keep the comments above in mind or try some mercy-building of your own. Then write down the results in your journal, focusing more on how you improved yourself and less on how you judged the "offender."

Follow-up Protocol

For best results, write down your impressions of this activity in your journal using the Heartwood Path Follow-up Protocol found in the Appendix. Afterwards, consider sharing your interpretations with others.

Heartwood Path Axioms

Key Assertions From Waypoint 2.25

2.25.1.

Displaying mercy is one of the best ways to practice being moral.

2.25.2.

Mercy keeps you focused on what you are for rather than on what you are against.

2.25.3.

Mercy encourages one to find loving solutions rather than angry reactions.

2.25.4.

Mercy helps you rectify affronts rather than exacting retributions.

2.25.5.

Seek to relieve the suffering that is likely to be behind bad actions.

Nocturnal Pilgrimage 2.25

For best results, write down your impressions of each night's dreams in your journal using the Heartwood Path Dreaming Time Protocols found in the Appendix. Afterwards, consider sharing your Dream Tending with others.

Be sure to maintain your nocturnal pilgrimage as you proceed down the Heartwood Path. By attending each evening to the Nocturnal Pilgrimage sections at each waypoint, you will discover wisdom and guidance that will change your life for the better.

Dream before moving forward. Continue to practice dream tending, as instructed. When ready, move to the waypoint: "Ideals."

26

Ideals

SPREAD TOUGH ETHICS, THEN SEEK WAYS TO PREVENT HAVING TO ACT ON THEM

Abraham Lincoln said: "As our case is new, we (have to) think and act anew. We (have to) disenthrall ourselves…" That is precisely what I hope to do here: help the course participant become disenthralled with some commonly held ethical assertions and help the course participant replace certain outmoded and discredited views with new ways of seeing, thinking, being, and acting.

Great improvements in deeds require great changes of mind. We may think that we are entitled to grow richer, consume more, and generate large amounts of waste. Such thinking leads to problems. Nature will show us that we cannot grow as a species indefinitely. Everyone causes resource depletion.

The world's ecosystem cannot support the consequences of our old line of thinking. Even the human right to reproduce without limits is questionable when such a right contributes to ecological collapse. The sooner we humans limit our reproduction through voluntary personal decisions based on individual intentions the less likely it is that we will all be subjected to involuntary social controls based on collective rules or laws.

Actual factual consequences of our old line of thinking will determine the viability of old-time moral and ethical codes. Actual consequences can nullify value judgments.

Moral theories that lead to ecological demise are counterproductive. Any ethic is doomed if its practice causes those who live by it to perish and take their cherished moral notions with them.

To The Dictates Of Conscience...

HumaNatureConnect Activity

Start-up Protocol

If this is not a day when you prefer to spend time in nature without an agenda, do the Heartwood Path Start-up Protocol found in the Appendix. Then return here to do the remaining portion of this activity:

Pertaining To You, Principles, And Tough Ethics

For this activity, look around for examples of the following principles in nature: oneness, dynamic balance, cyclical growth, and harmonious action. Then, look for examples of the following six ethical subjects in your chosen natural scene or in your memories from your own life: selflessness, moderation, embracing the mystery, non-contrivance (best summarized as a warning about consciously manipulated morality), detachment, and humility.

By reading the results of juxtaposing the principles to the ethic and by recording examples of your own related experiences or ideas, this exercise will be both systematically broad and comprehensive yet reflective of your own unique experiences and ideas.

1. The principle of oneness, when juxtaposed to the topic of self-lessness leads to the following nature-based ethic, that: ***it is best to keep your attention on the greater whole.*** Add your own related ethic, experience, or idea. *This juxtaposition of principles and ethics reminds me, for example of a dilemma I have faced numerous times: should I keep myself largely anonymous as a way to keep from making the issues about me and as a way to protect my family from the retributions often faced my activists or should I openly assume a leadership position knowing that more people will follow a leader than will follow a cause. I offer no answer here and mention this dilemma to provide an example of the kinds of ideas suitable for inclusion in this activity.*

2. The principle of oneness, when juxtaposed to the topic of moderation leads to the following nature-based ethic, that: ***we ought to seek oneness, not "muchness."*** Add your own related ethic, experience, or idea. *A personal example: Given how good I feel about my conservation successes, successes that were good for the many, I cannot imagine ever seeking muchness more than oneness.*

3. The principle of oneness, when juxtaposed to the topic of embracing mystery leads to the following nature-based ethic, that **there is nowhere to run**. Add your own related ethic, experience, or idea. *A personal example, intended to help you with your own answers: A dream I had about my father the same night he suffered a fatal stroke, opened my eyes to the immediacy and ultimacy of the inner world. So powerful was this dream and it's timing, I had no choice but to learn as much as possible about the inner world.*

4. The principle of oneness, when juxtaposed to the topic of non-contrivance leads to the following nature-based ethic: that ***one ought to beware of consciously contrived morality.*** Add your own related ethic, experience, or idea. *Another personal example: I once had an unpleasant experience of leading a retreat where one of the participants took issue with me answering his probing by saying that*

the Heartwood Path helps people recollect their unity with the Absolute. He said there is only one God and would not want to participate with people who had not already found Him. I believe his contrived morality got in his way of finding a helpful path of transformation.

5. The principle of oneness, when juxtaposed to the topic of detachment leads to the following nature-based ethic, that: **two polarities override all of existence so clinging to one or the other leads to misunderstanding.** Add your own related ethic, experience, or idea.

6. The principle of oneness, when juxtaposed to the topic of humility leads to the following nature-based ethic, that: **one ought to remain detached from the outcome.** Add your own related ethic, experience, or idea.

7. The principle of dynamic balance, when juxtaposed to the topic of selflessness leads to the following nature-based ethic, that: **one ought to not think of oneself only this way or that way but a balance of opposing ways.** Add your own related ethic, experience, or idea.

8. The principle of dynamic balance, when juxtaposed to the topic of moderation leads to the following nature-based ethic, that: **one ought to balance individual agency with relating to the whole and the importance of the inner world as well as the outer world.** Add your own related ethic, experience, or idea.

9. The principle of dynamic balance, when juxtaposed to the topic of embracing mystery leads to the following nature-based ethic, that: **one ought not cling to fixed ideas, set plans, or rigid concepts.** Add your own related ethic, experience, or idea.

10. The principle of dynamic balance, when juxtaposed to the topic of non-contrivance leads to the following nature-based ethic, that: **stiff morals become unbalanced.** Add your own related ethic, experience, or idea.

11. The principle of dynamic balance, when juxtaposed to the topic of detachment leads to the following nature-based ethic, that: *life is a cycle and not a grand victory or a grand loss.* Add your own related ethic, experience, or idea.

12. The principle of dynamic balance, when juxtaposed to the topic of humility leads to the following nature-based ethic: *one ought to focus on balancing life with career.* Add your own related ethic, experience, or idea.

13. The principle of cyclical growth, when juxtaposed to the topic of selflessness leads to the following nature-based ethic, that: *no matter how much one grows, one ought to remain behind to get ahead.* Add your own related ethic, experience, or idea.

14. The principle of cyclical growth, when juxtaposed to the topic of moderation leads to the following nature-based ethic, that: *one ought to accept limits because there is no such thing as limitless freedom.* Add your own related ethic, experience, or idea.

15. The principle of cyclical growth, when juxtaposed to the topic of embracing mystery leads to the following nature-based ethic, that: *despite our growth we ought to remain focused on mystery.* Add your own related ethic, experience, or idea.

16. The principle of cyclical growth, when juxtaposed to the topic of non-contrivance leads to the following nature-based ethic, that: *we ought to focus on better living and not greater rigidness of control.* Add your own related ethic, experience, or idea.

17. The principle of cyclical growth, when juxtaposed to the topic of detachment leads to the following nature-based ethic: no matter how much one grows, one ought to still focus on having and not having, *being and not being, existing and not existing.* Add your own related ethic, experience, or idea.

18. The principle of cyclical growth, when juxtaposed to the topic of humility leads to the following nature-based ethic, that: *no*

matter how much one grows, one ought to focus on the process because there is no final outcome. Add your own related ethic, experience, or idea.

19. The principle of harmonious action, when juxtaposed to the topic of selflessness leads to the following nature-based ethic, that: *you ought to remember that you will always be a prisoner if you care about gaining others' approval of you.* Add your own related ethic, experience, or idea.

20. The principle of harmonious action, when juxtaposed to the topic of moderation leads to the following nature-based ethic, that: *one ought to remember that most of our fearful reactions are overreactions.* Add your own related ethic, experience, or idea.

21. The principle of harmonious action, when juxtaposed to the topic of embracing mystery leads to the following nature-based ethic, that: *one ought to enjoy the unknown, the misunderstandings, and the confusion.* Add your own related ethic, experience, or idea.

22. The principle of harmonious action, when juxtaposed to the topic of non-contrivance leads to the following nature-based ethic, that: *like the self control of nature, one ought to not seek control imposed by others.* Add your own related ethic, experience, or idea.

23. The principle of harmonious action, when juxtaposed to the topic of detachment leads to the following nature-based ethic, that: *since all beings return to the common source, one ought to not create things that are resistant to such recycling.* Add your own related ethic, experience, or idea.

24. The principle of harmonious action, when juxtaposed to the topic of humility leads to the following nature-based ethic, that: *one ought not expect too much recognition.* Add your own related ethic, experience, or idea.

Follow-up Protocol

For best results, write down your impressions of this activity in your journal using the Heartwood Path Follow-up Protocol found in the Appendix. Afterwards, consider sharing your interpretations with others.

Heartwood Path Axioms

Key Assertions From Waypoint 2.26

2.26.1.

For the same reason that one can never step into the same river twice (because there is always newness presenting itself) one has to always think and act anew.

2.26.2.

Great improvements in deeds require great changes of mind.

2.26.3.

The sooner we humans limit our reproduction through voluntary personal decisions based on individual intentions the less likely it is that we will all be subjected to involuntary social controls based on collective rules or laws.

2.26.4.

Actual factual consequences of our old line of thinking will determine the viability of old-time moral and ethical codes.

2.26.5.

Any ethic is doomed if its practice causes those who live by it to perish and take their cherished moral notions with them.

Nocturnal Pilgrimage 2.26

For best results, write down your impressions of each night's dreams in your journal using the Heartwood Path Dreaming Time Protocols found in the Appendix. Afterwards, consider sharing your Dream Tending with others.

Within the purely natural state of conscious dreaming—which we have been calling "Lucid Dreaming"—are many benefits. We will list them in the half dozen waypoints that follow. Keep going.

With the previous text and activity in mind continue Dream Tending. When you are ready to continue, move to the next waypoint: "Satisfy."

27

Satisfy

INDULGE IN EARTHLY PLEASURES

For those traversing the Heartwood Path, indulgence in earthly pleasures is not considered suspect, transient, impure, or worthless. In Proverbs 13: 12 it says: "Hope deferred makes the heart sick, but a desire fulfilled is a tree of life."

Indulgence along the Heartwood Path ought to always be life-affirming, positive, and ethical. Rather than suppressing desires, the Heartwood Path encourages you to move into your desires with full consciousness. The Soul craves what it is denied. By embracing and then overcoming (transcending) your desires, you can, if you wish, overcome them.

To A Real Blast...

HumaNatureConnect Activity

Start-up Protocol

If this is not a day when you prefer to spend time in nature without an agenda, do the Heartwood Path Start-up Protocol found in the Appendix. Then return here to do the remaining portion of this activity:

Indulging In Earthly Pleasures

For this activity, indulge in an earthly pleasure (these being eating, drinking, sex, enjoying natural scenes or natural beings, and more) and thus find enjoyment in aspects of the natural world. Seek to also transcend these sensual pleasures by also attaining the wisdom that is housed in the Dharma (the a set of universal truths that are excellent, cause no afflictions or defilements, and are permanent) and by attaining wisdom that comes from Nirvana. To find the wisdom that abides in Dharma during this activity, indulge and, as you do, consider the origins and causes of this delight and the effects of your chosen indulgence. To find the wisdom of Nirvana as you indulge consider how the source of your earthly pleasure--the enjoyable person, place, or thing--is impermanent.

Follow-up Protocol

For best results, write down your impressions of this activity in your journal using the Heartwood Path Follow-up Protocol found in the Appendix. Afterwards, consider sharing your interpretations with others.

Heartwood Path Axioms

Key Assertions From Waypoint 2.27

2.27.1.

The Soul craves what it is denied.

2.27.2.

By embracing and then transcending one's desires, one can, if one wishes, overcome them.

2.27.3.

Indulge and, as you do, consider the origins and causes of this delight and the effects of your chosen indulgence.

2.27.4.

As you indulge consider how the source of your earthly pleasure—the enjoyable person, place, or thing—is impermanent.

Nocturnal Pilgrimage 2.27

For best results, write down your impressions of each night's dreams in your journal using the Heartwood Path Dreaming Time Protocols found in the Appendix. Afterwards, consider sharing your Dream Tending with others.

If you want to add some fun to your life—and why not?—experience the fantasy and adventure that is available to you when you have lucid dreams. Even if one were not to gain a fresh perspective from a lucid dream—which is extremely unlikely if not impossible—dream lucidly just for pure enjoyment. Let others know what you experience.

With the previous text and activity in mind, after tending to your dreams, move to the next waypoint: "Consider The Ego." You are making good progress toward Gladandgreen Junction.

28

Consider The Ego

DISTINGUISH BETWEEN THE EGO AND IT'S SPOILS

While Ego drives one to excel, the spoils of the Ego such as the motivation to achieve or the motivation to make one youthfully attractive ought not be regarded as highly as the timeless rewards that are available as one develops spiritually. The spoils of the Ego are tools that can be used for immediate but temporary personal development, but they are not timeless. They will, in time, disappear.

Too many of us are taking life too seriously. As author Alan Watts says: "Man suffers only because he takes seriously what the gods made for fun" (Goodreads Website).

To Your Own Mixed Bag...

HumaNatureConnect Activity

Start-up Protocol

If this is not a day when you prefer to spend time in nature without an agenda, do the Heartwood Path Start-up Protocol found in the Appendix. Then return here to do the remaining portion of this activity:

Considering Your Own Shame, Good Deeds, And The Ego

For this activity, look for evidence of any lack of shame in your chosen natural being or its place. Then write down how your Ego makes you ashamed of things you do not know, ashamed for not being able, and ashamed for not being pure. After listing what you are ashamed of, think of the wisdom you would like to achieve, think of the vows you need to make or remake, and consider what you can do to be more compassionate towards all sentient beings. Are there apparent good deeds associated with your chosen natural being or its place? Find a giver and a receiver at your natural location. Do you see any psychological attachments to givers and receivers in Nature? Write down your answer. Make a list of ten planned good deeds. Write down how reacting to your shame by seeking wisdom, making vows, and planning good deeds allows you to counter the negativities of shame that come from your Ego. If you are attracted to take an extra step, write down how nature handles the act of giving and receiving in terms shame; diligence; accommodation; the impermanence of the giver, receiver, and thing given; and non-attachment to results.

Follow-up Protocol

For best results, write down your impressions of this activity in your journal using the Heartwood Path Follow-up Protocol found in the Appendix. Afterwards, consider sharing your interpretations with others.

Heartwood Path Axioms

Key Assertions From Waypoint 2.28

2.28.1.

Distinguish between the Ego and its spoils.

2.28.2.

The motivation to achieve or the motivation to make one youthfully attractive ought not be regarded as highly as the timeless rewards that are available as one develops spiritually.

2.28.3.

Since pain forces us to learn, a common impetus for most spiritual journeys is some form of suffering; and, ironically, the more pain one is willing to take on the greater the joy.

Nocturnal Pilgrimage 2.28

For best results, write down your impressions of each night's dreams in your journal using the Heartwood Path Dreaming Time Protocols found in the Appendix. Afterwards, consider sharing your Dream Tending with others.

Some people may shun the Nocturnal Pilgrimage sections of the Heartwood Path because they do not like thinking about dreams. For many of these people, dreams turn into nightmares. Here's how lucid dreaming can be used to neutralize and even reverse the negative impacts of bad dreams: when you are conscious that you are dreaming, as you are during lucid dreaming, one has a chance to use the event for healing; one has a chance to use the event to uncover what is plaguing you in your waking life; and one has the power to change what happens in the night time reveries, making them less difficult to experience.

With the previous text and activity in mind, tend to your dreams. Then, continue your pilgrimage down the Heartwood Path by moving to the next waypoint: "The Deepest Self." There, you will learn about how to gain a deep ecological consciousness by adopting a wider identification.

29

The Deepest Self

CONSIDER ONENESS

A wider identification, the realization of the "Deepest Self," and a deep ecological consciousness all refer to essentially the same perspective—the one that minimizes boundaries and separateness. I like the term "Deepest Self" because it implies a self with depth. This "Deepest Self"—often referred to as the "Highest Self," the "Higher Self," or the "Greater Self"—is not interested only in acquiring things, is not interested in being better than anyone else, and is not interested in defeating others. Acquiring things, outdoing others, and defeating enemies are some of the defining interests of the Ego. The Deepest Self may enjoy possessions, but will never be possessed by them. Make sure it is the Deepest Self and not the Ego that is running your life. You know it is the former when you feel expansive.

It is next to impossible to realize your Deepest Self when you are angry, when you are stressed, when you are not thinking clearly, when your speaking is ineffective or hurtful, and when you are excessively tired. During these times you may feel that your breathing is shall, rapid, tight, or tense. The following activity, adapted from the book **Stress Free For Good** by Dr. Fred Luskin and Dr. Kenneth R. Pelletier, will help you improve your breathing so that you can lower your stress enough to perhaps realize your Deepest Self.

To The Breath Of Stress-relief...

HumaNatureConnect Activity

Start-up Protocol

If this is not a day when you prefer to spend time in nature without an agenda, do the Heartwood Path Start-up Protocol found in the Appendix. Then return here to do the remaining portion of this activity:

Understanding Belly Breathing And Stress Relief

For this activity, lower stress enough to realize your Deepest Self. To begin, inhale and imagine that your belly is a balloon filling with air. To add to this sensation, place your hands on your belly as you inhale slowly. Watch your hands rise with your inhalations and fall with your exhalations. Do this at least two or three times, always focusing your attention on the rise and fall of your belly. Doing so will teach you a simple form of stress management, remind you that it is possible to teach yourself to relax, help you balance your nervous system, and help you think in productive ways. Do this belly breathing often, especially when you feel scattered or stressed as you approach your chosen natural beings in the activities that follow.

Follow-up Protocol

For best results, write down your impressions of this activity in your journal using the Heartwood Path Follow-up Protocol found in the Appendix. Afterwards, consider sharing your interpretations with others.

Heartwood Path Axioms

Key Assertions From Waypoint 2.29

2.29.1.

Acquiring things, outdoing others, and defeating enemies are some of the defining interests of the Ego.

2.29.2.

The Deepest Self may enjoy possessions, but will never be possessed by them.

2.29.3.

Make sure it is the Deepest Self and not the Ego that is running your life.

2.29.4.

It is next to impossible to realize the Deepest Self when you are stressed, angry, tired, not thinking clearly, or using hurtful speech.

Nocturnal Pilgrimage 2.29

For best results, write down your impressions of each night's dreams in your journal using the Heartwood Path Dreaming Time Protocols found in the Appendix. Afterwards, consider sharing your Dream Tending with others.

Knowledge and inspiration come to those who master the skill of lucid dreaming. Use this power to increase your creativity.

With the Deepest Self, Oneness, and the previous activity in mind, after you sleep tend to your dreams. Then, continue your pilgrimage down the Heartwood Path by moving to the next waypoint: "The Dark Side."

30

The Dark Side

CONSIDER SUFFERING

A common impetus for most spiritual journeys is some form of suffering. This suffering may come from distant, abusive, or alcoholic parents; warring family members; or a variety of misfortunes. Think of the Heartwood Path as a great errand you are about to perform as a way to confront and then move away from past suffering.

Confronting the dark side of life is important as an early step in spiritual growth because there is a big psycho-spiritual payoff when life's problems are overcome. Since pain—physical, mental, and emotional—is inevitable it ought to be accepted with the knowledge that its purpose is to awaken and to help with spiritual growth. Pain often teaches what one needs to know. It often seems to be brutishly designed to force us to learn. Ironically, the more pain one is willing to take on, the greater the joy.

When grief is only an inner experience of sadness it immobilizes. Within darkness is a bright spot, a blessing. There can be an improved response to despair, as evident in the following practice. Here is how to make that response:

Feel your loss. Express it. Then look for the hidden blessing. Give it time. All losses are part of the divine order. Determine what is the source of your sorrow. Pay attention to your own state of suffering. Look for the hidden lesson in the suffering.

To The Prerequisites For Compassion...

HumaNatureConnect Activity

Start-up Protocol

If this is not a day when you prefer to spend time in nature without an agenda, do the Heartwood Path Start-up Protocol found in the Appendix. Then return here to do the remaining portion of this activity:

Responding To The Suffering Of Others

For this activity, determine how set up you for increasing your compassion by answering the following questions and marking down your answers in your journal:

Macy and Johnstone say, "the greatest danger of our times is the deadening of our response . . ." How have your responses been either deadened or quickened concerning the plight of nature? (2012, p. 2).

In what ways, if any, are you hopeful about solving major environmental issues such as global climate change, the safe storage of nuclear waste, overpopulation, or species loss?

In what ways, if any, have you become an active participant in solving local or global environmental problems?

In what ways, if any, are your actions to make the world better so enlivening that they make you feel better?

In what ways, if any, are you a participant in the following cycle: Honoring the Pain of the World > Seeing With New Eyes > Going Forth > Coming From Gratitude . . .?

In what ways, if any, are you involved in each of the following dimensions of the Great Work!: 1) campaigning in defense of life on

Earth, 2) developing new economic and social structures, 3) changing people's perceptions, thinking, and values?

Look over your answers and determine if there is more you want or need to do to foster the development of compassion within yourself. If you uncover room for growth, write down in your journal specifically what you plan to do. Doing so will help to bring out the best in you.

Follow-up Protocol

For best results, write down your impressions of this activity in your journal using the Heartwood Path Follow-up Protocol found in the Appendix. Afterwards, consider sharing your interpretations with others.

Heartwood Path Axioms

Key Assertions From Waypoint 2.30

2.30.1.

Consider suffering.

2.30.2.

A common impetus for most spiritual journeys is some form of suffering.

2.30.3.

Confronting the dark side of life is important as an early step in spiritual growth because there is a big psycho-spiritual payoff when life's problems are overcome.

2.30.4.

Pain often seems to be brutishly designed to force us to learn.

Nocturnal Pilgrimage 2.30

For best results, write down your impressions of each night's dreams in your journal using the Heartwood Path Dreaming Time Protocols found in the Appendix. Afterwards, consider sharing your Dream Tending with others.

Wouldn't it be nice if there was a place you could go to test your ideas and plans, to try out new skills, and to find inspiration and knowledge. It turns out that the setting of your lucid dreams, often full of the same wise natural beings you encounter during your Heartwood Path activities, is just such a place. Keep going and you will learn how to get to the fertile ground of lucid dreams, night after night. Go there with the intention of clarifying any guidance you may be receiving as a result of your time spent with attractive natural beings. Use the night time to refine the impressions you receive during the day time in nature. Important "how-to" information follows in this and the following Heartwood Path books and courses. With the subject of this waypoint and its activity in mind, sleep and dream.

Upon waking, tend to your dreams, as instructed. Then, continue your pilgrimage down the Heartwood Path by moving to the next way-point: "Essential Deeds." There, you will find the subjects of gratitude, relaxation, visualization, affirmations, and the destruction of negative behaviors.

31

Essential Deeds

FEEL THE LIFE-ENHANCING
SENSE OF GRATITUDE

At least once per week, make realistic changes in the way you relax, make affirmations, visualize, and eliminate self-destructive behaviors. A quick look at each of these changes will make it easier for you to feel that life-enhancing sense of gratitude.

Relax periodically. That way, when you come back to work your judgment will be better. When you do relax, put some actual distance between you and your work. During your time of relaxation, consider making some non-work related affirmations. Relaxing away from work and doing non-work affirmations will help you keep work in proper proportion to the rest of life.

Affirmation is stating what you want—stating it to yourself or, preferably, out loud. The sentence of affirmation needs to be in the present tense, as if it has already occurred—such as, "I am fit and trim."

Visualize what you would like to be and keep a hold on that picture for a long time. Doing so, you will soon materialize what you are thinking. Along with this mental picture of your goal, wish it, desire (which is wishing for it plus asking for it), intend it (which is wishing for it, desiring it, and framing it into a statement of intention) and put passion to it (which hardens the Will).

Eliminate self-destructive behaviors by creating tranquility whenever you are upset. Spend time appreciating your awesome mind. Remind yourself that nothing beyond yourself can make you unhappy unless you allow it to do so. Build within yourself the habit of developing one of the best antidotes to self-destructive behaviors: gratitude.

To More Thankfulness...

HumaNatureConnect Activity

Start-up Protocol

If this is not a day when you prefer to spend time in nature without an agenda, do the Heartwood Path Start-up Protocol found in the Appendix. Then return here to do the remaining portion of this activity:

Making A Change This Week, Beginning With Gratitude

For this activity, begin a practice of regularly showing gratitude. To do so, recall something that happened earlier in this day or week that pleased you. Then say out loud or to yourself: "I am happy that _____ happened." Then give thanks to whatever or whoever helped this happy moment occur.

Follow-up Protocol

For best results, write down your impressions of this activity in your journal using the Heartwood Path Follow-up Protocol found in the Appendix. Afterwards, consider sharing your interpretations with others.

Heartwood Path Axioms

Key Assertions From Waypoint 2.31

2.31.1.

Feel the life-enhancing sense of gratitude.

2.31.2.

Plan for and make at least one realistic change each week.

2.31.3.

Remind yourself that nothing beyond yourself can make you unhappy unless you allow it to do so.

Nocturnal Pilgrimage 2.31

For best results, write down your impressions of each night's dreams in your journal using the Heartwood Path Dreaming Time Protocols found in the Appendix. Afterwards, consider sharing your Dream Tending with others.

It will take a passionate and courageous love for the planet, including its people, to solve the environmental crisis. I am not only speaking of superficial pleasurable love nor narcissistic blissful love; I am talking about tough love, love with muscle, the kind that can arouse whole nations and heal the planet. This love is serious and active, but also hopeful and playful. It is a kind of love that heightens some of the central powers of the human species—the capacity for play, imagination, creativity, fantasy, and the endless search for possibilities. These powers are restored through sleep.

With the information and inspiration just received, Dream while sleeping before continuing. Tend to your dreams, as instructed. Then, continue your pilgrimage down the Heartwood Path by moving to the next waypoint: "The Critical Chronicle."

32

The Critical Chronicle

TAKE CARE OF YOUR SELF BY JOURNALING WELL

You have been asked numerous times already to make journal entries, thereby recording your love for yourself and the rest of creation. Now it is time to get serious about these entries, to improve your journal writing, and to make the most of your time journaling. The following activity, inspired by a book about journal writing written by Joan R. Neubauer (1985), will help.

To Better Journal-making...

HumaNatureConnect Activity

Start-up Protocol

If this is not a day when you prefer to spend time in nature without an agenda, do the Heartwood Path Start-up Protocol found in the Appendix. Then return here to do the remaining portion of this activity:

Journaling As A Way To Record The Results Of Heartwood Path Activities

For this activity, answer the following questions intended to help you with your journaling?

1. What do you need to do to make doing the Heartwood Path activities and writing the results in your journal a regular part of your everyday existence?

2. What do you have to do to create a scheduled time and a quiet spot for your journaling? Write down how you think journaling will foster your power to change for the better? Add how you are feeling each day in your journal entries so that you can compare how you are feeling as you engage in each activity, and how your activities changed how you feel, if at all. Focus on your goals. Use your journal to track your progress. Write down what are your goals with your journal writing. Use your journaling to state your goal, devise plans, and to track how you are progressing. Write down whenever you change your plans. Write down what, if anything, you need to get off your chest. Use your journal as a catharsis. Write down your pains, and the sources of your pains.

3. How do you feel right now?

4. What is making you angry, sad, hurt, and/or uncomfortable?

5. If you are lonely, what are you going to do about it?

6. What would you do differently?

7. How can you diffuse a current negative situation?

8. Do you feel afraid or frustrated? How can you change things?

9. How can you use journaling to vent, deal with emotions, and prepare for future experiences?

10. What would you say in a letter in your journal that you do not intend to send? Write down if you think this is a useful way to express emotions, to get your thoughts together, and to create a priceless legacy.

11. How can you use journaling to connect with the divine and with nature? How can journaling bring more joy into your life? How can your journaling help others? How can journaling bring to you a sense of peace? How can journaling help you find your reason for being?

12. Will you share your journal entries with others? If so, whom and how?

13. How can journaling take the content of your subconscious mind or the messages behind your dreams and put these inklings into expression or reality in your life?

14. How can you make your journal entries an informal autobiography?

15. What hopes and dreams do you hope to record in your journal?

16. What portrait do you seek to paint when you are making your journal entries?

17. What upcoming special events and what little things in your life do you hope to capture in your journal-writing?

18. What life reversals or new beginnings do you wish to record in your journaling?

19. What plans do you hope to develop in your journaling?

20. Do you know the difference between active and passive voice? With the active voice, the subject performs the action stated by the verb, as in the sentence: "Playful otters swim in the river." In passive voice sentences, the subject is acted on by the verb, as in the sentence: "The river is crowded with playful otters." Write in the active voice.

21. In what ways do you hope journaling will make you a better person?

Follow-up Protocol

For best results, write down your impressions of this activity in your journal using the Heartwood Path Follow-up Protocol found in

the Appendix. Afterwards, consider sharing your interpretations with others.

Heartwood Path Axioms

Key Assertions From Waypoint 2.32

2.32.1.

Take care of yourself by journaling well.

2.32.2.

Record the results of your Heartwood Path activities in a journal.

2.32.3.

Use a journal to save a record of your impressions, thought and dreams.

Nocturnal Pilgrimage 2.32

For best results, write down your impressions of each night's dreams in your journal using the Heartwood Path Dreaming Time Protocols found in the Appendix. Afterwards, consider sharing your Dream Tending with others.

By continuing down the Heartwood Path, you will soon discover how to dream consciously. Such lucid dreaming will be healing. It will contribute to your happiness. It will make you whole. The emotional baggage you carry—the one that is limiting the success of all of your endeavors—will be removed as you continue. The combination of the

Natural Systems Thinking Process during your day time pilgrimage and lucid dreaming during your night time pilgrimage will together move you forward to Gladandgreen Junction. Enjoy the ride!

With the information you found at this waypoint fresh in your mind, dream while sleeping before heading to the next learning station. Tend to your dreams by recording them in your journal. Then, continue your pilgrimage down the Heartwood Path by moving to the next waypoint: "Ease Of Heart." There we will address the important topic of choosing peace over conflict as a way to refresh the "brain in the heart." That puzzled look you have on your face right now will diminish soon enough.

33

Ease Of Heart

CHOOSE PEACE

Seek a wide embrace of compassion by being intimate with all beings in the timeless present. Doing so allows one's mind to give up (for even a brief moment) worrying about the past or planning for the future. In this way, one tends to awaken from the delusion that one is separate from the environment. Once the "capacity for presence" is expanded you will find an intensely comforting ease of heart. Nothing that is timeless loses its beauty, nor does it die. Feelings about problems pass, and that's a good thing. Sometimes one's feelings about a problem make you feel worse than the problem itself. This holds true about other people's feelings about your problems, as well. Regardless of the fleeting feelings of others or your opinions of others, live the truth as you see it. Choose that which brings you and others a sense of peace.

This sense comes from the heart, which, besides pumping blood, also

"sends us emotional and intuitive signals that help govern our lives (Childre and Martin, 1999, p. 23). The heart has its own independent nervous system, known as "the brain in the heart" which stimulates the release of the hormones of action and releases the body's inner systems, "thereby increasing its effectiveness" (Childre and Martin, 1999, p. 23).

When we feel happiness, appreciation, compassion, care, and love, we improve our hormonal balance and the responsiveness of our immune system. These benefits are especially true when we "learn to listen more deeply to our own hearts" (Childre and Martin, 1999, p. 23). Our "heart rhythms affect the brain's ability to process information, make decisions, solve problems, and experience and express creativity . . . Because the heart is the strongest biological oscillator in the human system, the rest of the body's systems are pulled into entrainment with the heart's rhythms. When subjects in research studies achieve entrainment of the brain with the heart, they report heightened intuitive clarity and a greater sense of well-being. By intentionally altering one's emotional state through certain heart-focused techniques, one modifies one's signals from the heart to the brain. "The changed information flow from the heart to the brain can facilitate higher brain function" (Childre and Martin, 1999, p. 23). One's emotional state is reflected in one's heart rhythms, which are shown in heart rate variability measurements. To begin to learn more about how to benefit from focusing on the heart, the first of several activities, inspired by the work of the Institute of Heartmath, will be presented below.

Along this portion of the Heartwood Path you are frequently asked to stop your daily commotion and thoughtfully pause with a natural being to do a HumaNatureConnect Activity. In the Freeze Frame activity that follows, you are asked to stop watching the movie of your life and to instead focus on one frame in that movie—your connection experience with a natural being, for example. In the next activity you will learn how to "call a time-out to gain a clear perspective on whats happening in a single frame. By helping you align your head and your heart, it gives you a quick and efficient access to heart intelligence . . . . It helps us reduce stressful self poisoning and gives us poise instead" (Childre and Martin, 1999, p. 66).

To Heart Intelligence...

HumaNatureConnect Activity

Start-up Protocol

If this is not a day when you prefer to spend time in nature without an agenda, do the Heartwood Path Start-up Protocol found in the Appendix. Then return here to do the remaining portion of this activity:

Putting A Stressful Feeling In The Freeze Frame

For this activity, put stressful feelings on hold and tap into heart intelligence and to return to high performance. There will be five steps in this activity, ones that can be used on the spot, whenever you are feeling out of sorts:

> 1. Recognize a stressful feeling, something that makes you feel out of balance emotionally or mentally. It is important to take this moment to focus on your stressful feeling because it may be buried under a mountain of stressful feelings that, because of your busy life, you simply do not devote the time to process. Signs of this inattention are your own abruptness and taking too many things personally.

> 2. Shift your attention away from your wandering mind or the stressful emotion to the area around your heart.

>> "Pretend you're breathing through your heart to help focus your energy in this area. Keep your focus there for ten seconds or more . . . While it's true that this step helps pull mental focus away from the problem, there's more in it than that. Shifting focus from head to heart improves nervous system balance, heightens cardiovascular efficiency, and enhances

communication between heart and brain, bringing more coherence (increased emotional "stability and . . . increased synchronization and harmony in the functioning of physiological systems) to the mind and emotions" (Childre and Martin, 1999, p. 68-69).

3. Recall a fun, positive feeling during a past time in your life. Remember the relaxation, love, joy, compassion, care, or appreciation you experienced during this previous time. Focus on the memory of the feelings and not what the life event looks like in your memory.

4. Use your intuition, sincerity, and common sense as you ask your heart the following question: "What would be a more efficient response to the situation, one that would minimize future stress?" (Childre and Martin, 1999, p. 70). Good answers to this question come after some repeated practice, always remaining focused on the area around the heart.

5. "Listen to what your heart says in answer to your question" (Childre and Martin, 1999, p. 70). As your mind becomes quiet, the answer will come as a "still, small voice." Remain still and heart focused. (Use) your heart time to entrain your biological, mental, and emotional systems. Doing so will make your system more coherent, as previously described. Sometimes the answer will be fleeting. Other times, you will not immediately like the answer. In your journal, write down the situation you recalled, the head reaction, the intuitive response from the heart, and state how the Freeze frame shifted you from _____ to _____.

Describe any feelings of clarity, inner security, and peace, if any.

You are now getting closer to finding revelations from your dreams. Such revelations will need to be perceived, as sometimes they are as allusive as a tiny warbler in in huge forest. To begin picking out bits of revelations from your dreams, it is necessary to engage in . . .

"subtle perception, I mean a kind of seeing in which we are aware of both our peripheral vision and our focused, core vision at the same time . . . When we do this, the living image often will reveal its innermost self, its soul" (Aizenstat, 2009, p. 48).

Follow-up Protocol

For best results, write down your impressions of this activity in your journal using the Heartwood Path Follow-up Protocol found in the Appendix. Afterwards, consider sharing your interpretations with others.

Heartwood Path Axioms

Key Assertions From Waypoint 2.33

2.33.1.

Choose peace.

2.33.2.

By being intimate in the timeless present and allowing your mind to give up (for even a brief moment) worrying about the past or planning for the future you will tend to awaken from the delusion that you are separate from the environment.

2.33.3.

Nothing that is timeless loses its beauty, nor does it die.

2.33.4.

Choose that which brings you and others a sense peace.

2.33.5.

Put stressful feelings on hold by asking the following question: "What would be a more efficient response to the situation, one that would minimize future stress?" and listen to what your heart says in answer to your question.

Nocturnal Pilgrimage 2.33

For best results, write down your impressions of each night's dreams in your journal using the Heartwood Path Dreaming Time Protocols found in the Appendix. Afterwards, consider sharing your Dream Tending with others.

I got good at subtle perception during my early days as a bird watcher. Now it is your chance to practice seeing both the small uniquenesses and the totality of the dreamscape. As you dream, or as you remember your dream just after waking up, focus on the particulars but also engage your peripheral vision in a way that allows you to see Dream Characters' surroundings. Write down both the details of the Dream Characters and the setting in your next journal entry.

With the intension to use your peripheral vision in your dream tending, sleep and dream. Upon waking, before your morning movements erase the memories of your dreams, make careful and systematic entries into your journal. Don't let the wisdom in your dreams evaporate with the morning mist. A few minutes of dream journaling first thing every morning will pay huge dividends later on.

With the content of this waypoint and your impressions of the previous activity fresh in your mind, after you sleep and dream, tend to your dreams. When ready, move to the next waypoint: "Immortal Guides." There, you will become more acquainted with Theos, Eros, and Ecos or, said another way, the Three Graces: Spirit, Sex, and Nature. You will also discover the three tickets needed to visit these forever living Holy Advisors.

34

Immortal Guides

USE THE HEARTWOOD PATH'S THREE GRACES: SPIRIT, NATURE, AND SEX

This powerful combination will take you to that special liminal "place" where feeling and imagination are, at once, ordinary and extraordinary. The Heartwood Path's Three Graces (Theos/Spirit, Ecos/Nature and Eros/Sex) will transport you on a rite of passage that will make you more susceptible to positive influences and beneficial changes.

The "tickets" for this journey to the liminal world that is not quite earthly and not quite heavenly are sensation, passion, and imagination. The use of these "tickets" in loving ways leads to an erotic morality that affects deeply all that is—from the *heart* within to the *wood* without. Lovingly using sensation, passion, and imagination encourages a slower pace—the use of time that allows for the development of wisdom. Use a slower pace to be wise and the rat race to be otherwise. A slower pace is helpful because it gives you time to listen.

Science amasses knowledge faster than society collects wisdom. The trouble with this inequity arises when science, using its rapid acquisition of knowledge, runs amok faster than society can find the wisdom to control it. So give the development of wisdom some time. Since knowledge speaks and wisdom listens, take time to hear the messages of the wise and thereby prevent yourself from speaking your knowledge while revealing your lack of wisdom. Speak, not only with your words (talk is cheap, until lawyers get involved); speak also with your actions.

As we all know, if you do speak, do not use double negatives. They are a complete no-no. And never, never, never repeat yourself.

Of the three tickets to the liminal world, now is the best time to discuss sensation. One of the best ways to develop your ability to sense the real world is to bring mindfulness into your daily activities. The following activity, inspired by a book written by Jan Chozen Bays, MD, (2011) will help you sing with the Three Graces of Spirit, Nature, and Sex.

To Live Life More Fully...

HumaNatureConnect Activity

Start-up Protocol

If this is not a day when you prefer to spend time in nature without an agenda, do the Heartwood Path Start-up Protocol found in the Appendix. Then return here to do the remaining portion of this activity:

Singing With The Three Graces: Spirit, Nature, And Sex

For this activity, begin living life more fully. This activity will help you become joyfully mindful. Ask the questions that follow to your chosen natural object but do not expect it or you to be able to answer the questions immediately. Just ask for permission to ponder these questions on site in nature; immerse yourself in the qualities of the natural being and its natural surroundings; use one or more of your natural senses; think of your chosen being as an emissary carrying the wisdom of nature to you after granting you its consent to have this connection experience by remaining attractive; resonate with the underlying tone or rhythm you feel in your heart as you sit, stand, or lie next to your chosen natural being; allow the questions to be processed (answered) in the natural realm of your unconscious mind overnight; after a night's sleep, return to this activity and write out your answers. Doing so allows the intelligence of nature to silently or perhaps in your dreams work its magic on you so that you can then write out answers that are not overly mental, piously heady, or tainted by fluctuating social pressures or willy-nilly moods. Take your time and, in your journal, write out your answers to each of the following questions (or as many as you like).

1. Do I ever use my non-dominant hand as a way to sharpen my beginner's mind?
2. Wherever I go, whenever possible, do I leave no trace or improve the natural condition of the place?
3. Do I work to rid my speech of filler words such as "um" and "like" as a way to practice ridding myself of entrenched unconscious behaviors?
4. Do I look at my hands daily as if they were a stranger's and marvel at how well they work together without getting in each others' way?
5. Do I just eat when I eat as a way to practice enjoying each moment of life?
6. Do I create wealth in my heart by complimenting someone every day?
7. Do I adjust my posture to alter my moods?
8. Do I fight unhappiness by being grateful for something each day?
9. Do I stop and just listen, listen to the sounds in the silence, as a way to quiet my mind?
10. Do I stop and take three cleansing breaths before I answer the phone as a way to refresh myself?

11. Do I regularly lovingly touch inanimate objects as a way to remind myself that I too am a fellow being of the earth?

12. Do I fight annoyance when waiting by practicing mindfulness, prayer, or meditation?

13. Do I replace the time I spend listening to the media with time spent in silence, contemplating beauty, or sharing in loving friendship?

14. Do I add love to the universe by looking at people, things, and pets with loving eyes?

15. Do I practice generosity by giving anonymously?

16. Do I ask the inner voice to be silent for at least three breaths as a prescription for health and happiness?

17. Do I appreciate each mind space by carefully closing doors before entering new space?

18. Do I remind myself that I am not alone by noticing trees?

19. Do I regularly relax my hands as a way to relax by whole mind and body?

20. Do I overcome greed, avarice, and ignorance by, whenever it is safe to do so, saying "yes?"

21. Do I break out of my self-absorbed mind by looking for the color blue in nature but not in the sky?

22. Do I work on my mental stability and emotional stability by placing my awareness on the bottoms of my feet?

23. Do I help my mind become spacious by attending to the space around objects rather than just the objects themselves?

24. Do I participate in the party in my mouth by putting down my utensils after each bite?

25. Do I increase my happiness by not clinging to desires?

26. Do I motivate myself to change and give myself the gift of empathy by noticing suffering in all its forms?

27. Do I do a silly walk when I need to lighten up?

28. Do I cultivate a light, flexible mind by opening my awareness to water, in bowls, in glasses, in lakes, in the ocean, and flowing in streams?

29. Do I expand my perspective by looking up?

30. Do I challenge my definition of my "self" by not defending or defining my personal territory or public labels attached to myself, such as Liberal (which, as we all know, you can tell by when one's heart starts bleeding), Midwesterner, Man, Independent?

31. Do I take the time to smell the smells around me?

32. Do I make each moment with someone vivid by reminding myself that this could be the last time I see this person?

33. Do I challenge what it means to be "too cold" or "too hot?"

34. Do I practice loving kindness as an antidote to aversion?

35. Do I pay attention to the movement of air as a way to expand my awareness?

36. Do I listen like a sponge without judging as a way to foster acceptance?

37. Do I appreciate life, my own and the one life of every being?

38. Do I ever pretend that I have one week to live and make a list of what I would do during that week?

39. Do I focus on breathing, listening, and feeling as a way to deal with impatience?

40. Do I stick to thoughts of the present, knowing that anxiety is usually about the past or the future?

41. Do I feel off center?

42. Do I focus my attention on my core?

43. Do I ever regularly direct loving kindness to myself?

44. Do I remember to smile often?

Follow-up Protocol

For best results, write down your impressions of this activity in your journal using the Heartwood Path Follow-up Protocol found in the Appendix. Afterwards, consider sharing your interpretations with others.

Heartwood Path Axioms

Key Assertions From Waypoint 2.34

2.34.1.

The Heartwood Path's Three Graces (Theos/Spirit, Ecos/Nature and Eros/Sex) will transport you on a rite of passage that will make you more susceptible to positive influences and beneficial changes.

2.34.2.

Use a slower pace to be wise and the rat race to be otherwise.

2.34.3.

Science amasses knowledge faster than society collects wisdom.

2.34.4.

Since knowledge speaks and wisdom listens, take time to hear the messages of the wise and thereby prevent yourself from speaking your knowledge while revealing your lack of wisdom.

2.34.5.

Never, never, never repeat yourself.

Nocturnal Pilgrimage 2.34

For best results, write down your impressions of each night's dreams in your journal using the Heartwood Path Dreaming Time

Protocols found in the Appendix. Afterwards, consider sharing your Dream Tending with others.

For tomorrow's Dream Tending, continue to practice perceiving the dream with subtle perception, using both your core vision and your peripheral vision to see both the unique details and the totality of the setting.

Also, begin looking at your dreams as mirrors reflecting yourself. As this reflection begins to include more and more of the setting around you, you can be assured that your More-Than-Individual-Self is developing.

With the concepts in the text of this waypoint and your impressions of the activity of this waypoint both in mind, sleep, form an intension to have a certain dream of your choice, dream, and, upon waking, tend to your dreams.

After your journal writing, begin all of the normal activities of your day. At some point, be sure to engage in the next waypoint, titled "Ready, Aim, Desire." There, you will learn to apply the particular power needed to reach the specific goals embedded within the basic urges. The reason for this "mouth-full" title of a branch of knowledge —this "glass-full" subject, so to speak—will become clear as the mud settles at the next learning station. With the clarity found at the next waypoint, you will see what is needed at each of the eight stages of human need.

35

Ready, Aim, Desire

APPLY TARGETED POWER

Apply the particular power needed to reach the specific goals embedded within the basic urges. The goal of the urge to live, for example, is meaning, and the power needed in the search for meaning is hope. The goal of the urge to be free is self-determination, and the power needed in the search for self-determination is courage. The goal of the urge to understand is knowledge, and the power needed in the search for knowledge is curiosity. The goal of the urge to create is originality, and the power needed in the search for originality is imagination. The goal for the urge to enjoy is happiness, and the power needed in the search for happiness is enthusiasm. The goal of the urge to connect in life enhancing ways is love, and the power needed in the search for love is caring. The goal of the urge to transcend is unity, and the power needed in the search for unity is openness.

With these powers you do not have to listen to those who try to influence you with their pessimism. People with mediocre minds are always opposed to those who possess great spirit.

The seven urges above are responses to human needs. We will be augmenting Abraham Maslow famous five-stage Hierarchy of Needs model, we with three additional stages of needs/urges. Maslow's five stages include (Stage 1) Biological and Physiological Needs; which, once met, allows one to reach (Stage 2) Safety Needs; which, once met, enables one to focus on (Stage 3) Belongingness and Love Needs; which, once met, makes it possible to arrive at (Stage 4) Cognitive Needs; which, once met, allows one to attain (Stage 5) Self-Actualization Needs. We will be inserting between Maslow's Stages Four and Five two additional stages: 1) Cognitive needs for knowledge and meaning and 2) Aesthetic Needs for appreciation and search for beauty, balance, and form. After Maslow's Fifth Stage we will be adding a stage called "Transcendence Needs," which has to do with helping others achieve self-transcendence. These three additional stages are borrowed from Alan Chapman (2003) and the activity below is inspired by and adapted from his work.

To Urges That Satisfy Needs...

HumaNatureConnect Activity

Start-up Protocol

If this is not a day when you prefer to spend time in nature without an agenda, do the Heartwood Path Start-up Protocol found in the Appendix. Then return here to do the remaining portion of this activity:

Satisfying Eight Human Needs

For this activity, determine what *human needs* you have already satisfied and, assuming you have not met all your needs, what are the next urges you can expect to emerge.

First Stage Of Human Need

Begin by asking yourself if your *biological needs* are being met. If not, you will likely have the urge to make sure you have food and shelter.

Second Stage Of Human Need

If these needs are met, you will likely have the wherewithal to address your likely need for *belongingness and love.*

Third Stage Of Human Need

If not met and the previous two needs are met, you will likely have *the urge to be loved,* to be a part of a family, to have adequate relationships with colleagues and friends, and to be accepted for who your are.

Fourth Stage Of Human Need

If these needs are met you may be able to move up the hierarchy of needs to the *esteem needs* stage. If the previous three needs are met but this one is not you will likely feel the powerful urge to be successful in life and work, to be recognized by your peers, to be satisfied with your responsibilities, roles, status, and reputation.

Fifth Stage Of Human Need

Once the previous four needs are satisfied, you will likely have the urge to satisfy your *cognitive needs.* If these needs are not met you will like feel the chief urge to improve your self-awareness, to pursue knowledge and the meaning of things beyond the necessities of work.

Sixth Stage Of Human Need

Once all the previous five needs are met you may feel the urge to satisfy your *aesthetic needs.* If these needs are not met and all the previous needs are met, you may be feel compelled to actively seek beauty and balance and to engage in the arts.

Seventh Stage Of Human Need

Once the six previous levels of needs are satisfied you will likely feel the urge to satisfy your *need for self-actualization.* If this need is not met but the previous needs are met you will likely have the chief aim of self-knowledge and enlightenment. You will feel that the most important thing to you is to have "peak experiences" and to realize your ultimate personal potential.

Eighth Stage Of Human Need

Once all the previous stages of needs are met you will likely feel the luxury of being able to focus chiefly on the *need to help others achieve their ultimate potential.* You will feel the need to do so, no matter what it takes. This is the level of needs aspired to by eartHearts. The Heartwood Path leads to this level of needs satisfaction. From this summary, determine your level of needs.

Write in your journal how you plan to address the urges that correspond with your level of need. Be grateful for the needs you have already achieved and be thankful for the opportunity to transcend to the need to be a helper of others without crashing.

Follow-up Protocol

For best results, write down your impressions of this activity in your journal using the Heartwood Path Follow-up Protocol found in the Appendix. Afterwards, consider sharing your interpretations with others.

Heartwood Path Axioms

Key Assertions From Waypoint 2.35

2.35.1.

Apply targeted power.

2.35.2.

People with mediocre minds are always opposed to those who possess great spirit.

2.35.3.

(Stage 1) Biological and Physiological Needs; which, once met, allow one to focus on (Stage 2) Safety Needs; which, once met, encourage one to focus on (Stage 3) Belongingness and Love Needs; which, once met, make it possible to focus on (Stage 4) Cognitive Needs; which, once met, enable one to focus on (Stage 5) Self-Actualization Needs. We will be inserting between Maslow's Stages Four and Five two additional stages: 1) Cognitive needs for knowledge and meaning and 2) Aesthetic Needs for appreciation and search for beauty, balance, and form.

2.35.4.

Once all stages of needs are met one will likely feel the luxury of being able to focus chiefly on helping others achieve their ultimate potential.

Nocturnal Pilgrimage 2.35

For best results, write down your impressions of each night's dreams in your journal using the Heartwood Path Dreaming Time Protocols found in the Appendix. Afterwards, consider sharing your Dream Tending with others.

The next nighttime step down the Heartwood Path has to do with learning how to engage in deep listening to Dream Figures. Such deep listening requires "emptying your mind of all responses. To listen carefully without reacting allows a Dream Figure to continue uninterrupted and to reveal from the inside out what it has to say" (Aizenstat, 2009, p.48). Do not finish the Dream Figures' sentences. Ban from your mind already prepared responses. Simply listen to the voice of the Dream Figure, without diminishing the message into what you want to hear. "When we listen to a living image in this way, its revelation is not barred by our expectations, judgments, or agenda" (Aizenstat, 2009, p. 48).

After listening deeply to your Dream Character, continue by moving to the next waypoint: "Usual Hazards." There, you will learn about the common pitfalls found along spiritual paths. It will be reassuring for you to know that the Heartwood Path is charted to enable you to go around such dangers.

36

Usual Hazards

AVOID THE COMMON PITFALLS
FOUND ALONG SPIRITUAL PATHS

These pitfalls include demanding instant results and following the wrong teachers (authoritarian "masters" who may be practicing "spiritual fascism," or cult leaders bent on satisfying their own ends rather than on promoting the interests of their flocks). Unlike a philosopher who confuses you sufficiently to make you think he knows what he is talking about, a good guru (spiritual teacher) acts like a guide who prevents his or her students from self-delusion; getting too "blissed out;" thinking that all is controlled by fate, destiny, and karma; believing too much in miracles and not enough in everyday life; and not following the Middle Way (a spiritual path that leads to neither too much indulgence nor too much asceticism in one's behaviors and neither too much externalism nor too much nihilism—skepticism in one's views). We trust that you will feel secure that the Heartwood Path is charted around such pitfalls.

The following activity is inspired and adapted from the book **The Seeker's Guide**, by Elizabeth Lesser (2009).

To A Safe And Appropriate Spiritual Path...

HumaNatureConnect Activity

Start-up Protocol

If this is not a day when you prefer to spend time in nature without an agenda, do the Heartwood Path Start-up Protocol found in the Appendix. Then return here to do the remaining portion of this activity:

Avoiding The Pitfalls Of Spiritual Paths

For this activity, help yourself avoid the pitfalls of spiritual paths. In the presence of your chosen attractive natural being, ask yourself the following questions. Wait until after you sleep and dream before writing down your answers to give your subconscious mind a chance to process the information and present it to you as feelings or dreams. Process any related emotions or mental images with your conscious mind before writing the answers in your journal.

1. As a result of going down a spiritual path, are you becoming more free, more loving, and more wise or are you really just hovering or going backwards? Explain your answer.

2. Is there a questionable disparity between the teachings along your path and the behaviors of your spiritual leader? Do you witness any abuses of power? Do you notice any of the following warning signs: any extravagant claims of enlightenment or healing, the minimizing of hard work, excessive commercialism that betrays the spiritual message, any blind adherence of followers, or any double standards?

3. Do you notice any shallow treatment of spiritual traditions and little respect for the depth behind them?

4. Do you hear claims that prayers will be answered the way the praying person wants them to be answered? This would negate the spiritual wisdom behind a negative answer to a prayer.

5. Do you see undue romanticizing about the spiritual teachings of foreign or indigenous cultures?

6. Do you see others or yourself being grandiose? Beware of unbearable profundity, feeling different from others, or being supposedly destined for sainthood.

7. Do you notice any so-called magical cures or claims of being a magical person? Look out for any claims of so-called all-powerful or all-knowing teacher who may be blinding you to the magic of everyday existence.

8. Do you witness claims of instant transformation? Remember that spiritual awakening takes hard work, patience, and the grace of the Absolute Spirit.

9. Do you feel caught in a never-ending course of self-improvement? Does your path have a myopic kind of focus on your individual self without encouraging you to help others seek improvements, as well?

10. Are the answers you hear superficial or too optimistic? Does the path obscure the necessity for grappling with complexity or feeling some pain?

11. Does your path negate the need to work on the greater good, focusing instead on only following your bliss or excessive self-centeredness?

Answer the following questions about the worthiness of your spiritual path:

1. Are you encouraged to have the essence of being human, are you encouraged to be gentle and kind, and are you encouraged to help others?

2. Can you recognize when the message of the spiritual path works? Is your life beginning to get better? Is drama becoming tiresome? Are disagreements and chaos used as opportunities for improvement? Are you surrounded by goodness and peace?

3. Are you no longer fighting the nature of life? Are you working with the principles of the universe? Are you getting on with living?

4. Are you experiencing honesty in relationships? Does your energy seem to be unblocked? Do you have passion? Are you proud of yourself? Are you unafraid to reveal what you want and need? Do you bear the consequences of telling the truth?

5. Do you keep from creating the additional burden of suffering by not resisting pain? Do you greet pain with calm curiosity?

6. Do you serve others, not because you have to, but because your heart leads you to the hearts of others?

7. Are you becoming more aware of your interconnectedness with all beings?

8. Do you resist the societal urge to acquire and use more and more?

9. Do you reach out for others for love and companionship yet know that abiding love comes from the Absolute Spirit? Can you perceive that love and loneliness are both states of grace?

10. Do you perceive that just to be is a blessing? Do you see the marvelous structure of the universe in the mundane?

11. Can you allow yourself not to be someone special but to simply be one of Nature's many creatures?

12. Do you feel friendliness towards change? Do you have faith in the principles of the universe even when the road is rough? Do you see how goodness fuels justice and beauty?

Explain your answers in your journal. Take appropriate actions, as inspired by your answers.

Follow-up Protocol

For best results, write down your impressions of this activity in your journal using the Heartwood Path Follow-up Protocol found in the Appendix. Afterwards, consider sharing your interpretations with others.

Heartwood Path Axioms

Key Assertions From Waypoint 2.36

2.36.1.

Unlike a philosopher who confuses you sufficiently to make you think he knows what he is talking about, a good guru (spiritual teacher) acts like a guide who prevents his or her students from self-delusion; getting too "blissed out;" thinking that all is controlled by fate, destiny, and karma; believing too much in miracles and not enough in everyday life; and not following the Middle Way (a spiritual path that leads to neither too much indulgence nor too much asceticism in one's behaviors and neither too much externalism nor too much nihilism—skepticism in one's views).

2.36.2.

Listen to what is said, not just what you want to hear.

Nocturnal Pilgrimage 2.36

For best results, write down your impressions of each night's dreams in your journal using the Heartwood Path Dreaming Time Protocols found in the Appendix. Afterwards, consider sharing your Dream Tending with others.

Dream. Engage in deep listening to the Dream Character. Write down what is said, not what you want to hear.

Go to the next waypoint, entitled "Simplify," to continue your pilgrimage down the Heartwood Path. As you move there, remember to also move outside. The Heartwood Path will not lead you to happiness and environmental sustainability if you stay in you chair looking at this screen. If your computer is an IBM let it stand for "I Better Move" outside.

37

Simplify

BRING CLARITY TO YOUR LIFE

Fruitfulness requires pruning. My time as a barn manager in the wine country of Missouri taught me that fruitful grape vines do not go off in all directions at once in an attempt to gather their sustenance of sunshine from as many places as possible. Instead, at the end of each growing season, the vines are cut back, way back. The owners of the vineyards have discovered the secret to a bountiful harvest. Each Spring the grape vine, pruned all the way back to the main stem, sends out new growth. From these limited, new branches comes the most bountiful harvest. The lesson here is clear: in life, as in grape production, simplification is fruitful.

To An Uncluttered Life...

HumaNatureConnect Activity

Start-up Protocol

If this is not a day when you prefer to spend time in nature without an agenda, do the Heartwood Path Start-up Protocol found in the Appendix. Then return here to do the remaining portion of this activity:

Simplifying Your Life

For this activity, begin working on simplifying your life. Ask the questions that follow to your chosen natural object but do not expect to receive or be able to answer the questions immediately. Just ask for permission to ponder these questions on site in nature; immerse yourself in the qualities of the natural being and its natural surroundings; use one or more of your natural senses; think of your chosen being as an emissary carrying the wisdom of nature to you after granting you its consent to have this connection experience by remaining attractive; resonate with the underlying tone or rhythm you feel in your heart as you sit, stand, or lie next to your chosen natural being; allow the questions to be processed (answered) in the natural realm of your unconscious mind overnight; after a nights sleep, return to this activity and write out your answers. Doing so allows the intelligence of nature to silently (and perhaps in your dreams) work its magic on you so that you can then write out answers that are not tainted by fluctuating social pressures or willy-nilly moods. Here are some good boldness-related questions, adapted from a book by Leo Babauta (2009):

1. Do I identify what is essential and eliminate the rest?
2. Do I set limitations on email, daily tasks, time spent on the phone, projects, subscriptions, time on the Internet, and things on my desk?
3. Do I focus on one task or one goal at a time?
4. Do I create simplifying habits?
5. Do I start small?
6. Do I focus on long-term recognition?
7. Have I identified the areas of my life that are overwhelming?
8. Do I limit my number of possessions?
9. Have I established my values, determined whom I love, what is important, and what has the biggest affect?
10. Do I distinguish needs from wants?
11. Do I single-task (which is usually more effective) or multitask?

12. Do I post my goals publicly?
13. Do I have a good filing system at home, at the office, and for the Internet?
14. Do I know what is important?
15. Do I reduce my incoming stream of emails and paper?
16. Do I empty my in-basket or incoming emails daily?
17. Do I keep my writing short?
18. Do I eliminate distractions by breaking one-addiction per week?
19. Do I know how to say no? (Try: "I simply cannot do it. I'd love to. I don't have time right now.")
20. Do I make time for the people and activities I love?
21. Do I prepare for the next day?
22. Have I decided to wake up at least fifteen minutes earlier to supercharge my day with a better morning routine? (cook, clean, exercise, meditate, make love, have a conversation, de-clutter the house, etc.)
23. Have I slowed down, giving time for meditation, planning, enjoying eating, driving safely, and saving gas and my sanity?
24. Do I start small, focus on one goal at a time, examine my motivations, determine what I really want, hold back, begin, remain accountable, find like-minded friends, read for inspiration, take a class, and work with a life coach?

Follow-up Protocol

For best results, write down your impressions of this activity in your journal using the Heartwood Path Follow-up Protocol found in the Appendix. Afterwards, consider sharing your interpretations with others.

Heartwood Path Axioms

Key Assertions From Waypoint 2.37

2.37.1.

Fruitfulness requires pruning; that is to say, in life, simplification is fruitful.

2.37.2.

Practice finesse, sensitivity, and spaciousness by making sure your eye gazing is not intimidating.

Nocturnal Pilgrimage 2.37

For best results, write down your impressions of each night's dreams in your journal using the Heartwood Path Dreaming Time Protocols found in the Appendix. Afterwards, consider sharing your Dream Tending with others.

Along with deep listening, it is important while Dream Tending to have an eye-to-eye meeting with the Dream Character. As a Living Image, it is important to engage in eye contact in a delicate and respectful way. Do not, for example, demand that the Dream Character reveal some sacred truth to you. Eye-to-eye contact helps encourage you not to make the interaction a search for the Holy Grail nor the plundering of the King's treasures. You are seeking a connection with the Dream Character that leads to a well of timelessness and presence. Practice finesse, sensitivity, and spaciousness. Make sure your eye-gazing is not intimidating. "Entering the portals of the soul opens us ever more deeply into our own soul life and to the mysteries of the dreamtime" (Aizenstat, 2009, p. 49).

After practicing "eye-to-eye" conversation with your Dream Character, continue on your pilgrimage down the Heartwood Path by moving to the next waypoint: "Gusto." There, you will take important steps towards healthfulness.

38

Gusto

SEEK GOOD HEALTH AND A ZEST FOR LIFE

The Heartwood Path seeks to foster good health and a zest for life by encouraging its travelers to develop and clarify goals and values, exercise daily, pay attention to nutrition, work to deserve the respect of the community in which one lives, appreciate beauty, have fun, relax effectively, enjoy humor, appreciate and use the power of music, reduce stress, and have a healthy sex life.

To put the wisdom of seeking good health and having zest for life to work, do the following activity.

To Healthfulness…

HumaNatureConnect Activity

Start-up Protocol

If this is not a day when you prefer to spend time in nature without an agenda, do the Heartwood Path Start-up Protocol found in the Appendix. Then return here to do the remaining portion of this activity:

Seeking Health And Zest

For this activity, list ten things you are doing to maintain your health and ten things you are doing to have zest for life. Then describe what you do to keep these things in your life. Next, list ten things you do that are not good for your health and ten things you do that show little or no zest for life. Then describe what you can do to rid yourself of each of these unhealthy behaviors.

Follow-up Protocol

For best results, write down your impressions of this activity in your journal using the Heartwood Path Follow-up Protocol found in the Appendix. Afterwards, consider sharing your interpretations with others.

Heartwood Path Axioms

Key Assertions From Waypoint 2.38

2.38.1.

Seek good health and a zest for life.

2.38.2.

Develop and clarify goals and values.

2.38.3.

Exercise daily and pay attention to nutrition.

2.38.4.

Work to deserve the respect of the community in which one lives.

2.38.5.

Appreciate beauty, have fun, relax effectively, enjoy humor, appreciate and use the power of music, reduce stress, and have a healthy sex life.

Nocturnal Pilgrimage 2.38

For best results, write down your impressions of each night's dreams in your journal using the Heartwood Path Dreaming Time Protocols found in the Appendix. Afterwards, consider sharing your Dream Tending with others.

Be patient, it may take a month or two to begin to be able to have lucid dreams suitable for eye-to-eye contact with Dream Characters. Or, it could happen for the first time the next time you dream. Tips for developing these skills will follow. Continue practicing both lucid dreaming and eye-to-eye contact with your Dream Characters. Make sure you sleep at least once before continuing.

When you are ready, move to the next waypoint: "Bearing" where you will begin charting your own course.

39

Bearing

SET YOUR OWN COURSE

To improve your wellbeing, realize that opportunities go through three stages: ridicule, opposition, and acceptance. Listening to friends, family members, and neighbors is often a big mistake for anyone trying to chart a nontraditional method of earning a living such as being a professional eco-centric life coach or being some other form of positive difference maker. The best way to inoculate yourself from the possible poor advice and influence of friends, family, and neighbors (who will likely have their own agendas) is to create for yourself a mastermind group (described subsequently) of people who share your vision.

To Chart Your Own Route...

HumaNatureConnect Activity

Start-up Protocol

If this is not a day when you prefer to spend time in nature without an agenda, do the Heartwood Path Start-up Protocol found in the Appendix. Then return here to do the remaining portion of this activity:

Setting Your Own Course

For this activity, develop your ability to take self-responsibility. Aimed at helping you set your own course, go through the following list, inspired by the book **Taking Responsibility**, by Nathaniel Branden, Ph.D (1996):

1. In what ways, if any, do you take responsibility for your own life—physically, intellectually, emotionally, and spiritually?
2. Have you ever felt compelled to say "yes" to an unreasonable request rather than to remain attached to your own interests and responsibilities. If so, describe the occurrence and give reasons.
3. In what ways, if at all, do you feel that you are the cause of the effects you want, as compared to hoping someone else will do the job for you?
4. Do you think one is ready for love if one has not made peace with aloneness and has accepted responsibility for his or her own existence?
5. How do you feel regarding ability to produce desired results? When, if at all, have you felt powerless?
6. Describe for whom or for what (if at all) you are willing to assume responsibility?
7. Describe ways that you demonstrate, if at all, that you own your own life.
8. How do you, if at all, share happiness rather than expect someone else to make you happy?
9. In what ways, if at all, have you ever took responsibility for someone or something beyond your control?
10. Can you describe an occurrence where someone suffered from a cause beyond their control? If so, write it down in your journal.
11. Are there times when you have not brought appropriate awareness to your activities? Are there times when you did? If so, jot down a summary in your journal.

12. Can you describe an occurrence when you have, if at all, been empathetic with another person? Describe the situation in your journal.

13. How would you complete the following sentences:
    a. Self-responsibility, to me, means . . .
    b. Independence, to me, means . . .
    c. I need to become more aware of . . .
    d. I need to be more self-assertive about . . .
    e. If I am more accepting of my feelings today . . .
    f. If I learn to manage my desire for approval . . .
    g. If I deny my Deepest Self . . .
    h. If I betray my thoughts and feelings in action . . .
    i. If I honor my judgements today . . .
    j. If I bring more integrity to my relationships . . .
    k. If I lived more authentically . . .
    l. If I hold myself accountable to my promises and commitments . . .
    m. If I am honest and straightforward today . . .
    n. If I want to outgrow my dependency I will need to . . .
    o. I feel most proud of myself about . . .
    p. I feel least proud of myself about . . . and
    q. As my understanding and individuality deepens . . .

Follow-up Protocol

For best results, write down your impressions of this activity in your journal using the Heartwood Path Follow-up Protocol found in the Appendix. Afterwards, consider sharing your interpretations with others.

Heartwood Path Axioms

Key Assertions From Waypoint 2.39

2.39.1.

Opportunities go through three stages: ridicule, opposition, and acceptance.

2.39.2.

Listening to friends, family members, and neighbors is a big mistake for anyone trying to chart a nontraditional method of earning a living.

2.39.3.

The best way to inoculate yourself from the poor advice and influence of friends, family, and neighbors (who will likely have their own agendas) is to create for yourself a mastermind group.

2.39.4.

Not to be confused with a very vivid dream, a lucid dream is the present-moment realization that you're dreaming.

2.39.5.

Connect with your archetypal self—one that seems to be of a mythic or universal nature.

Nocturnal Pilgrimage 2.39

For best results, write down your impressions of each night's dreams in your journal using the Heartwood Path Dreaming Time

Protocols found in the Appendix. Afterwards, consider sharing your Dream Tending with others.

As an eartHeart you are also an "oneironaut"—someone who has learned to move about consciously in the dream world. Here are some dream traveling tips:

If your Dream Image/Character for tonight's reverie does not have eyes, then accustom yourself to looking into the eye of the storm, or the hole in the tree, or the crevice of the stone. Give your Dream Character an imaginal eye. Connect with your archetypal self--one that seems to be of a mythic or universal nature. You will know when you have brought forth your archetypal self during your Dream Tending when the Dream Character turns to face you. Keep trying to entice your Dream Character until you are face-to-face (front). If the Dream Character does not respond, move on to another Dream Character or return to the previous Dream Character on another day. When a Dream Character does turn to you, thank it for responding to your Archetypal Self. Then,

> "ask permission to look directly into its eyes. Once you feel some form of assent (continued attraction, for example), imagine its eyes as the portals of its soul. Do not proceed with the need to know or the need to find an answer. Rather feel received and allow yourself to travel deep inside the figure. Pause here. Take this experience and become aware of your state of being. What has shifted? How are you breathing?" (Aizenstat, 2009, p. 50).

When one is experiencing consciousness in the dream world, one is experiencing what is called a "lucid dream." This type of dream, a type sought each night you dream during your Heartwood Path pilgrimage, is "one in which you become aware that you're dreaming. Not to be confused with a very vivid dream, a lucid dream is the present-moment realization that you're dreaming . . ." (Tucillo, Zeizel & Peisel, 2013, p. 6).

After tending to your dream in the way described in the previous activity, continue your daytime jaunt down the Heartwood Path by moving to the next waypoint: "Good Filter." We will be providing instruction in lucid dreaming throughout this series of books and courses.

40

Good Filter

USE THE APPROPRIATE EYE FOR SEEING

Modernity differentiates what is Good (morals and religion) from what is Beautiful (art) from what is True (science). These distinctions were all fine and good until they went too far, until differentiation became disassociation. Differentiation is necessary for integration (a process described earlier in our discussion of transcendence) but disassociation can lead to the kind of repression that allowed the Church to prevent Galileo from discussing what he saw through his telescope.

Where there was once (before Modernity) considerations of quality and quantity, disassociation reduces this wholesome coupling to mere quantity. How significant a thing or action may be is replaced with how costly or big a thing may be.

In both science and Modernism, moral considerations of better and worse are replaced with scientific considerations of bigger and smaller. This replacement occurs in the ways we "see."

For each of these ways to see we have, in effect, different eyes. We use "the eye of the flesh" to see that which we can sense, hold, or feel; we use the "eye of the mind" for mental pictures (images that you see only in your mind); and we use the "eye of contemplation" when we ponder significance, moral meanings, and the relative "rightness" or "wrongness" of things, thoughts, or actions.

Modernity relies almost entirely on the "eye of the flesh," which cannot see significance very well. Modernity mainly focuses on magnitude. This limited way of "seeing" works well for empirical science and industrial production but not at all for matters of "rightness" and "wrongness."

To What Is, To What Could Be, And To What Ought To Be...

HumaNatureConnect Activity

Start-up Protocol

If this is not a day when you prefer to spend time in nature without an agenda, do the Heartwood Path Start-up Protocol found in the Appendix. Then return here to do the remaining portion of this activity:

Using The Appropriate Eye To See

For this activity, learn to use your triple vision. Pick something to view with your physical eyes (the eyes of the flesh). Determine what this thing is and, if possible, what it contains. Now use the eye of the mind to look within yourself to the seat of your reasoning to determine what, in your imagination, the thing you saw with your eye of the flesh could be. Witness the conversation that occurs in the mind about various options. Last, look that the thing as seen with the eye of the flesh (the thing outside, seen monologically—without a dialogue—in the Realm of Exteriority) and the thing as seen by the eye of the mind/reason (the thing inside, seen with a dialogue running in the mind, in the Realm of Interiority) and determine what this thing or mental image ought to be (in the Realm of the Spirit, taking into account More-Than-Individual, More-Than-Human, transpersonal considerations, inspired by The Absolute Spirit). In other words, determine with your eye of contemplation whether the thing and your mental image of it is "right" or "wrong." Try to see other objects with these three eyes.

Write down your impressions in your journal, clearly identifying your use of each of the three eyes--flesh (what is), mind (what could be), and contemplation (what ought to be).

Follow-up Protocol

For best results, write down your impressions of this activity in your journal using the Heartwood Path Follow-up Protocol found in the Appendix. Afterwards, consider sharing your interpretations with others.

Heartwood Path Axioms

Key Assertions From Waypoint 2.40

2.40.1.

These distinctions—what is Good (morals and religion) from what is Beautiful (art) from what is True (science) are all fine and good until they go too far, until differentiation became disassociation.

2.40.2.

Differentiation is necessary for integration (a process described earlier in our discussion of transcendence) but disassociation can lead to the kind of repression that allowed the Church to prevent Galileo from discussing what he saw through his telescope.

2.40.3.

In both science and Modernism, moral considerations of better and worse are replaced with scientific considerations of bigger and smaller.

2.40.4.

We have, in effect, different eyes: we use "the eye of the flesh" to see that which we can sense, hold, or feel; we use the "eye of the mind" for mental pictures (images you see only in your mind); and we use the "eye of contemplation" when we ponder significance, moral meanings, and the relative "rightness" or "wrongness" of things, thoughts, or actions.

2.40.5.

Modernity relies almost entirely on the "eye of the flesh," which cannot see significance very well.

Nocturnal Pilgrimage 2.40

For best results, write down your impressions of each night's dreams in your journal using the Heartwood Path Dreaming Time Protocols found in the Appendix. Afterwards, consider sharing your Dream Tending with others.

As always, sleep and dream before continuing. Always ask permission from your Dream Character to gaze into its eyes or otherwise engage in a connection experience. When you feel comfortable with your Dream Character (or attracted to it), feel received through the portal of the eyes of the image. "This time, notice who or what greets you here. What do you become aware of? What feelings are evoked in you? Linger here for a while and notice everything that arises" (Aizenstat, 2009, p. 50).

With the topic of this waypoint and your impressions of the previous activity in mind, develop the intension to have a dream of your choice, dream, and make journal entries. When you are through Dream Tending, move to the next waypoint: "Rebel." Enjoy your next step down the Heartwood Path. It will help you deal with being what the world needs for it to become sustainable: a rebel.

41

Rebel

DO NOT CONFORM BLINDLY

Conformity to a sick society is a sickness. By killing morals and replacing them with science, the pathway to the Absolute Spirit becomes a blind alley. The Heartwood Path seeks to re-illuminate the path to the Absolute Spirit, without loosing the benefits of science.

The Heartwood Path ought to be viewed as an ally to both religion and science. There can be no integrity without both.

By furthering the purpose of the Heartwood Path—which is "the development of integrity"—pilgrims on the path can perhaps avoid some of the errors previous reformers of Modernity have made by learning from their mistakes. Learn from yours too.

When working on reform, prepare to be vilified, especially if you make trouble. Society seeks to put limits on personal liberty.

Do not concern yourself with fitting in to the expectations of others. Prepare yourself for the misunderstanding and wrath that will likely come your way if you are making trouble while seeking needed reforms. There is genius in everyone. Give other nonconformists and reformers words of encouragement. They too are likely to be experiencing the social burdens of being living agitators. By answering the questions in the following activity you will determine, by implication, ways to become a nonconformist.

To Become A Maverick...

HumaNatureConnect Activity

Start-up Protocol

If this is not a day when you prefer to spend time in nature without an agenda, do the Heartwood Path Start-up Protocol found in the Appendix. Then return here to do the remaining portion of this activity:

Being A Nonconformist

For this activity, imagine that you have become an original, a free spirit, a rebel, a dissenter, an unorthodox person, or an eccentric. Being such a nonconformist will be helpful to you as you work to shed the shackles of the domineering culture, shackles that are likely keeping you to be an underpaid worker and an over-spending consumer. Answering the following questions in your journal will provide some ideas for how to become a nonconformist.

1. What were the circumstances of a time, if you have one, when you stopped caring about what people think and set about on your own course?
2. What were the circumstances of a time, if you have one, when you were accepted for who you are?
3. In your attempts to be a nonconformist, if at all, how would you describe your boundaries?
4. How are you natural and not contrived when you demonstrate, if at all, you nonconformity?
5. As a nonconformist, how would you describe your "less beaten" path, if you have one?

6. What can you say about a time when you demonstrated that you value opinions that are different from your own?

7. How would you describe your passion, the thing that makes you an individualist, if at all?

8. Many nonconformists are mostly takers. What would you say about your pattern of giving as well as taking, if at all?

9. What would you write down in your journal about aiming high, beyond where others think you can go, if at all?

10. What plans, if any, do you have now that demonstrate that you are a bit of a loose cannon?

11. What plans would you like to make?

Follow-up Protocol

For best results, write down your impressions of this activity in your journal using the Heartwood Path Follow-up Protocol found in the Appendix. Afterwards, consider sharing your interpretations with others.

Heartwood Path Axioms

Key Assertions From Waypoint 2.41

2.41.1.

Conformity to a sick society is a sickness.

2.41.2.

When working on reform, prepare to be vilified, especially if you make trouble.

2.41.3.

Give other nonconformists and reformers words of encouragement, for they are likely to be experiencing the social burdens of being living agitators.

Nocturnal Pilgrimage 2.41

For best results, write down your impressions of each night's dreams in your journal using the Heartwood Path Dreaming Time Protocols found in the Appendix. Afterwards, consider sharing your Dream Tending with others.

Now that you are developing a relationship with Dream Characters, be sure to write down what you have experienced. Even if what you come across does not make sense to you, write down your impressions so you can consider them at another time. Always thank your Dream Characters, as you would your chosen attractive natural beings in your daytime HumaNatureConnect Activities. Both Dream Characters and attractive natural beings, when tended to appropriately—that is, with respect, with consent, and with open-mindedness—are sources of imagination, inspiration, and wisdom.

After tending to last night's dreams, move to the next waypoint: "Actual Unity." There, you will find several important teachings—all having something to do with the abandonment of the separate sense of self, including the value of Eros, Thanatos, Awareness, and Equanimity; the futility of using food and fame and other stands for unitive experience; the important two poles of compassion; and how material objects do not originate independently but are rather arisings of awareness itself.

42

Actual Unity

USE THE POWER OF BOTH EROS/ THANATOS AND AWARENESS/ EQUANIMITY

To progress into the far reaches of the Heartwood Path, the eart-Heart takes a difficult and often terrifying step: the abandonment of the sense of a separate self. This step is difficult because the Ego repels one back to a lower level or tricks one into accepting false symbols of transcendence rather than actual unity. These ultimately unsatisfying stand-ins for true unitive experience include money, fame, power, profane sex, titles, drugs, and food. These enticing yet unrewarding tokens of non-dual awareness can be overcome through the power of both Eros and Thanatos.

Eros can be thought of as that positive, ontological hunger or force that draws a person toward non-duality. This force can lead one to a higher developmental stage.

Thanatos—death anxiety—does its part in the drive towards a higher developmental stage by encouraging the person not to commit physical suicide but to accept the death of the separate sense of self. One reason why so many people in Western society strive to control Nature—

including the female—is the fear of becoming separate and the view that Nature is the source of infirmity, finitude, and death.

Talk of the erotic and of death is disconcerting to some, a discomfort that is less than helpful in one's quest to grow, to be happy, and to live in a healthy environment. If such talk makes you squirm, I encourage you to get over it eventually; but for now, let us get right to the topic of the other key set of wings for one's practice down the Heartwood Path (which has a point of completion, much as house-building has a completion) and thereafter (which means the work of growing as a person using the Heartwood Path goes on after you finish these series of books, much as houses are always being remodeled and used in various ways far after they are built initially).

These wings of practice are vital tools for the worthwhile task of acknowledging, experiencing, and bearing reality--a primary goal of most worthy spiritual paths. I am speaking of *awareness* (seeing clearly) and *equanimity* (calm abiding). Care exists in the tension between these two poles of our practice. On one pole there is *awareness,* which has to do with clear seeing, the mind, wisdom, the no-self, seeing through the self, insight, acknowledging reality, and reliance on the Seer. On the other pole, there is *equanimity* which has to do with calm abiding, the heart, compassion, the self, building up the self, bearing up to reality, and relying on the Mother. The Heartwood Path—the practice laid out in this book—spans between both of these poles, as any good psychotherapy would.

For those of us who travel the Heartwood Path, as you are doing in a summary and additive way by reading this orientation, the mother is not just your maternal biological parent. Along with this mother, we will be describing the transformative role of both significant feminine partners—discussed in detail in The Heartwood Path for Couples book (**Eros**)—and the Mother Earth (described in the pages that follow). By spanning both poles--awareness and equanimity--we will make sure that we are not just relying on the mind but also on the heart.

My jobs working with people with special needs (mental illness and developmental disability), my comforting and consistent paternal grandmother, my loving mother, my time at the breast of Nature, and the significant female partners I have had in my life have shown me the value of the dual awareness/equanimity approach to personal growth. These relationships with the feminine have demonstrated to me clearly that, in personal transformation, the application of both mind and heart, working in tandem, is an important requirement. Anyone being cared for will do best when they are **both** . . .

—*informed by awareness,* which we will show to mean way more than seeing clearly or being book smart (we will, by the way, show that the world is awareness and that there is, therefore, no sense in quibbling over whether guidance from Nature comes from non-human natural sources or from the human mind), and when they are

—*assured by equanimity,* which comes, not from clear seeing or the libraries of schools and towns, but from the compassionate handshake of therapists, the laps of grandmothers, and the lips of lovers.

As you work toward your goal of finding happiness or improving environmental quality or attaining a state of non-duality (described next) you can apply your own individual mind and heart to the task of furthering your own growth. To this end, your mind does a fair enough job on its own but your heart does not do this work so well alone. A good way to your own heart is through the heart of another.

Here we come to a crucial lesson, and it has to do with non-duality. This lesson is illustrated by the falseness the duality inherent in my own (and probably most person's) choices. When it comes to choosing between clearness of awareness (seeing clearly) and equanimity (acts of compassion and nurturing), for example, I would like to have both but if I had to chose one, I would in a knee jerk reaction pick equanimity any day.

This choice is an illustration of both the allure and the falseness of duality. Compassion, and any of the other warm aspects of equanimity, tends to keep the person seeing clearly longer because it adds a welcome sense of calm abiding. It is, therefore, alluring to pick compassion but doing so is a false choice for two highly instructive reasons:

First. The loving embrace of the Mother, the Earth, the therapist, the grandmother or the lover is only knowable through awareness.

Second. As we will prove in certain clearly marked activities throughout this book, the appropriate arms of the guru or therapist, the lap of the loving grandmother, the guidance of the Earth, and the lips of the lover are not really warm things at all. They, like all other so-called things, are arisings of awareness itself. This is one of the biggest lessons in life and, in a smaller sense, it is instructive here because soon in this book you will likely encounter a quandary—am I guided by non-human natural objects (beings) or am I guided by my own brain? Like my quick desire to choose equanimity over clear seeing, such either/or questions are misleading because they stem from duality. They are answered by the non-dual reality that such things as attractions in nature are not physical objects (beings) but are arisings in the oneness of awareness itself and so, that being the case, why make the distinction? The guidance you will receive in doing the activities of this book series does not come solely from a natural being nor solely from your own mind. It is not one nor the other. It is all one and that one is awareness.

To Cognizance And Composure...

HumaNatureConnect Activity

Start-up Protocol

If this is not a day when you prefer to spend time in nature without an agenda, do the Heartwood Path Start-up Protocol found in the Appendix. Then return here to do the remaining portion of this activity:

Covering The Poles Of Transformation

For this activity, answer the following questions:

1. How do you define awareness?
2. What or who has helped you become more aware?
3. How has your awareness helped you to grow thus far in your life?
4. Where have you experienced calm abiding most in your life?
5. How has the feminine or "the Mother"--male or female--played a role in giving the kind of vital assurance that has helped you to grow as a person?
6. How would giving up both your awareness and your assurance affect you and your growth as a person?
7. How, if at all, can your effort to grow as a person be aided by awareness (clear seeing, the mind, wisdom, the no-self, seeing through the self, insight, acknowledging reality, and reliance on the Seer) and can your effort to grow as a person be aided by equanimity (calm abiding, the heart, compassion, the self, building up the self, bearing up to reality, and relying on the Mother or the Feminine).
8. What would be the positive or negative result of using awareness and equanimity to achieve personal transformation?

Write something down even if you are dissatisfied with your ability to answer such a question. It will be interesting to compare your answer now to your answer reading this book. To write out your answers, create a table like the one below in your journal:

Personal Growth	Positive Results	Negative Results
From Awareness		
From Equanimity		

Follow-up Protocol

For best results, write down your impressions of this activity in your journal using the Heartwood Path Follow-up Protocol found in the Appendix. Afterwards, consider sharing your interpretations with others.

Heartwood Path Axioms

Key Assertions From Waypoint 2.42

2.42.1.

The abandonment of the sense of a separate self is difficult because the Ego repels one back to a lower level or tricks one into accepting false symbols of transcendence rather than actual unity.

2.42.2.

Unsatisfying stand-ins for true unitive experience include money, fame, power, profane sex, titles, drugs, and food.

2.42.3.

Care exists in the tension between the two poles of compassion: on one pole there is *awareness*, which has to do with clear seeing and the mind; on the other pole, there is *equanimity*, which has to do with calm abiding and the heart.

2.42.4.

Not separate from the viewer, so-called "things" are not in-dependent material objects but arisings of awareness itself.

2.42.5.

In dream interpretation, do not rush in too quickly with your bright ideas of what the images mean; for doing so will rob them of their intelligence and replace this substantial capacity with your own, which may not be as revealing.

Nocturnal Pilgrimage 2.42

For best results, write down your impressions of each night's dreams in your journal using the Heartwood Path Dreaming Time Protocols found in the Appendix. Afterwards, consider sharing your Dream Tending with others.

As living images that are part of the inner world of nature and part of your inner nature, Dream Figures, like natural beings and nature itself, have their own intelligence. All living beings, imaginal and tangible, speak according to their own fashion. Some in vibes, some in symbols, some in pillow talk. Nature's intelligence, like your intelligence, lives, in part, in the images of the dreaming psyche. So this intelligence can be witnessed in dreams, and brought forth more fully during Dream Tending. This intelligence is not located in "a preexisting system of early family or symbolic explanation" (Aizenstat, 2009, p. 51), which is why Freud's dream association and Jung's dream amplification are likely to be true but partial, potentially accurate but not nearly complete enough for our purposes along the Heartwood Path. "When we rush in too quickly with our bright ideas of what the image means, we rob it of its native intelligence and replace it with our own, which may not be as illuminating. We want to hear its knowledge, not ours" (Aizenstat, 2009, p. 51).

I believe that during the day or whenever it is not presenting itself in someone's dream, the Dream Figure lives, in part, in the multitude of natural beings that give Nature its diversity and beauty. Being respectful to both natural beings and their Dream Characters takes the seeking of consent to engage in connection experiences with the former—the natural beings—and asking for permission for eye-to-eye contact during Dream Tending with the latter—the Dream Characters.

With the polite relational protocol described in this book (which includes asking for consent, as described), the sojourner has an excellent chance to obtain guidance from nature, which, as you will see, sometimes "speaks" more clearly in dreams than it does in the field. In any of your dreams, including the ones you may have tonight, are you seeing any Dream characters (humans, animals, supernatural beings, individual plants) that seem to be the same thing as or symbolically related to your chosen attractive natural beings? Write down your impressions and reactions to this section in your journal.

With the teachings of this waypoint and your impressions of your participation in the previous activity, move to the next waypoint: "Singularity." There, you will learn about masculinity, femininity, and the transcendence of duality. Happy traveling!

43

Singularity

TRANSCEND TO NON-DUALITY

The step that needs to be taken at this point along the Heartwood Path is a step from a rung of personal development characterized by *masculinity*—by which I mean, among other things, hyper-rationality, competition, and atomistic thinking (seeing everything as separate)—to a rung characterized by *femininity*—intuition, cooperation, and a focus on relationships. This contrast between *masculinity* and *femininity* has very little to do with femaleness and maleness. This step brings one to non-duality—the blending of you as a subject with your object of inquiry—but it ought to not mean that all parts are blended into a homogenous whole. There are still parts, just as there is also one whole and one individual self. The needed step leads to the realization of "self-in-relationship"—not an egoistic self that is merged with a separate other, but the one Self imbedded in a network of essential others.

We all know that men are like steel, they lose their worth when they lose their temper. Women are like telephones, they love to be held and talked to. The thinnest book I ever saw was on the subject of what men know about women. Whether you are a man or a woman, never marry for money. You will have to earn every penny. My ex-wife always had the last word in every argument with her father. Whatever was said after that was just the beginning of the next argument. This relationship training ground is where I learned about the possibility of projecting past grievances on to other people. Which is worse? Trying to live up to superheroes, as many men do; or trying to live up to Barbie, as many women do.

To Merge Subject And Object...

HumaNatureConnect Activity

Start-up Protocol

If this is not a day when you prefer to spend time in nature without an agenda, do the Heartwood Path Start-up Protocol found in the Appendix. Then return here to do the remaining portion of this activity:

Moving To Non-duality

With this activity, answer the following question: How, if at all, can your act of blending your Self as the subject with your object of inquiry--that is, attaining a sense of non-duality--be aided through awareness (clear seeing, the mind, wisdom, the no-self, seeing through the self, insight, acknowledging reality, and reliance on the Seer) and how can your act of blending subject with object be aided by equanimity (calm abiding, the heart, compassion, the self, building up the self, bearing up to reality, and relying on the Mother or the Feminine)? What would be the positive or negative result of using awareness and equanimity to achieve such non-duality? Write something down even if you are dissatisfied with your ability to answer such a question. It will be interesting to compare your answer now to your answer after reading this book. To write out your answers, re-create and fill out a table like the one below in your journal. To get you going with this exercise, look over a sample of what I wrote when I did this activity (back when the only ones tweeting were birds).

Working To-wards Non-duality	Positive Results	Negative Results
From Awareness	I once noticed what I thought looked like a huge number of swollen and red mosquito bites on a loved one's legs.	Not being educated in the matter nor equipped to do tests, I did not know that the leg marks were from lymph nodes affected by a very virulent form of lymphoma.
From Equanimity	The upbeat, humor-loving personality of the loved one with lymphoma taught me the power of positive thinking, love, and music to overcome worry and discomforts.	Had I not mentioned the leg marks to an-other loved one, who immediate sought medical analysis and treatment for the stricken loved one, the miracle of cold analyti-cal treatment may not have been started in time. Our mutual good natures helped enor-mously, but alone they would not have saved his life.

Follow-up Protocol

For best results, write down your impressions of this activity in your journal using the Heartwood Path Follow-up Protocol found in

the Appendix. Afterwards, consider sharing your interpretations with others.

Heartwood Path Axioms

Key Assertions From Waypoint 2.43

2.43.1.

Masculinity and *femininity* has very little to do with femaleness and maleness.

2.43.2.

Masculinity means, among other things, hyper-rationality, competition, and atomistic thinking (seeing everything as separate).

2.43.3.

Femininity means intuition, cooperation, and a focus on relationships.

2.43.4.

Femininity leads to the realization of "self-in-relationship"—not an egoistic self that is merged with a separate other, but the one Self imbedded in a network of essential others.

Nocturnal Pilgrimage 2.43

For best results, write down your impressions of each night's dreams in your journal using the Heartwood Path Dreaming Time Protocols found in the Appendix. Afterwards, consider sharing your Dream Tending with others.

Continue down the Heartwood Path as you dream tonight. Prepare for something important to happen. Look for the intelligence that seems to come from a living being other than yourself.

After Dream Tending, continue your pilgrimage to the next trailside waypoint: "Profundity." Enjoy your pilgrimage.

44

Profundity

HONOR ALL LEVELS OF DEPTH

Revere both the lower levels and the upper levels of a person's spiritual development without exceptions; as all material things, life, and mind are manifestations of Spirit. At the same time, be able to make distinctions in fundamental, built-in, intrinsic worth based on the gradations of depth—levels of spiritual maturity.

Spirit pervades all cosmic persuasions: matter, life, mind, and Soul. Humans are composed of Spirit, matter, life, mind, and Soul. They also can achieve high levels of spiritual maturity, becoming, if they wish and work to achieve it, the level of a secular saint.

This level is achieved by those who are driven easily to fight injustice for the sake of all sentient beings. Also, being self aware, they allow the Universe to achieve its own recognition.

Everything is to be honored, but humans hold a special place. They are the most significant performers of the symphony of the universe.

To Honor The Strands Of The Web Of Life...

HumaNatureConnect Activity

Start-up Protocol

If this is not a day when you prefer to spend time in nature without an agenda, do the Heartwood Path Start-up Protocol found in the Appendix. Then return here to do the remaining portion of this activity:

Honoring All Levels Of Depth

For this activity, honor the whole Chain of Being, from the simplest beings to the most complex beings. In this activity, we will be honoring for the sake of others and not just for the sake of you as a Heartwood Path participant. In order for this honoring to be felt beyond yourself and beyond other humans, it will be helpful to find sensitivities that other beings have that correspond with senses or sensitivities that you as a human being also have or can develop. Using Dr. Cohen's System of Natural Senses, we will provide you with a complete list of sensitivities that exist as the various strands throughout the natural web of life. It will be up to you to determine, through observation and imagination, what beings with a particular sensitivity you wish to honor, and how you wish to honor these fellow beings. Use the following set of questions as your guide:

After you answer each of the questions below determine how you could use your natural senses to honor the beings you identify? If you do honor one or more beings, write down your impressions in your journal.

What being do you see or know of that…

1. has the sense of light and sight, including polarized light?
2. has sense of seeing without eyes such as heliotropism or the sun sense of plants?

3. has sense of color?

4. has sense of moods and identities attached to colors?

5. has sense of awareness of one's own visibility or invisibility and consequent camouflaging?

6. has sensitivity to radiation other than visible light including radio waves, X rays, etc?

7. has sense of temperature and temperature change?

8. has sense of season including ability to insulate, hibernate and winter sleep?

9. has electromagnetic sense and polarity which includes the ability to generate current (as in the nervous system and brain waves) or other energies?

10. has hearing including resonance, vibrations, sonar and ultrasonic frequencies?

11. has awareness of pressure, particularly underground, underwater, and to wind and air?

12. has sensitivity to gravity?

13. has the sense of excretion for waste elimination and protection from enemies?

14. has the feeling sense, particularly touch on the skin?

15. has sense of weight, gravity, and balance?

16. has a sense of space or proximity sense?

17. has the Coriolis sense or awareness of effects of the rotation of the Earth?

18. has sense of motion, body movement sensations, and sense of mobility? How could you use this or any other natural sense to honor that being? If you actually do honor this being, write down your impressions in your journal.

19. has the sense of smell with and beyond the nose?

20. has the sense of taste with and beyond the tongue?

21. has an appetite or hunger for food, water, and air?

22. has the natural sense of hunting, killing, or food obtaining urges?

23. has the humidity sense including thirst, evaporation control, and the acumen to find water or evade a flood?

24. has the hormonal sense, as to pheromones and other chemical stimuli?

25. has the sense of pain, external and internal?

26. has the natural sense of mental or spiritual distress?

27. has the natural sense of fear, dread of injury, death, or attack?

28. has procreative urges including sex awareness, courting, love, mating, paternity, and raising young?

29. has the natural sense of play, sport, humor, pleasure, and laughter?

30. has the natural sense of physical place, navigation senses including detailed awareness of land and seascapes, of the positions of the sun, moon, and stars?

31. has the natural sense of time?

32. has the natural sense of electromagnetic fields?

33. has the natural sense of weather changes?

34. has the natural sense of emotional place, of community, belonging, support, trust, and thankfulness?

35. has the natural sense of self including friendship, companionship, and power?

36. has the domineering and territorial sense?

37. has the colonizing sense including compassion and receptive awareness of one's fellow creatures, sometimes to the degree of being absorbed into a superorganism?

38. has the horticultural sense and the ability to cultivate crops, as is done by ants that grow fungus, by fungus who farm algae, or birds that leave food to attract their prey?

39. has the language and articulation sense, used to express feelings and convey information in every medium from the bees' dance to human literature?

40. has the natural sense of humility, appreciation, or ethics.

41. has the natural senses of form and design? How could you use this or any other natural sense to honor that being?

42. has the natural sense of reason, including memory and the capacity for logic and science? How could you use this or any other

natural sense to honor that being? If you do honor this being, write down your impressions in your journal.

43. has the natural sense of mind and consciousness?

44. has the natural sense of intuition or subconscious deduction? How could you use this or any other natural sense to honor that being? If you do honor this being, write down your impressions in your journal.

45. has the natural aesthetic sense, including creativity and appreciation of beauty, music, literature, form, design, and drama?

46. has psychic capacity such as foreknowledge, clairvoyance, clairaudience, psychokinesis, astral projection, and possibly certain animal instincts and plant sensitivities?

47. has the natural sense of biological and astral time, awareness of past, present, and future events?

48. has the capacity to hypnotize other creatures?

49. has the natural sense of relaxation and sleep including dreaming, meditation, or brain wave awareness?

50. has the natural sense of pupation including cocoon building and metamorphosis?

51. has the sense of excessive stress and capitulation?

52. has the natural sense of survival by joining a more established organism. How could you use this or any other natural sense to honor that being? If you do honor this being, write down your impressions in your journal.

53. has the natural spiritual sense, including conscience, capacity for sublime love, ecstasy, a sense of sin, profound sorrow, and sacrifice? And

54. has the natural sense of aliveness?
    (Cohen, website: http://www.ecopsych.com/insight53senses.html).

Follow-up Protocol

For best results, write down your impressions of this activity in your journal using the Heartwood Path Follow-up Protocol found in the Appendix. Afterwards, consider sharing your interpretations with others.

Heartwood Path Axioms

Key Assertions From Waypoint 2.44

2.44.1.

Humans, composed of all levels of depth—Spirit, matter, life, mind, and Soul—are, thus, the most significant performers of the symphony of the universe.

2.44.2.

Humans allow the Universe to achieve its own recognition.

2.44.3.

A great source of knowledge is one's psyche during dreams, especially if one tends to them by making associations, by amplifying them, or by animating them.

Nocturnal Pilgrimage 2.44

For best results, write down your impressions of each night's dreams in your journal using the Heartwood Path Dreaming Time Protocols found in the Appendix. Afterwards, consider sharing your Dream Tending with others.

Before arriving at the next waypoint, sleep and dream. By being patient and respectful, you can witness your Dream Images (a sunset, for example) and your Dream Characters (a pelican, for example) being alive during your Dream Tending. Doing so will give you insight and a fresh perspective. You will be tapping into the intelligence of the sunset, the pelican, the tree, or the whale. The intelligence of such natural being Dream Images and Characters, especially if you first apply the Natural Systems Thinking Process to these beings during your HumaNatureConnect Activities, will likely come to you during your Dream Tending.

Why limit your source of intelligence strictly to yourself. The Images and Characters that present themselves to your dreaming psyche are a broad source of primal knowledge. Allow your dreams to help you better appreciate and understand those oft-vague feelings and vibes you probably experienced during your time involved in HumaNatureConnect Activities.

Resist the temptation to minimize the relative importance of Dream Characters when compared to natural beings; saying, for example, that dreams are not as real as natural beings. Dream Characters live in your psyche just as natural beings live in your impressions of them. Both have intelligence, conveyed in different ways.

Natural beings encourage the formation of wordless, sometimes vague, impressions. It is these impressions and not just the actuality of the natural being that we are seeking when communing with nature along the Heartwood Path.

It is the mental impressions such beings help to form that best serves our purposes. The impressions can come from Dream Characters or natural beings, Dream Images or natural landscapes. The natural being impression and the natural landscape is no more real than the Dream Image or the Dream Character. Very little that is perceived in dreams is unrelated to actual objects or natural beings.

The natural beings that appear in dreams and the natural beings encountered in Heartwood Path Activities have much in common.

Neither is separate from the influence of the mind. Neither is unconnected to the actual, formed world.

When the natural beings first encountered in the HumaNatureConnect Activities seem to reappear as Dream Images or Characters an opportunity arises to learn more from them.

Gold comes in lots of pots along the Heartwood Path. The richest treasures come in the pots that have natural beings first experienced as impressions formed during HumaNatureConnect Activities, and processed as part of the Follow-Up Protocol, later reappear in dreams and are further refined during Dream Tending. When finding these particular pots of gold, remember not to force interpretations upon the natural being impressions that reappear in your dreams. They offer gifts that are too deep and expansive for flippant explanations.

After continuing to practice Dream Tending, move to the "Rise And Fall." You will learn more about your ensouled physical manifestation.

45

Rise And Fall

BALANCE ASCENT TOWARDS SPIRIT AND DESCENT TOWARDS PHYSICAL MANIFESTATION

The body itself is a location for the unfolding drama of matter becoming Spirit and Spirit incarnating (embodying) in matter. Ascent towards Spirit is represented by ascent-oriented religions and philosophies that focus on death-denying, control over Nature, and a body-repudiating search for union with the divine Spirit. Modernists who focus on Spirit-denying immanence (the material world of Exteriority) or this-worldly naturalism practice descent toward immanence. We humans need to end our repression of Spirit and Interiority and foster within everyone the development of an inter-subjective rational Ego and a transpersonal econoetic Self—one that identifies not only with the physiosphere and biosphere but also with the noosphere (the thinking realm) and theosphere (the spiritual realm). This transformation—from contemporary egocentricism to transpersonalism—is the job of eartHearts.

Do the following set of activities to gain the wisdom of age while you are still young enough to enjoy it.

To An Ensouled Physical Manifestation...

HumaNatureConnect Activity

Start-up Protocol

If this is not a day when you prefer to spend time in nature without an agenda, do the Heartwood Path Start-up Protocol found in the Appendix. Then return here to do the remaining portion of this activity:

Balancing Ascent Towards Spirit With Descent Towards Physical Manifestation

For this activity, focus on descending towards your soul. Ascending towards Spirit has to do with going to heaven, salvation, and, for members of Judeo-Christian religions, establishing behaviors condoned by God. Since such topics are covered in depth by houses of worship and the literature of the world's religions extensively, this worthy part of the spiritual balancing equation is readily accessible.

For that reason, we will focus here on Descent Toward Physical Manifestation and the Soul. As will be our custom, by doing the activities and by answering the questions below, you will likely learn much about this topic and yourself.

According to **A Field Guide to the Soul** by James Thornton (1999),

"We humans have never yet risen from the primal urge to consume resources . . . We need to enter into a new consciousness, one befitting our new status as the dominant global species" (Thorton, 1999, pp. 15-35).

With this statement in mind, in what way is your happiness, if at all, dependent on what you buy? Record your impressions in your journal, including your reactions to Thornton's statement above.

Thornton (1999) states that . . .

"Wisdom... accretes slowly, grain by grain... We need to step aside from the onrushing currents of our thoughts and feelings, and this is not easy to do. Wisdom practices, therefore, take a patient and long term application" (Thornton, 1999, pp. 44-46).

Thornton says there are three ways of the soul. Each of these are useful in physical manifestation--living in your body in the world.

The Way Of The Mind

The first of these is the *Way of the Mind,* which relies on the "fundamental fact we become whatever we give our attention to" (Thornton, 1999), p.51). This way or method "trains us to remain present in the midst of distractions so that we can make the choices that are appropriate to the moment. . . Love is attention. When we are distracted we cannot love" (Thornton, 1999, pp. 51-53). Record your impressions of these statements in your journal and then do the following when you are troubled by obsessive thought, when you are agitated, or when you are crazed with loneliness, longing, or other problems: follow your breath into your body. Feel your breath and your body, and tell yourself, as Thornton recommends: "I am here now, in this body, and nowhere else" (1999, p. 57). A sub-category of the Way of the Mind is one's response to troubles—or attempts to gain answers to queries about troubles.

To respond to troubles, practice the Eureka Principle, which has the following steps: 1) being absolutely clear about the problem, 2) knowing all the relevant facts, 3) knowing all the relevant rules, 4) asking the question with absolute sincerity and resolve, 5) going into silence until the answer emerges, and 6) testing the answer analytically, before proclaiming it. You may want to use the steps of this Eureka Principle whenever you are seeking guidance from nature, and specifically whenever you bring a problem or query along with you when you connect with your chosen attractive natural beings in the activities that follow.

In these activities, do not expect immediate revelations. Allow the silence to include dream time during sleep. Sleeping on an issue may give your unconscious mind time to send pertinent, helpful, novel, innovative, and intelligent messages to your conscious mind.

The Way Of The Heart

The second methodology of the soul is the *Way of the Heart*. According to Thornton:

"The great systole and diastole of the heart are offering and asking. In the practice of offering we open everything we are, everything we have hidden from ourselves all our life long, and offer it to that which is greater than ourselves . . . In the practice of asking, we ask for absolute fulfillment in that which is ultimately real. And when we ask, it begins to come" (1999, p. 109).

Offering and asking each deserve more elaboration. Concerning offering, do it throughout your day. When you awaken, speak directly to a named divine being greater than yourself (such as God, The Absolute Spirit, Gaia, Mother Nature), and, if you are in earnest, say something like: "I give you _(named divine being)____ my mind, body, and soul completely; when you eat, say "I give you_ (named divine being)____this food; when you encounter a problem, say "I give you __ (named divine being)_____this mess; when you are in a meeting and an opportunity arises, say to yourself "I give you _ (named divine being)_____this opportunity; when you feel the love of another, say "I give you __ (named divine being)__this love; when you have an orgasm, say "I give this to you __ (named divine being)___." Be sure to regularly offer praise to all of Creation and the Creator. Concerning asking, go all out. Ask for grace in your endeavors. Again, speak directly. If you do not like using names, mimic the beating of your heart and use the drawn-out sound "Be-love-ed" instead. Be sure, when necessary, to ask your Divine Beloved, for the ability to meet and bear up to suffering, anger, sexual obsession, and despair. Do your asking slowly (giving it sufficient time) and in solitude (where distractions are minimized). Focus on asking the denied parts of yourself, such as your fear and your anger, to come forth so you can face them, bring them to life, and teach you the lessons hidden in the chaos they normally produce. Be sure to ask for the wherewithal to constantly offer praise to Creation, to The Absolute Spirit, to Loved Ones, to Colleagues, and to whatever or whomever you feel a sense of gratitude. Give or ask for the ability to give loving kindness to yourself, your loved one, your neighbors, and all you encounter, especially those with difficulties. Ask for the ability to leave your cares, as St. John encourages, "forgotten among the lilies" (Thornton, 1999, p. 170).

The Way Of Action

The third method of the Soul, according to Thornton, is the *Way of Action*. Says Thornton: "We are what we do. All the awakenings in the world mean nothing if we are not loving in our actions" (p. 170) Becoming confident and positive and helping others to do likewise has to be foremost on anyone's list of actions. Act in ways that help you and others trade anger—which can help us fight the good fights but also leave us worn out—for a sense of connectedness to the source of all being. Once this anger is sufficiently overshadowed by connectedness, take action to make the important changes the world needs. This action requires the activist to feel the pain of the world and to be motivated by this pain to seek corrective measures. When feeling pain in the world, be careful not to add to this pain the suffering that comes from making your own happiness dependent on the success of alleviating the suffering of others. Offer solutions, learn from the pain, be motivated by the pain, but give the pain and especially any suffering that may go along with the pain, away to The Absolute Spirit. Feel the pain, but avoid dwelling on it, avoid reliving it, avoid remembering it, and avoid recounting it, or your own suffering will result. Pain is inevitable and telling. Suffering is avoidable and tortuous. Never make your happiness dependent on your success, whether that success is in conservation battles or in the financial world. Be a savior of the world, but do not make yourself a bore in the process (we all know that any-one named Pierce is likely to bore). Do not allow the world to be jollier without you (Never let it be asked: Why does an eartHeart cross the road? Answer: to bore the people on the other side). You need not feel compelled to make others agree with you, and certainly you need not agree with all that is said here.

In your journal, write down your impressions about what is stated in this activity. Also, sit with the following questions in silence and sleep on them before answering them as entries in your journal:

What does economic growth mean to you?

What will make you happier: working harder to pay for more luxuries, or spending more time doing whatever you love to do?

Beyond satisfying your basic needs, what would you like to do with your life?

Follow-up Protocol

For best results, write down your impressions of this activity in your journal using the Heartwood Path Follow-up Protocol found in the Appendix. Afterwards, consider sharing your interpretations with others.

Heartwood Path Axioms

Key Assertions From Waypoint 2.45

2.45.1.

The body itself is a location for the unfolding drama of matter becoming Spirit and Spirit incarnating (embodying) in matter.

2.45.2.

We humans need to consider ending our repression of Spirit and Interiority and foster within everyone the development of an inter-subjective rational Ego and a transpersonal econoetic Self—one that identifies not only with the physiosphere and biosphere but also with the noosphere (the thinking realm) and theosphere (the spiritual realm).

2.45.3.

Feel the pain (which is inevitable and telling), but avoid dwelling on it, avoid reliving it, avoid remembering it, and avoid recounting it, or your own suffering (which is avoidable and tortuous) will result.

Nocturnal Pilgrimage 2.45

For best results, write down your impressions of each night's dreams in your journal using the Heartwood Path Dreaming Time Protocols found in the Appendix. Afterwards, consider sharing your Dream Tending with others.

Your dreams are a link to a subtle place where spirituality openly mingles with reality. Go in your dreams to this subtle realm by crossing over the bridge to the soul and finding connection to higher realities.

After visiting the often strange realm of the spirit, do another session of Dream Tending before going to the next waypoint: "Contrast & Affinity." You are making your way nicely down the Heartwood Path.

46

Contrast & Affinity

BALANCE AGENCY (INDIVIDUALITY) AND COMMUNION (UNIVERSALITY)

Those who write self-help books about the Ego (the noosphere) tend to focus on self-determination, independence and self-responsibility. This emphasis, for them, is valid. But it is not enough for eartHearts.

Those who write ecology books about the Eco (biosphere or ecosphere) tend to concentrate on unity, wholeness and harmony. Again, this is, for them, valid. But such concentration alone will not do for eartHearts.

Those who write relationship books about the Ero (one's yearning for another) tend to concentrate on polarity, give and take, and romance. Again, this is, for them, valid. But such concentration alone will not do for eartHearts.

For us in the Heartwood camp, however, these three seemingly divergent subjects are not wrong. They are incomplete.

The Heartwood Path, transcends self-help (A) ecology (B), and relationship improvement (C) and leads us to Self Ecology (A plus B plus C equals ABCD). Like any good transcendence, the parts are not lost but added to, with the result of creating a new entity—the "D" represents the uniqueness that comes with the transcendence.

Avoid validating yourself by copying the behavior and accomplishments of others. Learn from role models, but do not copy them blindly. Keep the making of comparisons out of your relationships and your life. Set a new course when your heart calls for it. Know that you will not likely have a chance to go back and try things you neglected to do earlier. Do things now, according to your true heart's desire.

To Your Uniqueness And Commonality...

HumaNatureConnect Activity

Start-up Protocol

If this is not a day when you prefer to spend time in nature without an agenda, do the Heartwood Path Start-up Protocol found in the Appendix. Then return here to do the remaining portion of this activity:

Summarizing Your Uniqueness And Commonality

For this activity, write the story of your life. In this story, emphasize key moments of growth, missed opportunities, or problems that may have encouraged you to seek out the Heartwood Path or other personal/spiritual quests. Include events in your own life that changed you dramatically, or set you on an important course in your own life. Include how you plan to differentiate from someone you use as a mentor, guide, or model in your work or lifestyle. Write down what differentiates you from others and what makes you similar to others.

Follow-up Protocol

For best results, write down your impressions of this activity in your journal using the Heartwood Path Follow-up Protocol found in

the Appendix. Afterwards, consider sharing your interpretations with others.

Heartwood Path Axioms

Key Assertions From Waypoint 2.46

2.46.1.

The Heartwood Path transcends self-help (A) and ecology (B), and relationship improvement (C) and leads us to Self Ecology (A plus B plus C equals ABCD); and, like any good transcendence, the parts are not lost but added to, with the result of creating a new entity—the "D" represents the uniqueness that comes with the transcendence).

2.46.2.

Learn from role models, but do not copy them blindly.

2.46.3.

Since you will not likely have a chance to go back and try things you neglected to do earlier, do things now, according to your true heart's desire.

Nocturnal Pilgrimage 2.46

For best results, write down your impressions of each night's dreams in your journal using the Heartwood Path Dreaming Time Protocols found in the Appendix. Afterwards, consider sharing your Dream Tending with others.

Do not think of your dreams as merely elaborate and mysterious ways to reconcile past grievances or to reveal and clear up unwanted previous yearnings. Dreams are as much about the present as they are about the past. They help us to uncover, both from the past and the present, previously unseen hindrances to our goals. And they can also reveal latent or suppressed aims.

With the subject matter of this waypoint fresh in your mind, set an intention to have some sort of dream, either related to the subject of this waypoint or not. Either way, the practice of incubating a dream, described in greater detail subsequently, will help you with the vital ability to have lucid dreams. For starters, as you lie in bed prior to sleeping, repeat over and over the topic you intend to include in your next dream. Sleep well. Dream. Do not worry about what sort of dream emerges.

Tend to all of your dreams. When you are ready, proceed to the next waypoint: "Pleasure Beyond." There, you will learn of the value of enjoying the blessings of creation.

47

Pleasure Beyond

ENJOY THE BLESSINGS OF
CREATION

One needs to learn to value the experience of pleasure as a way to create a neuropsychological predisposition for pleasure-seeking behaviors. Failure to do so could, in the extreme, lead to the predisposition for violence-seeking behaviors. Heartwood Path Creation Spirituality draws a distinction between bodily pleasure and promiscuity.

Unlike promiscuity, body pleasure, when guided by Heartwood Path Spirituality, is not promiscuous, does not promote violence, and does not condone materialism. Also, in Heartwood Path Spirituality, celebration of matter is seen as holy; celebration of materialism is seen as idolatry.

A chief symptom of living in the industrialized world of Modernity is pleasure-anxiety—the limiting of one's full enjoyment of life. One becomes anxious about experiencing pleasure as a result of society's myths, laws, and common belief system. Our society, having roots in Puritanism, tends to encourage us to feel ashamed, guilty, and deserving of self-punishment.

Throughout the Heartwood Path, pleasure-anxiety is thwarted by discussions and practices that are intended to make a person more likely to experience the pleasure of peak experiences. These intensely pleasurable times teach how good one can possibly feel by demonstrating one's own vast potential for experiencing pleasure. Peak experiences also momentarily erase self-doubt; increase inspiration, self-appreciation, and courage; enhance the feeling of love and empathy for others; and make one feel more hopeful, confident, and connected to the world-at-large.

The craziness of Modernity makes one think too often about peak performances and not often enough about peak experiences. The result is often frustration and bitterness. Choosing to focus on good experiences is not only its own reward, but also often leads to the achievement of goals.

When one is inspired by some great goal one's mind becomes freer as it transcends limitations. One's consciousness expands in all directions, revealing a wonderful world. Forces, faculties, and talents that have been dormant spring alive. One becomes ready to receive the guidance of teachers. One begins to co-create with Spirit. Such co-creation is pleasurable. Co-creation almost inevitably requires the use of, not only words, but also wordless expressions from your vocal chords.

To Your Thoughts On Nature's Destruction…

HumaNatureConnect Activity

Start-up Protocol

If this is not a day when you prefer to spend time in nature without an agenda, do the Heartwood Path Start-up Protocol found in the Appendix. Then return here to do the remaining portion of this activity:

Reacting To A Disturbed Place

For this activity, develop a memory of a disturbed or non-pristine place, write some words about your relationship to this place, and say something about your feelings about this disturbance (focus on any feeling of fear, despair, emptiness, and loss). I, for example, during my years at high school and then again, almost two decades later, when I found myself waiting to pick up my daughters at this same school, would sit among a small grove of black locust trees across the street from the school's main entrance. I was always comforted by this small grove and have, on occasion, been teased for talking to the trees there, now gone in the name of progress. One time, a school mate, later a mother of two children at our Alma Mater, asked me why I always liked to talk to those trees. In response, I smiled, and said: "Because plants have all the anthers." What do your memories of a disturbed place tell you about yourself as? Write your answer in your journal.

Follow-up Protocol

For best results, write down your impressions of this activity in your journal using the Heartwood Path Follow-up Protocol found in the Appendix. Afterwards, consider sharing your interpretations with others.

Heartwood Path Axioms

Key Assertions From Waypoint 2.47

2.47.1.

One needs to learn to value the experience of pleasure as a way to create a neuropsychological predisposition for pleasure-seeking behaviors.

2.47.2.

A chief symptom of living in the industrialized world of Modernity is pleasure-anxiety—the limiting of one's full enjoyment of life

2.47.3.

When one is inspired by some great goal one's mind becomes freer as it transcends limitations.

Nocturnal Pilgrimage 2.47

For best results, write down your impressions of each night's dreams in your journal using the Heartwood Path Dreaming Time Protocols found in the Appendix. Afterwards, consider sharing your Dream Tending with others.

Remember to continue asking, in each of your Dream Tending activities: "Who is visiting now?" Doing so will take away some of the uncomfortable feelings some people feel when encountering a living and intelligent Dream Character. Ask this question directly to the Dream Character. Listen to any response, which is likely to be scattered and incomplete. Each time you breathe, open yourself up to more receptivity. Doing so will make you image-centered. "As the image animates, what are you hearing, feeling, seeing? Do not wait for some lightning bolt of knowledge to illuminate you" (Aizenstat, 2009, p. 54). Write down every fragmented communication you receive from the Dream Character.

After doing so, move to the next waypoint: "Voice." During the next learning station, you will be improving your breathing.

48

Voice

IMPROVE YOUR BREATHING

An eartHeart's great asset is his or her voice. The Source gives her this personal attribute as a tool for empowerment, self-realization, and the expression of gladness.

As a Heartwood Path pilgrim, search deep within to that place that is One with the Absolute, One with God, and One with Awareness It-self and you will be able to give better expression to, not only yourself as a civilized person, but, more importantly, you will be able to give a voice to your Uncivilized Self. This is the part of you that is unencumbered by the stress of the modern world. It is the part of you that can best identify with The Absolute and provide the best healing to yourself and others. In some of the various activities that follow, you will be looking for, not words necessarily, but rather expressive utterances that are, among other things, the (illiterate/non-worded) raw sounds of emotions and feelings. At this inner place of non-worded expression, this place of inner sound, you will find the real you, doing what you always wanted to do, able to give voice to both the More-Than-Individual-Self and the individual self.

Words are too limited for our purposes here, for they are mere human symbols and thus contain all the ill-conceived aspects of our un-natural modern culture. In contrast, word-free vibrational sounds are the link between energy and material manifestation.

When one becomes literate one can use words to excel in society. This use of words—written, read, or spoken—is useful. Words are, however, not all that can be ascertained from sounds. In fact, words can be a hinderance for two reasons: 1) they are cultural symbols of the real thing rather than what is actual or true and 2) they require the use of the rational mind which too often prevents one from tapping into the non-rational mind so full of valuable feelings and useful emotions.

When one sings, tones, or chants word-free sounds, one can enter into an alpha state and experience the sacred realm of the perpetual now, of namelessness, of extraordinary intelligence, of attraction, of aliveness, and of unlimited love. Making wordless sounds in the presence of an attractive natural object (note that, rather than "object," we have been and will continue to use the more respectful term "natural being") one becomes both attuned to a broader perspective and also speaks on behalf of the more-than-human pairing, thus giving true (actual) and partial (incomplete and limited) expression to the Greater Self. This Greater Self includes your own individual self and your chosen natural being, acting (with your soon-to-become skilled help) as an emissary for the Whole.

Part of the skill required in getting the most out of vocalizing comes from realizing that, like the strings on a violin that produce thin sounds until they are amplified and beautified by the wooden body of the violin, it is one's larynx that makes the sounds which are amplified, made richer, and made more useful by the resultant vibrations of the vertebrae column and the axial bones. We will be learning how to tone and chant in ways that cause the kind of bodily vibrations that serve particular purposes, including those that lead to personal happiness, mental health, and planetary health. In doing so, we will be undoing the witch hunts, the inquisitions, and the whole host of other dreadful events in Europe and elsewhere between the Eleventh and Sixteenth Centuries that "destroyed the rites of exchanging sexual and erotic vitality between humans and nature" (Gardner-Gordon, 1993, p

53). We seek nothing less than a transformation of the human/earth relationship worldwide; in part, through "sounding."

For our purposes here, we need to make a distinction between two words:

1. "sounding" is the making of wordless sounds, without melody but with a rhythm and
2. "toning" is the "vibratory power of the voice by making long, sustained sounds, without the use of melody, beat, or rhythm. When we make "toning" sounds, they "cause vibrations which may create overtones (high sounds that emanate from a single musical note) that reverberate in a way that is incredibly penetrating" (Gardner-Gordon, 1993, p. 61).

Along the Heartwood Path, you will not need a good singing voice. You will also not need in-depth musical knowledge.

Low, soothing tones tend to slow down the heart. Pleasant low tones produce "a grounded, earthy practical sense of well-being. (Low tones are) good for getting into your body and getting things accomplished" (Gardner-Gordon, 1993, p. 61).

High, piercing tones tend to speed up the heart. Pleasing high tones can help you to release stress and transcend your day-to-day worries. They tend to produce a euphoric, angelic, other-worldly, or deeply relaxed feeling.

The oral production of sustained low or high notes require deep breathing, another aspect of toning that "contributes to health and a sense of peacefulness" helps eliminate the effects of stress, helps ameliorate heart disease, asthmas, bronchitis, and senility (Gardner-Gordon, 1993, p. 63). Prepare now to overcome any chronic lack of oxygen and to more freely express your emotions--two unfortunate results of that time during your youth when, if you are like most people, you were regularly forced to be quiet, still, and to hold back your feelings (happy or sad).

To Better Breathing...

HumaNatureConnect Activity

Start-up Protocol

If this is not a day when you prefer to spend time in nature without an agenda, do the Heartwood Path Start-up Protocol found in the Appendix. Then return here to do the remaining portion of this activity:

Creating The Breathy Foundation For Meditation

For this activity, stand near your chosen natural being with your feet a shoulder length apart. Take in a deep breath so that your lower abdomen (below the navel) and your upper abdomen expand like a balloon. If you breathe in sufficiently your shoulders will rise. Hold your breath for a count of five and then suck in your entire abdomen without exhaling. Then push your abdomen back out again, exhale, and relax. Repeat ten times. As you inhale think of how thankful you are to have fellow beings in your presence like the one you are standing next to. As you exhale, offer gratitude to your chosen natural being for participating with you in this connection experience (a connection between you and your chosen natural attractive being) that improves your breathing. Write down how, if at all, better breathing by you can be good for yourself and other beings.

Follow-up Protocol

For best results, write down your impressions of this activity in your journal using the Heartwood Path Follow-up Protocol found in the Appendix. Afterwards, consider sharing your interpretations with others.

Heartwood Path Axioms

Key Assertions From Waypoint 2.48

2.48.1.

The voice is a tool for empowerment, self-realization, and the expression of gladness.

2.48.2.

Search deep within to that place that is One with the Absolute, One with God, and One with Awareness Itself and you will be able to give better expression to, not only yourself as a civilized person, but, more importantly, you will be able to give a voice to your uncivilized self. This is the part of you that is unencumbered by the stress of the modern world.

2.48.3.

It is the part of you that is unencumbered by stress that can best identify with The Absolute (both Mystery and the Muse) and provide the best healing to yourself and others

2.48.4.

Words are not all that can be ascertained from sounds:

by making wordless sounds in the presence of an attractive natural being one becomes both attuned to a broader perspective and also speaks on behalf of the more-than-human pairing, thus giving true (actual) and partial (incomplete and limited) expression to the Greater Self.

2.48.5.

Words can be a hinderance for two reasons: 1) they are cultural symbols of the real thing rather than what is actual or true and 2) they require the use of the rational mind which too often prevents one from tapping into the non-rational mind so full of valuable feelings and useful emotions.

Nocturnal Pilgrimage 2.48

For best results, write down your impressions of each night's dreams in your journal using the Heartwood Path Dreaming Time Protocols found in the Appendix. Afterwards, consider sharing your Dream Tending with others.

After completing this waypoint, sleep, dream, and tend to your dream before starting the next assignment. During your Dream Tending, pay attention to every emotion inside of you. And feel free to make-believe.

When you are finished Dream Tending, move to the next waypoint: "Sounding." Enjoy the vibrational alignment and the healing vibes you will find there.

49

Sounding

ACHIEVE VIBRATIONAL ALIGNMENT

Sounds can be soothing and relaxing, cleansing and releasing, or re-generative. Humming is soothing and relaxing. Moans and groans are cleansing and releasing. Regenerative sounds vary. They are low and full-bodied when they are about sexual matter or survival. They are in the mid range when they are for self worth and love. When they are high and ethereal they open us up to spirituality.

Using sounds to release emotions can be scary for some people. The not-so-uncommon concern is that released emotions may encourage one to become violent or crazy. Have no fear. You will not become ill, mentally or physically, by expressing your emotions. Suppressing your feelings is another matter. It is good to get your feelings out in the open. If you are self-conscious about making sounds, then start by humming quietly, growing into more forceful sounds as you see that nothing bad happens. Give yourself permission to lose some control, as much as you are comfortable releasing at any moment. In time, you will be able to use your voice to rejoice. You will feel better.

We will be using the voice to produce a vibrational alignment. When I encourage you to go to a natural being when doing most of the activities, you may want to use this time to make personal adjustments.

You may remember our previous description of chakras. As a reminder, they are invisible vortexes of spinning energy that act as transformers of energy as it moves from body, to mind, to emotions, and to Spirit. Basically, chakras allow your biography to affect your biology. They are like an extension of the mind in that they are non-physical and give direction to the body and self.

Vibrational alignment is the use of vibrational tools such as sound and color to produce health and perfection. Through the use of their innate being, natural beings, from flowers to crystals, "share their energetic resonance with us, and by being in their presence, we remember our own perfection" (Gardner-Gordon, 1993, p. 118). Gardner and Gordon's eloquent and vital point is illustrated in the following activity.

To Vibrational Alignment...

HumaNatureConnect Activity

Start-up Protocol

If this is not a day when you prefer to spend time in nature without an agenda, do the Heartwood Path Start-up Protocol found in the Appendix. Then return here to do the remaining portion of this activity:

Breathing In The Healing Vibes Of Natural Beings

For this waypoint, prepare to make a tone and associate a color with each chakra. The exact tone is not crucial. If you can, however, start with middle C for the First Chakra, D for the Second, E for the Third, F for the Fourth, G for the Fifth A for the Sixth, and B for the Seventh. You can do vibrational alignment on all of your chakras, as a general boost, or focus on ones that seem to need alignment, as described below. If you cannot readily reproduce these musical notes with your voice easily, simply start your voice low with the First Chakra and raise your tone roughly up one note with each chakra--A low note for the lowest chakras and higher notes for each higher chakra. If you feel that your First Chakra, the one that helps you manifest what you desire in the physical world, is on the wane, find a red natural being, breathe in repeatedly and, as you do, imagine that you are breathing the red color directly into your groin, and tone an EE sound. If you feel the need to boost the Second Chakra near your belly button, which affects your sexuality, sociability, and friendliness, tone the sound O, find an orange natural being, breathe in repeatedly and, as you do, imagine that you are breathing the orange color directly into your belly-button region, When your power wanes your Third Chakra may need the influence of a yellow natural being and the tone AOM. Be sure to breathe in repeatedly and imagine that the yellow color is absorbed at the base of your sternum. When you need a boost in your compassion and uncon- ditional love--the main jobs of the Fourth Chakra at your heart center, say "Ah", breathe in repeatedly, imagining that the pink or green color of a natural being is being absorbed directly into your heart (which is most receptive to pink or green). The Fifth Chakra may need the pres- ence of a blue natural being and feel the vibrations associated with a UU tone if you are feeling difficulties with communication or opening to the spiritual realm. As you observe the blue colored natural being, breathe in and imagine that the blue vibrations are absorbed directly by your Throat Chakra. Breathe in the color repeatedly, imagine the color purplish blue directly entering your Third Eye Area, and say "MM" in the presence of matching colored natural being when you want to become more telepathic, more intuitive, less superstitious, less fearful, and balanced in your open-mindedness or skepticism. Your Seventh Chakra, on top of your head, helps you feel connected to the world and Spirit. If it needs a boost, breathe in the violet color or violet-colored natural being repeatedly, imagine that this color is being absorbed the

the top of your head, and say "EE" (Gardner-Gordon, 1993, p. 115-117). Write down how, if at all, better breathing by you can be good for yourself and other beings.

Follow-up Protocol

For best results, write down your impressions of this activity in your journal using the Heartwood Path Follow-up Protocol found in the Appendix. Afterwards, consider sharing your interpretations with others.

Heartwood Path Axioms

Key Assertions From Waypoint 2.49

2.49.1.

Achieve vibrational alignment.

2.49.2.

Sounds can be soothing and relaxing, cleansing and releasing, or regenerative.

2.49.3.

Music is a wonderful form of meditation because it keeps both the performer and the listener fully alert to the moment.

Nocturnal Pilgrimage 2.49

For best results, write down your impressions of each night's dreams in your journal using the Heartwood Path Dreaming Time

Protocols found in the Appendix. Afterwards, consider sharing your Dream Tending with others.

Look to your dreams for signs that can be associated with latent or suppressed yearns or desires. Write these associations in your journal.

After completing this waypoint, sleep, dream, and tend to your dream before starting the next assignment. When you are finished Dream Tending, move to the next waypoint, "The Hills Are Alive." There, you will learn about the positive effects of music.

50

The Hills Are Alive

KEEP THE HEART BLESSED
WITH THE SOUND OF MUSIC

When sounds are appreciated they are music. Whether coming from a live band, a recording, a bird in the hills, or a person, sounds that are appreciated have to be listened to and not just heard. Music is a wonderful form of meditation because it keeps both the performer and the listener fully alert to the moment. Variations in melody and rhythm stimulate the feminine brain where careful listening is processed. Listening comes in stages: 1) the level of meaning, 2) the level of feeling, 3) constant awareness, known as presence, and 4) soundless sound (these stages are described in more detail later in this series of books).

Regardless of which stage is being applied to the listening process, with the right attitude, all sounds are beautiful, good, and true. Judging sounds to be bad interferes with one's perception and the enjoyment of life.

Elemental Listening

Sounds rouse the imagination. How the sounds foster imagination depends on if and how the listener perceives the elements of the music.

These elements include Ether (which is space), air, fire, water, and earth. Each will be described subsequently.

Listening for the elements is a gut level primitive form of listening that requires "looking through the reality around a music to the elements that give rise to that reality" (Beaulieu, 1987, p. 16). We will be practicing and working with elemental listening later, a process that will include 1) hearing the sounds, 2) using your imagination with the sounds, 3) applying music to the realities of life, and 4) the silence that precedes and succeeds every sound plus offers untold guidance to the perceiver.

Like extracting medicine from a flower, elemental listening to music and toning is "vis medicatriz naturae." The healing power of nature does not just stem from nectars and minerals. Vis medicatriz naturae-- the healing power of nature --includes what music and toning -- two aspects of nature --can offer in the way of fostering personal happiness and planetary health.

Pythagoras's discovery of the hidden musical blueprint for the formation of physical reality and modern theories of quantum physics were our species' early warnings that the consumptive, un-thinking party of the Twentieth Century was about to end. Despite the warnings, our species still clings to its childish ways.

Now, after a period wherein our species grew to become, collectively, like a maladjusted adolescent, a new beginning is on the horizon. This dawning comes from our greater knowledge and acceptance of the kinds of solutions presented in this book. What is presented here has the potential to bring us out of our delusions of separation, beyond the notion of being mere united earthly brethren, to the responsibility of being co-creators of the future. We just have to learn to sing a different tune.

To The Impact Of Appreciated Tones...

HumaNatureConnect Activity

Start-up Protocol

If this is not a day when you prefer to spend time in nature without an agenda, do the Heartwood Path Start-up Protocol found in the Appendix. Then return here to do the remaining portion of this activity:

Being Affected By Music

For this activity, listen to the sounds of nature as if they are a musical composition. Along with this natural symphony, sing, whistle, or hum a made up tune or a familiar tune that you find pleasing. Keep the music going. When you return home, get out some music and prepare to receive any of the known positive affects music can have on your body:

1. Repair Brain Damage. Talk again after a stroke.

> "Melodic intonation therapy, or singing until you can talk, takes advantage of the fact that language functions are located in the left brain, but music lives over on the right side of the brain. So when that . . . stroke robs you of your ability to speak, you can train your brain to move those functions to the other side by associating music with language. . . . (Music) gives your brain a massage and fills it with happy chemicals . . ." (Jurado, Cracked.com Website).

2. Kick an addiction. Provide a distraction from withdrawal symptoms. "Introducing music can increase levels of some chemicals associated with . . . addictions, like dopamine and norepinephrine . . . In addition, certain music lowers things like heart rate, blood pressure, muscle tension, etc. . . . ." (Jurado, Cracked.com Website).

3. Boost your immune system. Recovery from . . .heart disease, lung ailments and even the common cold. (Music) "reduces stress by reducing cortisol levels, a chemical in your brain that causes you to feel stress in the first place" (Jurado, Cracked.com Website).

4. Prevent seizures. "(Music) by Mozart played on the piano reduces seizure -causing activity in the brain within five minutes . . ." (Jurado, Cracked.com Website).

5. Return lost memories. "When you listen to music you know, feelings associated with the song are returned by the hippocampus" (Jurado, Cracked.com Website).

6. Increase spatial reasoning. "Mozart music, especially piano music, can raise your spatial reasoning the equivalent of nine IQ points" (Jurado, Cracked.com Website)

7. Reduce Parkinson's symptoms. "Music can trick your broken unresponsive body into obedience" (Jurado, Cracked.com Website).

Practice making your own music with the sounds of nature. And enjoy recorded music. Notice any affects on your body.

Follow-up Protocol

For best results, write down your impressions of this activity in your journal using the Heartwood Path Follow-up Protocol found in the Appendix. Afterwards, consider sharing your interpretations with others.

Heartwood Path Axioms

Key Assertions From Waypoint 2.50

2.50.1.

Keep the heart blessed with the sound of music. Sounds can be soothing and relaxing, cleansing and releasing, or regenerative.

2.50.2.

Sounds can be soothing and relaxing, cleansing and releasing, or regenerative.

2.50.3.

Music is a wonderful form of meditation because it keeps both the performer and the listener fully alert to the moment.

2.50.4.

Vis medicatriz naturae—the healing power of nature—includes what music and toning—two aspects of nature—can offer in the way of fostering personal happiness and planetary health.

2.50.5.

The known positive effects music can have on your body include: repairing brain damage, kicking addictions, boosting the immune system, preventing seizures, returning lost memories, increasing spatial reasoning, and reducing the symptoms of Parkinson's disease.

2.50.6.

Now, after a period wherein our species grew to become, collectively, like a maladjusted adolescent, a new beginning is on the horizon.

Nocturnal Pilgrimage 2.50

For best results, write down your impressions of each night's dreams in your journal using the Heartwood Path Dreaming Time Protocols found in the Appendix. Afterwards, consider sharing your Dream Tending with others.

Sometimes images appear over and over in your dreams.

"These recurring dream elements are called dream signs, and they're a powerful stepping-stone to lucid dreams . . . (To facilitate lucid dreaming), Tell yourself before bed, 'The next time I see (whatever) I will realize that I am dreaming" (Tucillo, Zeizel & Peisel, 2013, pp. 79-80).

By checking on the reality of dreaming and by realizing the importance of your conscious observations in invoking realty, the primacy of reality over your impressions of reality will diminish and you will begin to see the oneness of awareness and how one's perceptions provide benefits in both the outer world and the inner world. After finishing your daily Dream Tending, continue on your pilgrimage down the Heartwood Path. To do so, go to the "Joy Columns" waypoint.

51

Joy Columns

WORK ON THE FOUR PILLARS OF PLEASURE

The Heartwood Path is not charted to provide its sojourners with mere fleeting moments of temporary giddiness. Instead, The Heartwood Path leads to Triple A Happiness; that is, a form of happiness that is abiding, abundant, and authentic. This form of happiness is the joy that is made more stable and long-lasting by what we shall call the "Four Pillars of Happiness." If there is contentment, enjoyment, amusement, satisfaction or gratification, the Four Pillars of Happiness become stalwart towers of strength that stabilize joy.

Let's take each of them in turn:

1. The Happiness Pillar of Excitement, for example, is a good remedy for loneliness, boredom, and depression. My example of this Happiness Pillar is playing drums in my band at a big new venue.

2. The Happiness Pillar of Challenge is overcoming obstacles and making improvements in one's life that require more than normal exertion. Such exertion may cause some stress but if one can stay expansive, open, and relaxed during difficult times,

improvements will come. My example of this Happiness Pillar is seeing the Heartwood Path released after over two decades of preparation.

3. The Happiness Pillar of Authenticity is being able to know one's true dislikes and true likes. My example of this Happiness Pillar is going to hear Eric Clapton perform live and realizing that I like his music ever so much more than today's rap music.

4. The Happiness Pillar Courage is facing one's fears. Courage comes from mastery—being positively motivated and capable at a level beyond just coping. My example of this Happiness Pillar is flying an airplane solo for the first time.

To The Supports For Contentment...

HumaNatureConnect Activity

Start-up Protocol

If this is not a day when you prefer to spend time in nature without an agenda, do the Heartwood Path Start-up Protocol found in the Appendix. Then return here to do the remaining portion of this activity:

Building The "Pillars" Of Authenticity, Courage, Excitement, And Challenge In The Pursuit Of Happiness

For this activity, write how you do or do not (or can or cannot) support your pursuit of happiness through authenticity, courage, excitement, and/or challenge. To help you with this exercise, consider using the following format:

My authenticity supports (or does not support) my happiness when I_____.

My courage supports (or does not support) my happiness when I_____.

Getting excited supports (or does not support) my happiness when I _____.

Challenging myself supports (or does not support) my happiness when I_____.

Follow-up Protocol

For best results, write down your impressions of this activity in your journal using the Heartwood Path Follow-up Protocol found in the Appendix. Afterwards, consider sharing your interpretations with others.

Heartwood Path Axioms

Key Assertions From Waypoint 2.51

2.51.1.

Work on the Four Pillars Of Happiness.

2.51.2.

The Happiness Pillar of Excitement is being able to dispense with loneliness, boredom, and depression.

2.51.3.

The Happiness Pillar of Challenge is overcoming obstacles and making improvements in one's life that require more than normal exertion (such exertion may cause some stress but if

one can stay expansive, open, and relaxed during difficult times, improvements will come).

2.51.4.

The Happiness of Authenticity is being able to know one's true dislikes and true likes.

2.51.5.

The Happiness Pillar of Courage is facing one's fears.

Nocturnal Pilgrimage 2.51

For best results, write down your impressions of each night's dreams in your journal using the Heartwood Path Dreaming Time Protocols found in the Appendix. Afterwards, consider sharing your Dream Tending with others.

To get the most from your dreams, you will need to set an intention before you go to sleep and, in doing so, you can have some of the richest experiences of your life. Columnist Sheila Graham says: "You can have anything you want if you want it desperately enough. You (have to) want it with an inner exuberance that erupts through the skin and joins the energy that created the world" (Tucillo, Zeizel & Peisel, 2013, pp. 55-57).

To set an intention, do not make it into a cold equation. Make it a heartfelt desire." Phrase "your intention in the present tense . . . engage all five senses . . . go to bed looking for a lucid dream . . . (and concentrate) on your intention until sleep pulls you under. This way your desire will carry over into the dream world and produce the exact results you are hoping for" (Tucillo, Zeizel & Peisel, 2013, pp. 55-57).

With this in mind, set an intention, sleep, dream, and write down your dreams in your dream journal.

After tending to your dreams, when ready, continue to the next waypoint: "Octagon Of Joy."

52

Octagon Of Joy

PLAY WITH THE EIGHT FORMS OF PLEASURE

The Pillars Of Happiness described previously apply to the eight forms of pleasure: primal, pain relief, elemental, mental, emotional, sensual, sexual, and spiritual. Without each of these forms of pleasure one will not have the steadfastness to endure the pilgrimage to Gladandgreen Junction. Instead of being carried forward by your pleasure, one will likely become weary, distracted, or disinterested. Without pleasure any endeavor becomes a tedious chore and the positive results are left to those who, instead of focusing on the languor and length of the pilgrimage, find some sort of delight in each step along the way.

Here are our substitutes for longueur (fatigue from lengthiness)—our ways to keep any pathway of growth from seeming to be protracted, dragged-out, or interminable: Primal pleasure is feeling good by going with the flow; walking on air; and feeling buoyant, elated, exulted, and high. Soothing aches and pains through therapeutic or emphatic touch is the pleasure of pain relief. Elemental pleasures include play, movement, and making pleasing sounds. Curiosity, the craving for information, and learning are all mental pleasures. Love, avoidance of fear, and moving away from threats as a result of anger are the components of emotional pleasure. Love moves one toward what promises emotional nourishment. Love sires all positive emotions: including liking something or somebody; feeling thankful, hopeful, trusting, eager, and enthusiastic; and feeling exultation, awe and bliss. One experiences sensual pleasures when one lingers over and enjoys a stimulus. Spiritual pleasures need not be limited to relating to God or cultivating the immortal Soul. While religious fervor can certainly be a form of spiritual pleasure, what is really producing the pleasure is the feeling of being a part of or connected to something that is larger than one's self. Fulfillment comes from coming to terms with deep spiritual matters such as life; death; one's place in the whole scheme of things; and being a part of something good, larger than one's self, and divine.

Limiting your capacity to experience any one of the eight forms of pleasure will, in turn, limit your capacity to enjoy all the other delights. Also, cultivating your capacity to enjoy some of the more basic forms of pleasure—such as laughing or feeling buoyant—adds to your ability to heighten your response to more complicated forms of pleasure—such as sexuality.

Laughter creates the shortest bridge between two individuals. It does so because it brings forth the kind of joyousness that counters contempt and indignation. When you are sad you attract emptiness. When you are happy, the world laughs with you.

To Eight Forms Of Pleasure...

HumaNatureConnect Activity

Start-up Protocol

If this is not a day when you prefer to spend time in nature without an agenda, do the Heartwood Path Start-up Protocol found in the Appendix. Then return here to do the remaining portion of this activity:

Assessing How You Are Supporting (Or Not Supporting) Your Pursuit Of Pleasure

For this activity, determine how you are using authenticity, courage, excitement, and challenge to support your pursuit of the eight forms of pleasure. Do so systematically by recreating the table shown below in your journal and filling in your responses.

Statement				
Assess and write down how you are or how you are not supporting your pursuit of happiness with one or more of the eight forms of pleasure and their sub-categories, as listed below:	Authenticity	Courage	Excitement	Challenge
	Pertaining to each statement, I do (or do not) support my deep pursuit of happiness with the Pleasure Pillar of Authenticity in the following ways:	Pertaining to each statement, I do (or do not) support my deep pursuit of happiness with the Pleasure Pillar of Courage in the following ways:	Pertaining to each statement, I do (or do not) support my deep pursuit of happiness with the Pleasure Pillar of Excitement in the following ways:	Pertaining to each statement, I do (or do not) support my deep pursuit of happiness with the Pleasure Pillar of Challenge in the following ways:

I experience primal pleasure by "going with the flow."			
I experience primal pleasure by, as the expression goes, "walking on air."			
I encounter primal pleasure by feeling buoyant.			
I encounter primal pleasure by feeling elated, exalted, and/or high.			
I experience the pleasure of pain relief by therapeutic or emphatic touch.			

I come face to face with elemental pleasure through play.			
I encounter elemental pleasure through movement.			
I experience elemental pleasure through making pleasing sounds.			
I encounter mental pleasure through learning.			
I meet mental pleasure through curiosity.			
I experience mental pleasure through craving information.			

I meet emotional pleasure through love.			
I encounter emotional pleasure through moving away from fear.			
I experience emotional pleasure through moving away from threatening anger.			
I encounter sensual pleasure by lingering over and enjoying a stimulus.			

I experience spiritual pleasure by being a part of something good, bigger than myself, and/or divine.				

Follow-up Protocol

For best results, write down your impressions of this activity in your journal using the Heartwood Path Follow-up Protocol found in the Appendix. Afterwards, consider sharing your interpretations with others.

Heartwood Path Axioms

Key Assertions From Waypoint 2.52

2.52.1.

Laughter creates the shortest bridge between two people.

2.52.2.

Love sires all positive emotions: including liking something or somebody; feeling thankful, hopeful, trusting, eager, and enthusiastic; and feeling exultation, awe and bliss.

2.52.3.

While religious fervor can certainly be a form of spiritual pleasure, what is really producing the pleasure is the feeling of being a part of or connected to something that is larger than one's self.

2.52.4.

Fulfillment comes from coming to terms with deep spiritual matters such as life; death; one's place in the whole scheme of things; and being a part of something good, larger than one's self, and divine.

2.52.5.

Limiting your capacity to experience any one of the eight forms of pleasure will, in turn, limit your capacity to enjoy all the other delights just as cultivating your capacity to enjoy some of the more basic forms of pleasure—such as laughing or feeling buoyant—adds to your ability to heighten your response to more complicated forms of pleasure—such as sexuality.

Nocturnal Pilgrimage 2.52

For best results, write down your impressions of each night's dreams in your journal using the Heartwood Path Dreaming Time Protocols found in the Appendix. Afterwards, consider sharing your Dream Tending with others.

It is often difficult to remember your dreams. Elsewhere in this book there are suggestions for how to increase your chance for dream recall. Here is one tip not mentioned elsewhere: " . . . try switching sleeping positions. Lie on your side, roll on to your back, go to your stomach, but do so slowly. You can often recall the experience (of the dream) more easily by lying in the position in which you had the dream" (Tucillo, Zeizel & Peisel, 2013, pp. 55-57).

With this in mind, sleep, dream, when you wake up get back into your sleeping position to help you remember your dream. Then record your dreams in your journal. Whatever your intentions were for your dreams, phrase them in the present tense. If you are looking to, in effect, wake up in your dreams while you are asleep, and thereby become aware that you are dreaming and possibly control your dreams, have the intention (before falling asleep) to have such a lucid dream and state that intention in the positive, using a phrase such as "I am lucid and aware in my dream" (Tucillo, Zeizel & Peisel, 2013, pp. 57-68).

When ready, move to the next waypoint: "Sound Wellness." Keep heading to Gladandgreen Junction.

53

Sound Wellness

CHANNEL THE ENERGY

As you seek wholeness (perfection), experience pleasure, and laugh you begin to perceive wellness. Perfection-seeking, as long as it is pleasurable and lighthearted as opposed to excessively concerned with a preconceived preoccupation with a goal imposed by others, moves a person along Dr. John Travis' Wellness Continuum; that is, away from premature death, disability, symptom of illness, and signs of ill-health to education, growth, self-actualization and a high level of wellness. "Wellness," writes Travis, "is an efficient channeling of energy--energy received from the environment, transformed within you, and sent on to affect the world outside" (Beaulieu, 1987, p. 22). This channeling is precisely what happens along the Heartwood Path. We will be using sound to find the wellness that comes from elemental flexibility, the flexibility to change, the ability to convert the stress of this change into euphoria.

In many of the activities that follow you will be asked to hum a tone or say "Om." This sound is the king of mantras. It is an ancient resonance that provides a sort of sonic womb. It is recommend that you say "Om" in a droning or muttering fashion that generate undertones— which commonly occur when you speak in a low voice, whisper, or mutter (vocalize under your breath). "Om" can be orally drawn out in a series of three sounds "A," "U," and "M." But let us not forget that there is an important silence after the droned "OM. " "A" corresponds to the waking state, "U" to the dream state, "M" to deep sleep, and the silence after the "OM" to "the state of *turiya*, a field of spacious consciousness considered vital to the development of yogic power because it encompasses waking, dream, and deep sleep states in concurrent continuity" (Paul, 2004, 180).

In order for "anything to exist it has to be in motion, vibrating" (Paul, 2004, p. xx). If "any object is in motion, it is producing a frequency—a specific tone" (Paul, 2004, p. xx). "Life is vibration, tone, and rhythm. In this sense, everything is alive."

Music "is the organization of specific tones or frequencies, located at specific distances—or musical intervals—from each other" (Paul, 2004, p. xx). Music is "the perception and understanding of the underlying order and relationships among all these vibrations, expressed in melody, rhythm, and harmony" (Paul, 2004, p. xx). Unpleasant (discordant) vibrations "will configure our inner world. Conversely, inner turmoil manifests as a manic outer world" (Paul, 2004, p. xx).

Treading down the Heartwood Path enables you to become a postmodern sonic yogi. You will become aligned with the harmony of the universe through the use of postures and mantras. You will be appreciative of the sacredness of all parts of the human body. You will become devoted to humaNature, to one's neighbors, and to the Divine. And, you will become complete with a crucible-like heart that is capable of transforming the self and the world.

Mantras, both the articulated external sounds one hears with one's ears and the radiant power awakened in one's heart when the sounds resonate rightly, awaken us to vast fields of consciousness. They connect one's soul to the energy that emanates from the governing vortexes of energy called "chakras." Such connecting allows us to absorb Divine attributes into ourselves and, in so doing, aspire to our highest good. Mantras are specific tones or tone phrases which are a means to good ends, and these ends are wholeness, happiness, perfection, and health.

These sacred sounds are, thus, an important augment to medicine and any program of personal or social improvement.

We will use mantras as an antidote to the right-brain, ego-dominated lives that one's reliance on sight exaggerates. The ego-controlled analytical right brain is about doing, often doing that which one ought not to do. We will be using mantras to activate the soul-controlled artistic left brain, which is more about being, being in touch with the soul, and being the way one ought to be. Such ways of being involve ethics, a major theme of this book series.

Our use of mantras will focus on the vibrations of the sounds and not their meaning. While many mantric phrases are Sanskrit words that are translatable into English, we are in this course of study focusing on the sound as an aspect of nature, as an aspect also of our deeper nature, and not as an aspect of human language. We will, therefore, be looking for Spirit in sound by toning sounds more than we will be chanting words—Sanskrit, English or otherwise. We are here connecting mostly with nature and not so much with man-made words, for reasons that will be presented subsequently. It is the sensual experience, the vibration, the music of the spheres, and not the linguistics or the human-oriented meanings that we will be highlighting. Nature does not need our words for its vibrations to work its magic.

In our yoga of sound, we will not be concentrating on human-generated words much at all. Such words are too often communicated without feeling, which will not work for what we are attempting to accomplish—the attainment guidance from undivided humaNature. We will instead employ the deeper significance of "Vak," the sounded "speech of all things"—the underlying "language" of nature. It comes in levels of manifestation that correspond with states of consciousness. There are four levels, only one of which is the audible sound normally associated with oral speech, music, and other vibrations that resonate in the ears.

The first stage mentioned here we shall call the *Articulation Level Of Vaikari Vak*. It is the one where manifested beings make audible sounds: people gives speeches, turtles make short "Whoosh" sounds when they close there shells, trees "creak," in the wind, and humpback whales "sing."

The second stage is more subtle. Here, the vibrations from the Source present themselves as images and thoughts. We shall call this stage the *Thoughts and Images Level Of Madhyama Vak*. Preceding this level is the next step in the unfolding of the manifest world.

The third stage presents to the meditative and still Heartwood Path wayfarer perceptions on the inner world stages of their awareness. We shall call this stage in the unfoldment of nature's speech (vibrations, including sound) the *Perception Level Of Pashyanti Vak* Coming from the undifferentiated, unformed Source, the vibrations of our next stage actually starts this whole process of unfoldment.

As the primordial I-Am, the forth stage presents the wholeness of all potentiality. It precedes perceptions, thoughts, images, articulated sounds, and formed things. We shall call this stage the *All Potentiality Level Of Paraa*. This stage is pure awareness, the Self, in which ever of these ways you chose to think about it is often overlooked, Paraa—the silent background from which all expression (and all differentiation) emerges is largely forgotten because we devote so much of out time witnessing manifest vibrations such as sounds from commercials on television.

The diversity that emerges from the oneness of everything springs from the way each aspect or being within the universal field expresses itself, sometimes through sound, sometimes through thoughts and images, and sometimes through perceptions.

The "Vak" sounds we will be using are like preprogrammed vessels guided in their sonic meter and nuance to merge with the sound of The Absolute Spirit known as "Shabda Brahman." In doing so, we will be replacing words, often laced with negativity, with the Vak sounds of Shabda Brahman that are positive and engender peace, trust, universal belonging, and love.

Given the condition of the world, we can no longer communicate solely in a medium that relies on the abstract form of words, on a medium that allows us to converse without feeling. The job for eartHearts will be to rebuild our lives with the signifying sounds of "Vak," sounds that allow us to feel fully as we communicate with audible sounds, with comprehended gestures in silence (nodding of heads, for example), and even with the ultimate vibration, our own echoing of the "Huge Hum" (also known as the Big Bang), used by the Divine to evoke creation. Within this hum is the harmony the world needs.

The need for mantras is great. Their power is needed now.

We are using sounds that come from humaNature. Be open to using mantras inspired by nature sounds. Feel the mantras as vibrations.

Focus on the effects of the mantra and not so much on what they mean in human words. To translate the mantra is to bring into the process the distraction of applying concepts when really it is feelings that ought to be examined.

Translating mantras brings in the complication of reflecting in a narrow and shallow human way. These sounds deserve more. They are, after all, sounds that come from a broad and deep More-Than-Human source.

Pay attention to how, if at all, they pull together various aspects of your self into a state of wholeness. Pay attention to how, if at all, the mantras reconnect you with your highest truth. Judge for yourself their usefulness and truth.

Certain sounds or sound phrases, some of them musical, are useful; but if you want to pinpoint the emotion, feeling, or ailment you are dealing with, use the following system to create your own mantras out of the "Bija" or "seed sounds" (listed in the paragraphs that follow). Each seed sounds evokes a chakra and a particular transcendental element, allowing it to go to work on the job of healing.

Bijas used to facilitate the flow of energy in the lower three chakras are "lam," "vam," and "ram." Bijas used to facilitate the flow of energy in the fourth, fifth, and sixth chakras are "yam," "ham," and "om." The crown chakra responds to silence—the Sonic Absolute.

Mudra Hand Gestures

To strengthen the power of the mantra consider using hand gestures. When doing so know that the thumb represents the Divine and the index finger—the one next to the thumb—represents the human soul. There are too many mudras to describe here. We will, however, point out the mudra where the thumb and the index finger are joined, indicating the act of yogic union or the yoking of the individual with the collective. The other fingers represent aspects of nature: the middle finger, purity and light; the ring finger passion and fire; and the little finger, darkness and inertia. For receptivity or to facilitate the flow of energy from the base of the spine to the top of the head, place the hands, thumbs touching the index finger, on the thighs with palms facing up. For groundedness or to facility the flow of energy in the other direction, place the hands on the knees with the palms facing down. Use the palms down mudra if you feel too flighty and need to become grounded. Use the palms up mudra if you feel too drained and need to raise your energy.

Conscious Breathing

Through a certain form of intentional breathing one can release the most primal form of the life force—kundalini (described in detail in the Heartwood Path for Couples book). Like a river flooding fields after gathering water from tributaries on its way to the sea, the kundalini fertilizes every level of one's being.

We will be working directly with the Vak speech of nature in Waypoint 2.56. But before you get to a portion of the Heartwood Path that could give you a glimpse of what it would be like to be an enlightened sage, there is important work to be done. Namely, use the following practice...

To Revitalize Your Nervous System...

HumaNatureConnect Activity

Start-up Protocol

If this is not a day when you prefer to spend time in nature without an agenda, do the Heartwood Path Start-up Protocol found in the Appendix. Then return here to do the remaining portion of this activity:

Flooding The Fields Of Your Nervous System With Vitality

For this activity, revitalize your nervous system using the following method: Sit on the ground next to your chosen attractive natural being. Relax. Pay attention to the breath entering and leaving your body. Take in one long breath (all the way down to the body) and hold it for an instant. When exhaling, let out your air controllably through the mouth, first from the top of the chest and lastly from the belly, forcing the last of it out by contracting your abdomen. The breath coming out of the mouth is made audible by maintaining "a slight pressure in your throat so that the contracted glottis can regulate the outflowing air . . . The effect is like the sound of an ocean wave" (Paul, 2004, p. 167). This "great yogic breath is essential to deriving the maximum energy from toning vowels—particularly when intoning the sacred syllable "Om" (Paul, 2004, p. 183).

Follow-up Protocol

For best results, write down your impressions of this activity in your journal using the Heartwood Path Follow-up Protocol found in the Appendix. Afterwards, consider sharing your interpretations with others.

Heartwood Path Axioms

Key Assertions From Waypoint 2.53

2.53.1.

Use sound to find the wellness that comes from elemental flexibility, the flexibility to change, and the ability to convert the stress of this change into euphoria.

2.53.2.

Use mantras, conscious breathing, and hand gestures to create a more harmonious inner world, which will then improve the outer world.

2.53.3.

Promote samadhi not because you care little about this world but because it helps to liberate oneself from self-induced suffering and because, once suffering is minimized, one can devote more attention to helping others, including all sentient beings.

2.53.4.

When you use mantras focus on the vibrations of the sounds and not their meaning.

2.53.5.

Certain sounds or sound phrases, some of them musical, are useful; but if you want to pinpoint the emotion, feeling, or ailment you are dealing with, use or create your own mantras out of the Bija Mantras or "seed sounds."

Nocturnal Pilgrimage 2.53

For best results, write down your impressions of each night's dreams in your journal using the Heartwood Path Dreaming Time Protocols found in the Appendix. Afterwards, consider sharing your Dream Tending with others.

Many people need to be reminded or convinced to start an actual dream journal. For the remainder of this course of study, at least, you will be exploring your dreams. All great explorers always keep a log of their adventures. You ought to, as well.

No need to write long passages. Just follow your attractions and do your Journal your own way.

With this and the and the rest of the subject matter of this waypoint in mind, after you sleep and dream, record whether you have had a lucid dream, and, when ready, move to the next waypoint, "Bija Strings;" but also be sure to treat your mind to some time in nature today. The sensory inputs you receive on your nature walk creates a brain state that is similar to the one that occurs during lucid dreaming. Whether you are turning your attention to external stimuli in nature or to the internal stimuli found during your lucid dream state, your brain will react in the same way. That is why it is possible to make headway down the Heartwood Path at night while you dream, just as you do during the day while you attend to attractive natural beings. Knowing this, your impressions rise in importance. Keep track of them in your daytime and nighttime journals.

54

Bija Strings

SAY THE MANTRAS

Certain sounds such as "ah," "bam,", or "da," cannot be translated into a literal meaning but have the power to create great transformative growth and expansion in humans at the physical, emotional and spiritual levels. Such sounds are called "Bija" or **Seed** Mantras—mantras being sounds that are repeated for meditation purposes.

Our use of seed mantras is based, in part, on the concept of the Five Elements as described in the Vedas, perhaps the Earth's oldest literature, dating back 5000 years. Once you know the subtleties of the Five Elements, even a brief time in nature will confirm that Ether (the space in which anything happens, the Void), Air (anything that is in motion and eternally dynamic, gives movement to biological systems), Fire (the power to transform, burn, and illuminate, the heat and radiant energy that exists in all metabolic and chemical reactions), Water (unstable, continuously flowing, the life-sustaining nectar), and Earth (the solid state of all matter, the source of all nourishment) together provide the building blocks of all material existence. Every object is unique because it contains a particular mixture of these Elements. To have a mantric impact on anything, therefore, one will need a system for saying a series of mantras—hence the need for Bija strings. Bija strings affect what is outside of you and what is inside of you, which is only natural based on one of the most important lessons to be learned along the Heartwood Path:

The outside is inside all of us.

Given the pervasive and interconnected aspects of the Five Elements, usually you will need to employ the powers of more than one element through the use of mantras. This requirement is true whether you are working to create (Fire makes Earth, for example) or destroy (Water quenches Fire). Affecting the multifaceted nature of life and the interactions of all things requires the stringing together of various sounds in a long strung-out mantra. If you wish to string more than one Bija Mantra together, say them in descending order; by which I mean, start with the sounds associated with the Ether, then descend to the Air, then descend to Fire, then Water, and finally to Earth. The mantras for the elements and the chakras are presented below now so that you will be prepared for the following activity, which will also demonstrate why you need to know about seed sounds:

Ether

Like a vessel that contains everything, our first transcendental element, Ether, is space. More specifically for our purposes here, Ether is the shape of the musical octave where all tones exist. It is perceivable when we experience the noiseless sound behind silence. Witnessing this sound will be covered later in this book. Being the shape of the octave and not the notes, or rhythms, or volume, exhibited by the other elements, Ether is either silent or open and resonate. Some associated seed sounds are "om," and "ah."

You are the space that is ether. To help remember this association, activate the throat chakra (Fifth Chakra) by repeating the correlated mantra: "ham," pronounced "hum."

Air

Volatile, shifty, breezy, and transparent, the transcendental element of Air is more commonly called the "mind" and the "intellect." When a person is controlled more by their rational mind than by their emotions, when a person is philosophical and full of ideas, that person exhibits the element of Air. Air has speeds that are fast to very fast, a volume that is loud to very loud, and a pitch that is high to very high. Some associated seed sounds are "gam," "nam," "cam," "jam," "tam," and "kam."

You are air. To help remember this association, activate the heart chakra (Fourth Chakra) by repeating the correlated mantra: "lam," pronounced "yam."

Fire

Bring light into darkness through your vision, burn with enthusiasm, be volatile or out of control and you will be exhibiting the transcendental element of Fire. Fire is present when you move with purpose in a single direction. The speed of the element of Fire is moderately fast to medium. Its volume is moderately loud to medium. Its pitch is moderately high to medium. Some associated seed sounds are "dah," "na," "ta," and "da."

You are fire. To help remember this association, activate the power chakra (Third Chakra) by repeating the correlated mantra: "lam," pronounced "lum."

Water

Water manifests itself as flowing creativity. When you are involved with reproduction and sexuality you are up to your navel in the transcendental element of water. When the speed is moderately slow and the volume is medium to low, and the pitch is medium to low, you are likely exhibiting or experiencing the element Water. Some seed sounds associated with water are "ba," "ma," "ya," "ra," and "la."

You are water. To help remember this association, activate the sex chakra (Second Chakra) by repeating the correlated mantra: "vam."

Earth

As the foundation for the other transcendental elements, Earth is exhibited when you are real and have your "feet on the ground," when you are solid, when you are factual and when you are reliable. Without this transcendental element there is fear and insecurity—two emotional conditions that force a person to compensate by being rigid, dogmatic, and opinionated. The speed of the rhythm associated with Earth is slow to very slow. Its volume is low to very low. And its pitch is low to very low. Associated seed sounds are "va," "sah," and "say." You are the Earth. To help remember this association, activate the root chakra (First Chakra) by repeating the correlated mantra: "lam," pronounced "lum."

Sometimes saying the mantras—words or sounds repeated to aid concentration—may evoke or present an action that is too powerful or too soon. To soften the effects of mantras, to use the mantras as a sweet devotion, or to create a sort of time-release effect: place the mantra "Om" before and the mantra "Namaha" after certain pure mantra sounds. Here are some examples of how to buffer or give a time-release effect when tired and at the same time do some other things:

- to slowly infuse strength and stability into your soul say "Om Hoom Namaha,"
- for a slower development of wisdom and learning say "Om Aim Namaha,"
- to slow down the pace of new beginnings say "Om Gam Namaha," and

- to awaken passion gradually or to bring satisfaction into your life at a slower pace say "Om Kleem Namaha."

To The Sounds Of Healing...

HumaNatureConnect Activity

Start-up Protocol

If this is not a day when you prefer to spend time in nature without an agenda, do the Heartwood Path Start-up Protocol found in the Appendix. Then return here to do the remaining portion of this activity:

Creating Your Own Healing Mantras

For this activity, work out some mantras for you to use for specific healing purposes. Think about what you need right now in terms of physical or emotional healing. If you cannot decide, talk out loud to your chosen natural being, telling it how you feel about whatever is going on in your life presently. Listen to yourself talk. Note if your speed of expression is fast or slow, if your volume is high or low, and if your pitch is high or low. Make needed adjustments in your emotional state based on the following question for you to use regularly on yourself and, later on, with others: Is the quality inherent in a transcendental element, as imparted to yourself or others through the Bija Mantra (seed sound) for the highest good of the individual (and for the highest good of the Greater Self which is that person and his or her associates and environment)? If the tone, speed, and volume of your voice is too high pitched, fast-paced and loud, and if what you are saying is not very creative, then you may want to evoke the elements of Earth (for solid steadiness) and Water (for the flow of new ideas) by using the mantra "ba va" or "ma sah." In making your strings of mantras, apply the transcendent element needed and arrange the sounds in descending order as described above (Ether> Air>Fire> Water> Earth. Before using a mantra whisper it to yourself to see if it resonates properly, based on your intuition. Make sure the sounds you are using match with your intention. Also, make sure the sounds chosen come from the transcendental elements needed for the highest good rather than for some transitory or inappropriate purpose. To make this activity more effective, say the Bija Mantra in the speed, pitch, and volume of the transcendental elements you are evoking by using the seed sounds. Here's a quick summary:

> Ether is silent or open and its associated seed sounds are "om," and "ah."

> Air has speeds that are fast to very fast, a volume that is loud to very loud, and a pitch that is high to very high. Some associated seed sounds are "gam," "nam," "cam," "jam," "tam," and "kam."

> Fire has speeds that are moderately fast to medium, it's volume is moderately loud to medium, it's pitch is moderately high to medium and associated seed sounds are "dah," "na," "ta," and "da."

> Water is moderately slow, it's volume is medium to low, its pitch is medium to low and its associated speed sounds are "ba," "ma," "ya," "ra," and "la."

> Earth is slow to very slow, its volume is low to very low, its pitch is low to very low, and its seed sounds are "va," "sah," and "say."

I understand any skepticism about the effectiveness of the Bija Mantras. Trust what I have presented here, but verify it yourself. Having tried the seed sounds myself, I can report that they were helpful for me. Saying "Va, Sa, Say," slow, low, and quietly, for example, helps me to keep my heart from falling out of rhythm (as it sometimes does when I am exhausted from overwork or emotionally strained by a loved one). The mantras seem to work surprisingly fast.

Follow-up Protocol

For best results, write down your impressions of this activity in your journal using the Heartwood Path Follow-up Protocol found in the Appendix. Afterwards, consider sharing your interpretations with others.

Heartwood Path Axioms

Key Assertions From Waypoint 2.54

2.54.1.

Sometimes saying the mantras may evoke or present an action that is too powerful or too soon.

2.54.2.

Sometimes you may wish to employ the powers of more than one chakra through stringing various sounds together in a long strung-out mantra.

2.54.3.

If you wish to string more than one Bija Mantra together, say them in descending order; by which I mean, start with the sounds associated with the Ether (such as "om," "ah," or "hum."): then descend to the Air (using "gam, "nam," "cam," "jam," "tam," and "kam." and "yam"); then descend to Fire (using "dah," "na," "ta," and "da," and "lum"); then to Water (using "ba," "ma," "ya," "ra," and "la," and "vam"); and finally to Earth (using "va," "sah," and "say," and "lum."

2.54.4.

To buffer or give a time release effect to your search for wisdom and learning say "Om Aim Namaha;" to buffer or give a time-release effect to remove obstacles in your life say "Om Aim Namaha;" to buffer or give a time-release effect to your efforts to remove obstacles in life or bring new beginnings say "Om Gam Namaha;" to buffer or give a time-release effect to your efforts to awaken passion or bring satisfaction into your life say "Om Kleem Namaha."

2.54.5.

To overcome any skepticism about the effectiveness of the Bija Mantra verify their effectiveness for yourself.

Nocturnal Pilgrimage 2.54

For best results, write down your impressions of each night's dreams in your journal using the Heartwood Path Dreaming Time Protocols found in the Appendix. Afterwards, consider sharing your Dream Tending with others.

"As your dream journal grows, so will your relationships with your dreams. You'll soon be dreaming more, having longer and richer dreams, and a wonderful list of common themes and symbols will start to take shape. Hey, you may even learn a thing or two about yourself along the way" (Tucillo, Zeizel & Peisel, 2013, pp. 80-81).

Here's a little activity to do that will help you understand how mantras work. You can actually do this activity or just imagine doing it. Before it gets too dark, take a rope measuring twenty-five feet or so to a nearby tree or shrub. Tie one end of the rope to a branch of the tree or shrub. The branch will have to be thick enough to avoid breaking if you pull on it slightly but still pliable enough to move easily. Hold the other end of the rope and walk away from the tree or shrub. Holding the free end of the rope, move your hand up and down so that it creates multiple waves in the outstretched rope. Consider your rope-clenching hand your mouth when it is making vowel sounds. Consider the rope a wave of sound that is normally produced by someone chanting or toning. And consider the branch where the rope is tied the body being affected by the mantra. Notice as you change the speed of your moving hand that the waves change on the rope and the impact changes on the branch. That's how mantras work. If you are toning vowel sounds, for example, the vowel sound "o" produces a different sound wave and has a different impact on the body of a nearby being than does the vowel sound "e." As you return home from your rope wagging exercise, tone the vowel sounds as you walk. Don't expect all the branches to wave at you. But be assured that you are generating effects on nearby bodies. Of course, some of these effects may be on the bodies of your neighbors, who, after seeing you wiggle your rope, are plotting to call for the padded wagon to transport you to Hotel California (if you know what I mean). So don't get too complacent: as the song—recorded a few blocks from where I sit—goes: "you can check out but you can never leave." More on mantras later. Go over in your mind what you now know about mantras as you prepare for sleep. Intend to dream about mantras.

As you tend to your dreams, you are continuing on your way to the junction of your own happiness and the world's greatest need, Gladandgreen Junction, the destination for the Heartwood Path. When ready, move to the next waypoint: "The Road To Sageness."

55

The Road To Sageness

SEEK ENLIGHTENMENT

The best word for what happens on avenues of pilgrimage such as the Heartwood Path is "sadhana," which is akin to the Sanskrit word sadhu, which means going straight to a goal. "Sadhana" is a Hindu or Buddhist spiritual practice through which an individual reveres a formed image as a mediate step—a connecting link, an intervenor— in the worship of a formless deity or principle. Sadhana is the Tantric evocation of a formless deity by means of ritual for the purpose of getting control of the deity. Sadhana is also a discipline through which an individual can attain enlightenment or samadhi—the state of deep concentration resulting in union with the ultimate reality. This state is achieved by worshipping (we could say revering, venerating, adoring, exalting, or admiring) the image of a formed thing as a mediate step (a connecting link, an intermediary) to the worship and use of a form-less deity or principle (natural laws, the animating spirit . . . God). While sadhana is a Hindu and Buddhist spiritual practice, there are traces of this custom in other religions and spiritual paths, as well. The worshipping of the image of Jesus by Christians is one such example. Our own picking of attractive natural objects (a form of praise), our seeking of consent (a form of reverence and honor), and the repetition of visiting natural beings (a form of devotion) makes the Heartwood Path at least reminiscent of a sadhana. Certainly our chosen attractive natural beings are mediate steps (intervenors, resolvers) leading to the praise of the Absolute and the reception of its guidance, information, and healing.

A formed thing to be worshipped along the Heartwood Path as a mediate step is one's own "self," which we shall define as that which is considered all that is of a singular character, united, and not separated as would be an "other" (we shall see subsequently how this self is expanded as a Sacred or Greater Self which includes more than what is enclosed in one's own bag of skin). Also included in our definition, therefore, are two other significant adornments to the "self," namely: Nature and a lover.

I use the word worship carefully. When I use the term worship in the context of the Heartwood Path, which is not a religion, I mean an act, process, or instance of expressing veneration by taking part in exercises or rituals in an effort to realize the real presence of the Divine. This presence along the Heartwood Path comes as the excellent guidance, information, and healing one receives with the help of attractive natural beings from the Absolute—that which is complete, pure, consummate, boundless, and universal. I could replace the word "worship" with the word "devotion," and, thereby, minimize the chances that the participant will react negatively to "worshipping" in unfamiliar or religiously forbidden ways.

The formed things of primary interest along the Heartwood Path are not considered the Divine. Rather, the formed things are mediate steps that connect one through ritual to the Divine; they reconcile and interpret for us Its (or His or Her) Ultimate Reality.

In addition to our sadhana-like practices of visiting attractive natural beings, the stage will be set for your possible illumination or enlightenment during your time on the Heartwood Path through a curious but time-tested mixture of practices that includes Shabda Yoga (the Yoga of Sound), the attainment of tranquility, the retention of childhood innocence, boldness, and the seeking of justice (each covered in the waypoints that follow).

To The Yoga Of Sound...

HumaNatureConnect Activity

Start-up Protocol

If this is not a day when you prefer to spend time in nature without an agenda, do the Heartwood Path Start-up Protocol found in the Appendix. Then return here to do the remaining portion of this activity:

Taking The Four Steps Of Shabda Yoga

Think of something you want very much. Encode this heartfelt desire in the short phrase " I want to feel _____ " Then start the four steps of Shabda Yoga:

1. Get in touch with your feelings by articulating what you feel clearly and confidently. Say your phrase three time. This step will activate the dense physical form of the physical plane (which is material) and cause it to conform to your statement.
2. Soften the sound of your phrase by whispering it three times. This step will bring your message to the subtle plane (which is emotional-energetic) and cause it to conform to your statement.
3. Say the phrase slowly, confidently, and clearly three times in your mind. This step will affect the substructures of your self, reconfigure your system of core beliefs system, and activate the causal plane of existence (which is spiritual). And
4. Just listen to the silence. Feel the affects of this practice. Perceive your soul "speaking" in the silence to the Divine, who is listening with you in silence.

To strengthen the force of this mantra, say "I want" in the comfortable fundamental tone--one that feels best in your heart chakra (fourth). Then, to move the power from the heart to the head (throat, third eye, and crown chakras) say "to feel" in a note slightly higher in pitch. To move the power to the belly (first, second, and third chakras) say what you want in a tone slightly lower than the first fundamental tone.

Follow-up Protocol

For best results, write down your impressions of this activity in your journal using the Heartwood Path Follow-up Protocol found in the Appendix. Afterwards, consider sharing your interpretations with others.

Heartwood Path Axioms

Key Assertions From Waypoint 2.55

2.55.1.

Seek enlightenment.

2.55.2.

"Sadhana" is a Hindu or Buddhist spiritual practice through which an individual worships a formed image as a mediate step in the worship of a formless deity or principle.

2.55.3.

The formed things to be worshipped along the Heartwood Path as a mediate step include the Self and its significant adornments; namely: Nature and a lover.

Nocturnal Pilgrimage 2.55

For best results, write down your impressions of each night's dreams in your journal using the Heartwood Path Dreaming Time Protocols found in the Appendix. Afterwards, consider sharing your Dream Tending with others.

The route to becoming a true sage is different from the Heartwood Path. Those who seek to become a sage focus most of their meditations on formlessness. By comparison, those who seek to become better helpers hone their skills at universities; vocational programs; and, through trial and error, while on assignment. They tend to focus their thoughts on formed beings, mostly themselves and those under their care.

Those who travel the Heartwood Path are not seeking to become sages nor are the seeking to become typical helpers. EartHearts—those who follow the Heartwood Path—are seeking to become secular saints, meaning that they are uncanonized helpers with many sage-like qualities. The Heartwood Path leads its followers to become elders with prophetic abilities to help others without crashing themselves.

Heartwood Path Saints—eartHearts—stand up against injustice and, while not sages themselves, they have many sage-like qualities—many learned by following the Heartwood Path. To become a sage-like saint while heading down the Heartwood one seeks guidance, information, healing, and spiritual insight by looking in two directions: 1) outwardly, often to attractive natural beings in nature; and, for clarity and additional inspiration, 2) inwardly, often to Dream Characters in dreams. Whichever way they turn, their development and the quality of their service is improved by the Yoga of Sound—Shaba Yoga. Review the four steps of Shaba Yoga before you prepare for sleep.

After tending to your dreams continue on your way to the junction of your own happiness and the sustainability of the environment. When ready, move to the next waypoint: "The Yoga Of Sound."

56

The Yoga Of Sound

CREATE AND TRUST YOUR OWN MANTRAS

At this point in your Heartwood Path pilgrimage you know where you are heading (to a state of being an enlightened prophet, armed with a sonic staff, and prepared to serve the greater whole happily and persistently) but you do not yet know how to get there. You are not yet prepared to speak and respond to Vak sounds and so you are still dependent on words. Meeting you where you are in your dependence on words, the Heartwood Path now takes you to the four steps in our yoga of sound protocol. Note in the activity below that we will still be using words. This is done for two reasons: 1) right from the start we want you to become accustomed to creating and trusting your own mantras (even if they are words rather than sounds) as that is what you will be doing often as you proceed down the Heartwood Path and 2) using unfamiliar sounds, at this step, will take the focus away from the four steps in the following activity (1.listening to sounds, 2. building a bridge of awareness and avoiding attachment to thoughts, 3. absorbing thought-fresh impressions, and 4. remaining still in the silence) and put your attention too much on the newness of the Vak sounds. Later, mantric sounds will replace the words and you will, possibly, enter into the state of samadhi and become a saint.

To A Greater Likelihood Of Illumination...

HumaNatureConnect Activity

Start-up Protocol

If this is not a day when you prefer to spend time in nature without an agenda, do the Heartwood Path Start-up Protocol found in the Appendix. Then return here to do the remaining portion of this activity:

Working With Vak Vibrations

For this activity, try a four-step process that uses the speech (vibrations) of nature.

1. Applying the Articulation Level Of Vaikari Vak. Listen to any sounds emanating from your chosen Natural being or the attractive natural landscape that surrounds it. Using your own voice, out loud, imitate the Vak sound you heard from your chosen attractive natural being. Using your strong and confident voice, repeat what you heard three times. By imitating the sound from your chosen being you are making a mantra that comes, not from a guru but from nature. To strengthen the force of this mantra, as before, say the natural sound in the comfortable fundamental tone--one that feels best in your heart chakra (fourth). Then, to move the power from the heart to the head (throat, third eye, and crown chakras) say the natural sound in a note slightly higher in pitch. To move the power to the belly (first, second, and third chakras) say the natural sound in a tone slightly lower than the first fundamental tone. Repeat this approach with at least three natural sounds heard while you were involved in this

activity. Remember this approach. You are taking the power that manifests in thunder, lightning, and ocean currents, birds, mammals, insects and ingesting it in mantra capsules. Keep records of them in your journal.

2. Applying the Thoughts and Images Level Of Madhyama Vak. For the same natural being, shift your perspective away from its audible sound to its more subtle emanations, which can be noticeable by you as thoughts and images. To do so, follow our usual start-up protocol. As you remain close to the natural being, psychologically build a bridge of awareness between yourself and your chosen natural being. As before, refrain from attempting to understand any thoughts or images that come to mind, and do not bother trying to understand where your thoughts or images come from. You are generating these thoughts but not without the influence of the natural being. Do not attempt to understand the origin of Vak thoughts and images. If necessary, remind yourself that all is one so there is no reason to distinguish where the thoughts and images are generated. For our purposes with Vak Sounds here, it's does not matter if it is the natural being that is generating the thoughts and images. It also is not productive, for this sort of activity, to argue that it is really you alone that is creating the thoughts by your self in your own mind alone. It is very likely that your physical closeness to the natural being is, in a large or small way, affecting your thoughts. Rather than entertain such thoughts during the activity, for this exercise, set aside this explanation and focus on absorbing rather than on understanding. Absorb the Vak images and thoughts by doing no more than witnessing them and storing them in your memory. Any mental or audible running commentary (words running through your mind) gets in the way of the simple, unfettered absorption of thought and images that could provide you with guidance, information, and healing. Do your best to continuously limit the self-generation of any sort of words as you do this step of this activity. Simply absorb the pertinent thoughts and images—

those that have something to do with you, the natural being, guidance, information, or healing—and store them, as you did with the audible sounds, in your memory for later inclusion in your journal.

3. Applying the Perception Level Of Pashyanti Vak this step, move your perception away from audible sounds (which you absorbed in Step 1.) and away from thoughts and images (which you did did in Step 2). Instead, shift your perception to your consciousness without thoughts by building in your mind a bridge of awareness between you and your chosen natural being. Repeatedly practice being aware of your natural being without also generating thoughts about your companion. Once you can be aware without forming a mental commentary (consisting of thoughts and images), absorb your thought-free impressions and secure them away in your memory. Later, you can make notes about your impressions in your journal. I recommend letting your absorbed awareness (your thought and word-free impressions) percolate in your memory for a while before you encapsulate any impressions into words and lock them away in your journal. How much time do you need for this percolation? Long enough to do Step 4. below before making your Step 3. journal entries.

4. Applying the All Potentiality Level Of Paraa Vak. As you did in the "I want to feel ___" exercise, experience the silence surrounding your chosen natural being. You are at a level where the vibrations are beyond the senses. At this level, people with considerable training encounter spiritual revelations. Novices, with some practice, can find universal principles. Linger long in the silence. Absorb any spiritual insights you uncover. Absorb the universal principles you find within the silence. You are peaking into the world of the sage. Include what you experience in your memory. Later, write about the revelations in your journal.

Follow-up Protocol

For best results, write down your impressions of this activity in your journal using the Heartwood Path Follow-up Protocol found in the Appendix. Afterwards, consider sharing your interpretations with others.

Heartwood Path Axioms

Key Assertions From Waypoint 2.56

2.56.1.

Create and trust your own mantras.

2.56.2.

Imitate Vak Sounds.

2.56.3.

Absorb the Vak images and thoughts by doing no more than witnessing them and storing them in your memory.

2.56.4.

Absorb your thought-free impressions and secure them away in your memory.

2.56.5.

Linger long in the silence, absorb any spiritual insights you uncover, and absorb the universal principles you find.

Nocturnal Pilgrimage 2.56

For best results, write down your impressions of each night's dreams in your journal using the Heartwood Path Dreaming Time Protocols found in the Appendix. Afterwards, consider sharing your Dream Tending with others.

EartHearts meet with natural being outside and spend much of their time in a sort of dreamy existence. They also, paradoxically, meet with Dream Characters inside and spend much of this time awakened. Whether dreaming or awakened, EartHearts obtain both inspiration and solace by using Vak Sounds. Review what you learned about Vak Sounds before you prepare for sleep.

After you dream, tend to your dreams. Continue on your way to the Gladandgreen Junction. When ready, move to the next waypoint: "Abundant Tranquility."

57

Abundant Tranquility

FOCUS MORE ATTENTION ON THE PERSON INSIDE THE BODY

Sex lies at the core of one's identity and at the root of one's need to discover joy or avoid loneliness. Heartwood Path Sex, unlike conventional sex, is not mainly an outlet leading to a release of sexual pressure; but rather an inlet leading to relationship, enchantment, and the holding of sexual/physical/ spiritual pleasure. The wonderful results of Heartwood Path Sex have a lot to do with abundant tranquility and not very much to do with ambitious conquests or passing gratification.

To put this essential message to work for you, tell someone you like—your partner, maybe—the little things that you notice about their personality or shared inner world operations which make him or her appealing and attractive. Focus more attention on the person inside the body. Write a poem to your beloved. Develop your sense of humor. Laugh more, particularly on bad days. Look for the humor in the drudgery, the sad times, the moments that would otherwise evoke resentment. Be a little crazy once and a while. Write down ways to inspire laughter and craziness. Laugh at yourself and the things you do. That way you can nearly always be amused.

To A Greater Likelihood Of Illumination...

HumaNatureConnect Activity

Start-up Protocol

If this is not a day when you prefer to spend time in nature without an agenda, do the Heartwood Path Start-up Protocol found in the Appendix. Then return here to do the remaining portion of this activity:

Seeking Abundant Tranquility

For this activity, ask the questions that follow to your chosen natural object but do not expect answers the questions immediately. Just ask for permission to ponder these questions on site in nature; immerse yourself in the qualities of the natural being and its natural surroundings; use one or more of your natural senses; think of your chosen being as an emissary carrying the wisdom of nature to you after granting you its consent to have this connection experience by remaining attractive; resonate with the underlying tone or rhythm you feel in your heart as you sit, stand, or lie next to your chosen natural being; allow the questions to be processed (answered) in the natural realm of your unconscious mind overnight; after a night's dream-filled sleep, return to this activity and write out your answers. Doing so allows the intelligence of nature to silently (and perhaps in your dreams) work its magic on you so that you can then write out answers that are not tainted by fluctuating social pressures or willy-nilly moods. The following questions are adapted from a book by Taylor Clark(2011):

1. In what ways, if any, do I put fear to work for me?
2. Do I breathe slowly and deeply as a way to counter the negative effects of fear?
3. Do I write about my fears in a journal? If not, what would I say in such a log?

4. How, if at all, do I train, practice and prepare as a way to become tranquil in the face of fear?

5. When fearful, do I focus on the present moment and the task at hand or do I grow preoccupied with worries?

6. Do I postpone worries by writing them down and scheduling a time to deal with them later, perhaps when they are no longer so bothersome?

7. How do I expose myself to manageable fears in a way that builds up my ability to handle stressful fears?

8. In what ways have I, if at all, accepted uncertainty and lack of control?

9. In what ways, if at all, do I reframe fears in ways that lead to more tranquility?

10. In what ways, if at all, do I use humor to gain tranquility in the face of fear?

11. In what way, if at all, do I build faith in myself?

12. What principles, if any, have I used to lead myself into a sense of tranquility?

13. In what ways have I welcomed the inevitable fear, anxiety, and stress into my life as a way to make it more tranquil?

Follow-up Protocol

For best results, write down your impressions of this activity in your journal using the Heartwood Path Follow-up Protocol found in the Appendix. Afterwards, consider sharing your interpretations with others.

Heartwood Path Axioms

Key Assertions From Waypoint 2.57

2.57.1.

Focus more attention on the person inside the body.

2.57.2.

Sex lies at the core of one's identity and at the root of one's need to discover joy or avoid loneliness.

2.57.3.

Heartwood Path Sex, unlike conventional sex, is not mainly an outlet leading to a release of sexual pressure; but rather an inlet leading to relationship, enchantment, and the holding of sexual/physical/ spiritual pleasure.

2.57.4.

The wonderful results of Heartwood Path Sex have a lot to do with abundant tranquility and not very much to do with ambitious conquests or passing gratification.

2.57.5.

Tell someone you like—your partner, maybe—the little things that you notice which makes them appealing and attractive.

Nocturnal Pilgrimage 2.57

For best results, write down your impressions of each night's dreams in your journal using the Heartwood Path Dreaming Time Protocols found in the Appendix. Afterwards, consider sharing your Dream Tending with others.

In many of our Nocturnal Pilgrimage sections, it was suggested that you set an intention to have a certain dream while you sleep. Now that you have had experience either succeeding in choosing your dream in advance or failing to "incubate" a certain dream, it is time to expand on this vitally important topic.

Incubating Dreams—that is, choosing what you are going to dream about on any given night—is a very important key to your success in moving down the Heartwood Path, to finding Triple A happiness, and to living in a beautifully sustainable environment. Of all the ways to awaken within your dreams—to examine and control your dreams consciously while you are sleeping—incubating your dreams is most important. And all you have to do to choose your dreams is to have the intention to do so. The foundation of lucid dreaming is having the burning desire to become lucid.

The brain does not quibble over the difference between a thought and an action. For this reason, think about becoming conscious in your dreams and you will become lucent in your dreams. Likewise, think that you will receive guidance, information, and healing from nature and you will carry these benefits to you on the impressions that across the bridge of awareness you establish between the outer world natural being and your own inner world. Go over what you learned here about seeking lucidity and tranquility before you prepare for sleep.

After a dream filled night sleep and tending to your dreams, when ready, move to the next waypoint: "Childlike Innocence."

58

Childlike Innocence

STAY ACTIVE LIKE CHILDREN

Being childlike does not mean being childish, or immature, or undisciplined, or uneducated. It does mean to be nonjudgmental, accepting, and loving.

To be as perfect as a child, spend time with children. Just remember, as we all know, they are capable of disgracing you by demonstrating in public the example you set for them in private.

When you are being stodgy, convert to being childlike. Stay active like children. Keep moving. Write down how you will be childlike this week.

To Be Nonjudgmental, Accepting, And Loving...

HumaNatureConnect Activity

Start-up Protocol

If this is not a day when you prefer to spend time in nature without an agenda, do the Heartwood Path Start-up Protocol found in the Appendix. Then return here to do the remaining portion of this activity:

Maintaining Childlike Innocence

For this activity, consider the wisdom that comes from being child-like. Review the following statements and add some of your own. Record your impressions of these statements in your journal.

Statements Inspired By Looking Through Children's Eyes	What Do I Think Of Each Statement
When milk spills, what is done is done.	
I accept me for the way I am.	
Sharing time with loved ones is important. Most other things less so.	
My life is dedicated to ____.	
Life is a friendly sparring partner, not an enemy.	
I seek to fix the world for my own benefit more than for the world's benefit.	
It is often hard to accept that what is good for others is more important than getting what I want.	
Life has struggles and respites.	
Shouting does not work.	

Answer your own questions.

Fear, surprise, hesitation, and doubt prohibit progress.

It is better to be motivated by others than to be envious of others.

I get smarter after I count to ten.

Let go of what you cannot change.

Shoot for the top and accept failure.

Dream big. Plan smart.

Live in the moment.

Reality is as good as the dream.

Think before you act and speak.

Dress not so people react to you better.

Show it, don't explain it.

Give yourself space to do what you want.

Put plans to your dreams.

Laugh.

Make your own bed.

My rewards come from effort.

You feel better about yourself when your comfort zone is bigger.

Nurture me and do not break my will and I will have confidence, cooperation, and compassion.

Clarify your thoughts with questions. Ask "why?"

Self-esteem and self-respect lead to dignity.

It is good to be willful as long as you also, when appropriate, cooperate.

Release your feelings.

Do good. Don't try to convert others.

I will learn to listen to my parents by them listening to me.

People do not always make sense.

I can only learn to forgive when I have someone to forgive.

Often statements and feelings come from the distant past.

Let go.

I can only learn to be patient when I have to delay my gratification.

You're a grown-up when you are on your own.

Manners count.

I can only learn to cooperate by things occasionally not going my way.

Stuff grows to fill the space you give to it.

When lost, go back to where you were when you knew where you were.

I can best learn to be creative by having to do some things for my-self.

Being scared of other people diminishes when you set personal boundaries.

I can learn to be compassionate by feeling pain and loss.

Buy only what you can afford.

I can learn courage and optimism by facing adversity.

If you are worried, do something.

We all want to belong.

I can learn to persevere and de-velop my strength by facing things that are hard.

Music that lifts your spirits only makes you feel better when you play it.

Feeling guilty is a sign that you are being good.

I will learn how to self-correct by experiencing difficulty, failure, and mistakes.

After an argument, as long as we are talking we are making progress.

Rules are flexible.

I will develop my self-esteem and healthy pride by overcoming obstacles and achievement.

I am not responsible for everything that happens.

It is wonderful to have someone who is happy to see me.

I will become more self-sufficient by experiencing exclusion and rejection.

Everyone needs space to be themselves.

Be nice.

You are allowed to become an individual.

I will be more self-directed when I have opportunities to resist authority and not get what I want.

Apologize, when needed.

Everyone has the right to privacy.

Some of the best phrases for helping me overcome my resistance and to encourage me to participate are "will you . . ." and "would you . . ."

For a loved one, the important thing is to be there, and not just for the good parts.

Never be too busy for a loved one.

As a child, do not ask me what I want, or like, or need, or think, or even feel. Instead, make a suggestion and let me accept or resist.

Let others make some of their own mistakes so they can learn from them.

You cannot be skilled and enthusiastic about everything.

Only lend what you are not attached to.

The behavior may be bad, but never the child.

Lift the spirits, lift the gloom, lift the burden.

As a child grows, let them do more.

I will resist you if I do not feel heard or seen.

Allow the child to break free so they can come home as more than a child.

It is a good thing when the child is hanging out with people who test your tolerance. It shows they are not being judgmental and prejudiced.

Being heard is more important than being someplace on time.

Children have a duty to be courteous, respectful, and cooperative with their parents.

Forgive but do not allow yourself to be pushed around.

As a child, I need strong parents who know what is best more than I need more choices.

Play some part in your community.

Hang around with people who make you feel good.

As a child, I need a boss because I am too young to be self-employed.

As a child, I will learn to accept what has to be by expressing and then letting go of my resistance.

It is helpful and I like it when you pass along your skills.

The high ground tastes better than revenge.

Do not give up your life for God, live your life for Absolute Spirit (or God, if you prefer that name).

The television is rarely a good option.

Take some action.

Giving me more time with you encourages me to be cooperative.

Not everyone can be as green as we would like.

Add your own bit here.

Be resilient.

It is better that you remain strong after you use your command voice. It is better to leave emotional distress out of your expression.

If not now, when?

Be optimistic.

Lectures are boring and confusing and do not inspire cooperation.

Accept.

Put your own spin on it.

Be moderate, but not all the time.

As a child, I am small so you can put me in time out when I am out of control. Time out works fast.

Show up.

Join the party.

Find meaning.

As a child, you will spoil me if you give me more to avoid confrontation.

Crying makes me feel better.

If you want me to cooperate, ask and do not order.

Fixing is not as good as listening and nurturing when you want to minimize resistance and improve communication.

Rewarding works better than punishing if you want to increase my motivation.

A good leader commands rather than demands.

Time outs are better than spank-
ings if you want to maintain
control.

At any age, a masculine child needs
trust more and a feminine child
needs caring more.

It invalidates my feelings when you
say "Don't worry about it," or
That's ridiculous" or "just do it," or
"its not so important."

A feminine person knows that no
matter how good it gets, it can
always get better.

Sometimes people are shaped
round and that is ok.

Ad your statement here.

I do not want to learn more skills
because I might fail.

My mistakes are normal and inevitable.

My speed of learning may be
slower than yours and that is ok.

The younger I am the less responsible I am.

I will learn responsibility through
your example.

I will learn to love myself by the way you treat me.

Negative emotions are acceptable and thinking of them that way helps me learn to manage them.

Your reassurance and guidance opens me up to empathy, which can be expressed by silent caring and understanding.

I need a little expressed validation.

When you resist my feelings it is because I am expressing something you are resisting in yourself.

Know and recognize the difference between a manipulative whiner and a brilliant negotiator.

Set reasonable limits or I will become unreasonable.

Add some more statements of your own and record your impressions of them in your journal.

Follow-up Protocol

For best results, write down your impressions of this activity in your journal using the Heartwood Path Follow-up Protocol found in the Appendix. Afterwards, consider sharing your interpretations with others.

Heartwood Path Axioms

Key Assertions From Waypoint 2.58

2.58.1.

Stay active like children.

2.58.2.

Being childlike means being nonjudgmental, accepting, and loving.

2.58.3.

To be as perfect as a child, spend time with children.

2.58.4.

When you are being stodgy, convert to being childlike.

2.58.5.

Write down how you will be childlike this week.

Nocturnal Pilgrimage 2.58

For best results, write down your impressions of each night's dreams in your journal using the Heartwood Path Dreaming Time Protocols found in the Appendix. Afterwards, consider sharing your Dream Tending with others.

Tonight, let me suggest one thing to lose and one thing to retain. Experience tells me that those who commune with both Natural Beings and Dream Characters can achieve whatever they want. The

Heartwood Path can bring you many good things but that is not what the books or courses are for. Using personal development to gobble up all the goodies is the height of adult arrogance. That's what the earth needs you to give up. What you are encouraged to retain is your childlike innocence. Worthy elders are not like babies and they are certainly not like maladjusted teenagers. They are childlike in that they are nonjudgmental, accepting, and loving.

Go over what you learned about maintaining childlike innocence before you prepare for sleep. Dream. Tend to your dreams. Continue on your way to the Gladandgreen Junction. When ready, move to the next waypoint: "Do It, Do It Boldly, And Do It Now . . ."

59

Do It, Do It Boldly, And Do It Now

ASK YOURSELF: AM I IN EARNEST

To be bold, as all eartHearts will need to be, one has to be willing to be courageous, innovative, and confident. Boldness is the opposite of fearfulness. It is not a common quality because one has to overcome the risk of failure and face the risk of being considered insolent. Bold people are often thought to be this way because, in the course of being earnest, they tend to push too hard against commonplace standards. In doing so, they naturally rub up against the boundaries of proper etiquette and politeness. Despite the occasional criticism for being inappropriate, eartHearts who are bold are admired for both getting things done and instigating growth, progress and movement for themselves and others.

Goethe says: "Boldness has genius, power, and magic in it." True enough, as you will discover when you overcome procrastination. I ask you: "Are you in earnest? Your answer needs to be "yes!" I plead with you to "seize this very day." You do not have to have all the steps figured out in advance. Just start. Goethe says: "Only engage, and then the mind grows heated—Begin it, and then the work will be completed." Write down ten things you have been putting off. Despite any feelings of resistance, begin at least one of them now. Then begin each of the remaining nine items on each of the nine consecutive days. If this doesn't make you bold enough do not wait around for a bold person to provide the leadership. Here is what bold and earnest people do:

1. They know their own flaws and strengths.
2. They keep clear priorities so that they can seize opportunities.
3. They say what needs to be said.
4. They do their homework so that they can couple their knowledge with their action and lead their team.
5. They learn from their mistakes by allowing failure to be an acceptable part of the process.
6. They make the most of any given circumstances and they celebrate every small accomplishment as a stepping-stone to eventual victory.
7. They build momentum by crafting their plan so that every step leads to the next positive step. And
8. They assess themselves by constantly reviewing their answers to the kinds of questions posed the following activity.

To Boldness...

HumaNatureConnect Activity

Start-up Protocol

If this is not a day when you prefer to spend time in nature without an agenda, do the Heartwood Path Start-up Protocol found in the Appendix. Then return here to do the remaining portion of this activity:

Being Bold

Begin by examining the illusions you hold inside and consider the ways you change reality around you. The illusion to examine is not a delusion—a false image that prevents you from seeing the reality around you. A bold person, knowing that everything is an illusion, works to create themselves and their worlds according to the way they think and feel. In doing so, bold people endorse what Shakespeare says: "Nothing is but thinking makes it so." With these thoughts in mind, ask the following questions to your chosen natural being but do not expect to be able to answer the questions immediately. Just ask for permission to ponder these questions onsite in nature; immerse yourself in the qualities of the natural being and its natural surroundings; use one or more of your natural senses; think of your chosen being as an emissary carrying the wisdom of nature to you after granting you its consent to have this connection experience by remaining attractive; resonate with the underlying tone or rhythm you feel in your heart as you sit, stand, or lie next to your chosen natural being; allow the questions to be processed (answered) in the natural realm of your unconscious mind overnight; after a night's dream-filled sleep, return to this activity and write out your answers. Doing so allows the intelligence of nature to silently (and perhaps in your dreams) work its magic on you so that you can then write out answers that are not tainted by fluctuating social pressures or willy-nilly moods. The following questions are inspired by a book written by Christine Comaford-Lynch (2007):

1. What message about my boldness am I projecting through my self-image to others?
2. Do I feel powerful?
3. What do I have to do to change my self-image regarding boldness?
4. Do I get things done? If not, do I do any of the following to maximize forward motion efficiently: stop blaming others, write out your goals, solicit support, remove toxic influences such as alcohol or people who bring you down, use only talk (to yourself and others), focus on what you want to become, begin again

intelligently after learning from failure, focus on details yet also scan the surroundings, and give yourself appropriate rewards?

5. Do I overcome rejection by remembering that "some will, some won't, so what?, someone is waiting."

6. Do I remember that, no matter how late, I can still make a difference?

7. Do I convert in my mind the answer of "no" to "maybe?"

8. Do I avoid trying to change others?

9. Do I do volunteer work as a way to overcome negativity and to raise hope?

10. Do I periodically make a list of my own positive qualities?

11. Do I mentally equalize myself with others, thinking that every-one has the same measure of self-worth?

12. Do I constantly build my network by talking with people, making new friends, and offering compliments to strangers?

13. Do I randomly pick someone from my contacts file simply to check in?

14. Do I express appreciation to someone new daily?

15. Do I realize that there is more to life than having everything?

16. Am I progressing in my self-discovery?

17. Am I too swept up in daily details?

18. Am I my own best friend?

19. Am I authentic?

20. Am I stretching myself outside of my comfort zone?

21. What do I still fear?

22. How do I get to the next level?

23. Are my relationships fulfilling?

24. Do I realize that I am the only problem and the only solution?

25. Am I being patient?

26. Am I successfully balancing wealth, career, fun, health, appear-ance, relationships, personal development, and charity?

27. Do I work on a cause that feeds by soul?

28. Do I give one hour or more of my time (one hour's salary) per week to a cause?

29. Do I get others involved?
30. Am I caring or burdened with over care?
31. Do I realize that I am enough, do enough, and have enough?

Follow-up Protocol

For best results, write down your impressions of this activity in your journal using the Heartwood Path Follow-up Protocol found in the Appendix. Afterwards, consider sharing your interpretations with others.

Heartwood Path Axioms

Key Assertions From Waypoint 2.59

2.59.1.

Ask yourself: "Am I in earnest?

2.59.2.

Goethe says: "Boldness has genius, power, and magic in it."

2.59.3.

**Goethe says: "Only engage, and then the mind grows heated—
Begin it, and then the work will be completed."**

2.59.4.

Write down ten things you have been putting off; and, despite any feelings of resistance, begin at least one of them now.

2.59.5.

Seize this very day, even if you do not have everything figured out.

Nocturnal Pilgrimage 2.59

For best results, write down your impressions of each night's dreams in your journal using the Heartwood Path Dreaming Time Protocols found in the Appendix. Afterwards, consider sharing your Dream Tending with others.

Set the intention to wake up in your dream tonight. Dream lucidly. Walk around in your own inner universe. Keep an eye out for images of nature, especially the Natural Beings you encounter during your HumaNatureConnect Activities. Once found, seek the beings' consent by witnessing its enduring attractiveness. Once consent is established, ask: "Who is visiting here?" Listen respectfully. Then ask "What is happening here?" Ask the same two questions to the most exuberant Character in your dream. Pay particular attention to anything exuberant in your dreams. Intend to remember your encounters for your Dream Tending tasks when you wake up in the morning.

During your Dream Tending, go over what you learned about being bold. Continue on your way to the Gladandgreen Junction by moving to the next waypoint: "Prophets Of Change."

60

Prophets Of Change

SEEK JUSTICE

In the Bible it says: "let justice roll down like waters, and righteousness like an ever flowing stream." –Amos, 5:24. Free people need to agree on some ground rules in order to live together in harmony. Principles of justice are such ground rules. They point to ideas of fair treatment. These principles serve as guidelines that help to govern modes of exchange and interaction in society. Principles of seeking justice of particular interest to eartHearts include the following ethical guidelines: participation is to be voluntary and based on informed choice; there is no discrimination; help and advice is available to all; disputes are resolved through mediation or other nonviolent methods established by each participating group; personal safety is protected; vulnerable participants are supported; the civil rights and dignity of persons is respected; community safety and social harmony are promoted; help for the disadvantaged is made available; and cultural diversity is respected along with civil rights and the rule of law.

Fairness, equity, and moral rightness are the main aspects of justice, which can be defined as action in accordance with the requirements of some law, be it God's command, rules common to all humanity that emerge out of some consensus, or the edicts from society's legal system.

In a narrower sense, justice is action that pays due regard to the proper interests, property, and safety of one's fellows. The seeking of justice is the main job of eartHearts aspiring to be secular saints.

Here's what it mean to be a prophet:

1. They have a need to express their thoughts and ideas verbally.
2. They need to make sure they restore a wrong-doer to right living and not just expose the wrong-doer.
3. They tend to make quick judgments and, there, need to guard inspect themselves to guard against temptation.
4. They react strongly to dishonesty, indiscretion, or wrong-doing.
5. They need to guard against angry tirades and proud reactions
6. Thy are self-critical and open about their failures.
7. They are loyal to the truth and end relationships with people who fail to be truthful or righteous.
8. They feel responsible to speak out.
9. They are eager to embrace their own suffering.
10. They tend to embarrass themselves in their bluntness.
11. They have a special ability to define what is right or wrong.
12. Their judgments become fixed on their minds and they feel compelled to persuade other to agree with them.
13. They predict the future.
14. They receive visions and dreams from the Absolute.
15. When they receive a vision they have superhuman strength.
16. They are always accurate.
17. They seek only to glorify the Absolute.
18. Anyone can become a prophet.
19. They put themselves between the oppressor and the oppressed.
20. Unlike most saints—canonical or secular, eartHeart saints do not become martyrs.

To Become A Justice-seeking Prophet...

HumaNatureConnect Activity

Start-up Protocol

If this is not a day when you prefer to spend time in nature without an agenda, do the Heartwood Path Start-up Protocol found in the Appendix. Then return here to do the remaining portion of this activity:

Seeking Justice

To organize your thinking and acting regarding the seeking of justice, look over the statements below. In presenting the following seven statements, we are not endorsing any one religion or theology. Good statements from one religion can certainly serve as worthy guides or as food for thought to people who are members of a different religion or who endorse no religion. As instructed below, record your impressions, memories, concerns, and plans regarding each of the seven Themes from Catholic Social Teaching (2005):

1. Life and Dignity of the Human Person: The Catholic Church proclaims that human life is sacred and that the dignity of the human person is the foundation of a moral vision for society. This belief is the foundation of all the principles of our social teaching. In our society, human life is under direct attack from abortion and euthanasia. Human life is threatened by cloning, embryonic stem cell research, and the use of the death penalty. The intentional targeting of civilians in war or terrorist attacks is always wrong. Catholic teaching calls on us to work to avoid war. Nations need to protect the right of life by finding effective ways to prevent conflicts and resolve them by peaceful means. We believe that every person is precious, that people are more important than things, and that the measure of every institution is whether it threatens or enhances the life and dignity of the human person.

2. <u>Call to Family, Community, and Participation</u>: The person is not only sacred but also social. How we organize our society—in economics and politics, in law and policy—directly affects human dignity and the capacity of individuals to grow in community. Marriage and family are the central social institutions that have to be supported and strengthened, not undermined. We believe people have a right and a duty to participate in society, seeking together the common good and well-being of all, especially the poor and vulnerable.

3. <u>Rights and Responsibilities</u>: The Catholic tradition teaches that human dignity can be protected and a healthy community can be achieved only if human rights are protected and responsibilities are met. Therefore, every person has a fundamental right to life and a right to those things required for human decency. Corresponding to these rights are duties and responsibilities—to one another, to our families, and to the larger society.

4. <u>Option for the Poor and Vulnerable</u>: A basic moral test is how our most vulnerable members are faring. In a society marred by deepening divisions between rich and poor, our tradition recalls the story of the Last Judgment (Mt 25:31-46) and instructs us to put the needs of the poor and vulnerable first.

5. <u>Call to Family, Community, and Participation</u>: The person is not only sacred but also social. How we organize our society—in economics and politics, in law and policy—directly affects human dignity and the capacity of individuals to grow in community. Marriage and family are the central social institutions that have to be supported and strengthened, not undermined. We believe people have a right and a duty to participate in society, seeking together the common good and well-being of all, especially the poor and vulnerable.

6. <u>The Dignity of Work and the Rights of Workers</u>: The economy has to serve the people, not the other way around. Work is more than a way to make a living; it is a form of continuing participation in God's creation. If the dignity of work is to be protected, then the basic rights of the workers have to be respected—the right to productive

work, to decent and fair wages, to the organization and joining of unions, to private property, and to economic initiative.

7. <u>Solidarity</u>: We are one human family whatever our national, racial, ethnic, economic, and ideological differences. We are our brother's and sister's keepers, wherever they may be. Loving our neighbor has global dimensions in a shrinking world. At the core of the virtue of solidarity is the pursuit of justice and peace. Pope Paul IV taught that "if you want peace, work for justice." The Gospel calls us to be peace-makers. Our love for all our sisters and brothers demands that we promote peace in a world surrounded by violence and conflict.

Answer the following four questions for each of the above seven justice-seeking statements:

1. What is my general impression of the statement?
2. What memories are evoked by the statement?
3. What concerns inherent in the statement are currently being played out in my life?
4. What are my plans for seeking justice regarding the topic of the statement?

Follow-up Protocol

For best results, write down your impressions of this activity in your journal using the Heartwood Path Follow-up Protocol found in the Appendix. Afterwards, consider sharing your interpretations with others.

Heartwood Path Axioms

Key Assertions From Waypoint 2.60

2.60.1.

Seek justice.

2.60.2.

Principles of justice serve as guidelines that help to govern modes of exchange and interaction in society.

2.60.3.

Fairness, equity, and moral rightness are the main aspects of justice.

2.60.4.

Justice is action that pays due regard to the proper interests, property, and safety of one's fellows.

2.60.5.

The seeking of justice is the main job of eartHearts aspiring to be secular saints.

Nocturnal Pilgrimage 2.60

For best results, write down your impressions of each night's dreams in your journal using the Heartwood Path Dreaming Time Protocols found in the Appendix. Afterwards, consider sharing your Dream Tending with others.

Review the seeking of justice as a prophet before you prepare for sleep. Dream. For your next Dream Tending session, get curious about what intelligence came forward in your dream. Do not look for an answer, though. Just recall what the image revealed. Be sure to write down your notes in the present tense. Write down anything you perceive. It may not make sense or be presented in a rational order. Use sketches and words for your journaling. You are putting together a puzzle. You are letting the Dream Character's intelligence find you.

After your Dream Tending, continue your pilgrimage down the Heartwood Path. Prepare to start getting yourself right. When you are ready, proceed to the next waypoint: "Soul Steps."

61

Soul Steps

PUT YOURSELF RIGHT

To provide more equity, fairness, and moral rightness, humans need to, among other things, overcome the tendency, common in corporations, to subordinate eternal public values for expedient commercial priorities. When such subordination occurs, it is the environment, the community, the worker, the consumer, and democracy itself that pays the dearest.

If things are wrong in the world, it is because something is wrong with the individual. To save the world, put your self right first; then help other nearby individuals; and, only after attending to people, work on the non-human cause of concern.

You may feel that you are on a mission to save the world, and indeed you may be. This is joyous work because you feel you are on target. It is also terrible work because of the magnitude of the burden. As you develop as a person your heroic mission to save the world will not remain a burden because after you make your promise to work on a big cause overcoming hindrances becomes your simple way to participate in the world.

A better end product occurs when its initiation is right. Start your dreams in the dream world of The Absolute and keep them in this private, quiet, unseen place until you have gathered sufficient momentum to carve your own path.

To put yourself on course, do the five steps described by Jonathan Parker in his book The Soul Solution: Enlightening Mediations for Resolving Life's Problems (2011). These five step are: 1) grounding (quieting the mind), 2) centering (putting your attention on your heart region, 3) attuning (repeating a sound to connect to the divine presence of your Soul), 4) integrating (becoming still and feeling the expansiveness of peacefulness), and, 5) gratitude (basking in the light and beauty of your love). They are all described in detail in the following activity.

To Prepare To Help Solve The World's Problems...

HumaNatureConnect Activity

Start-up Protocol

If this is not a day when you prefer to spend time in nature without an agenda, do the Heartwood Path Start-up Protocol found in the Appendix. Then return here to do the remaining portion of this activity:

Putting Yourself Right

For this activity, work toward getting yourself closer to being just, suitable, correct, and prepared to participate in solving the world's problems. This process of getting yourself right takes five steps:

1. Grounding. Engage in conscious and controlled breathing. Quiet the mind. Focus your attention on your chosen attractive natural being. Form the intention to connect the base of your spine with the center of the Earth. Direct the energy of the First Chakra to flow to the center of the Earth. Send distracting thoughts and emotions down this flow of energy to the center of the Earth. Continue with this flow until you feel settled, relaxed, stable,

balanced, focused on the present, and grounded. Form the intention to maintain this connection to the earth always.

2. Centering. Put your attention on the place in your body where you most readily feel compassion, grief, sadness, emotional pain and love; namely, the heart region. To direct your consciousness at your heart area, place one or both hands on your upper chest. As you do so, repeatedly ask for your Soul to emerge in your heart. As your soul emerges you will first feel quietness, then a presence. At the first sign of quietness, say repeatedly something like: "I feel the divine presence of my Soul in my heart." Continuing to say this mantra will deepen your experience of Soul connection. This experience is your true nature, an expression of infinite love and light. As harmony and congruity grows sustainably within you over time, you will notice that you feel off track any other way. This is a sign that old programs and beliefs are giving way to the direction of the Soul. This direction heals any part of you that is maladjusted due to isolation or fear.

3. Attuning. Now you will use a repetition of a sound to connect to the divine presence of your Soul. Pick a name, word, or phrase for your connection, any such utterance that has a positive association for you. We all know any sounds will do, except for "I am sending all my money to Don." Repeat such mantras as "Yahweh —the Hebrews' Biblical name for God," "Allah," "Buddha," "NNI-AAL," or "I feel my Soul in my heart" for several minutes or until you feel supported, healed, and supported spiritually. Then sit in silent and attune yourself to the subtle impulses that arise. Keep judgements out. Just be aware of what arises within you. Do not give up if you do not immediately experience these arisings. If you feel stuck, go back to the grounding phase of this activity and continue with the centering phase. Reconnect with the Earth. Reestablish the connection between your Soul and your heart. Without delay, start the sounds again. Continue until you begin to really notice the inner arisings amid the vastness of the peaceful stillness.

4. Integrating. Relax your mind. Let go of the desire to bring questions to your Soul. Become still and feel the expansiveness of peacefulness. Stay peaceful for several minutes or as long as you like.

5. Expressing Gratitude. Simply express gratitude for your meditation session, regardless of your perception of its effectiveness. Feel how your repeated statements of gratitude open you up a little more each time. Perceive with your senses. Notice the details of your chosen attractive natural being and its surroundings. Notice how the more you connect with your Soul the limitations of your outer perceptions become apparent. Bask in the light and beauty of your love.

Once you finish these five steps, jot down your impressions in your journal. Be sure to not support any feelings of specialness. Despite your newly expanded inner connection and its glorious light and beauty, avoid boasting of your accomplishment. No matter how much deeper or brighter you feel, remain humble. Help in this matter follows.

Follow-up Protocol

For best results, write down your impressions of this activity in your journal using the Heartwood Path Follow-up Protocol found in the Appendix. Afterwards, consider sharing your interpretations with others.

Heartwood Path Axioms

Key Assertions From Waypoint 2.61

2.61.1.

If things are wrong in the world, it is because something is wrong with the individual.

2.61.2.

To save the world, put your self right first; then help other nearby individuals; and, only after attending to people, work on the non-human cause of concern.

2.61.3.

A better end product occurs when its initiation is right.

2.61.4.

Start your dreams in the dream world of The Absolute and keep them in this private, quiet, unseen place until you have gathered sufficient momentum to put yourself on course.

2.61.5.

The process of getting yourself right takes five steps:

1) grounding (quieting the mind),

2) centering (putting your attention on your heart region,

3) attuning (repeating a a sound to connect to the divine presence of your Soul),

4) integrating (becoming still and feeling the expansiveness of peacefulness), and

5) expressing gratitude (basking in the light and beauty of your love).

Nocturnal Pilgrimage 2.61

For best results, write down your impressions of each night's dreams in your journal using the Heartwood Path Dreaming Time Protocols found in the Appendix. Afterwards, consider sharing your Dream Tending with others.

Each night during your Heartwood Path pilgrimage you will be asked to sleep and dream. One way to expect to dream is our fifth way to put yourself right in the previous activity: to express gratitude, sometimes in advance.

Along with expressing gratitude, there is that previously-mentioned, time-tested, and effective way to get more out of your dreams. I am speaking, once again, about "Wake-Back-To-Bed." This technique will help you zoom in your consciousness on that time when you are past the period of deep sleep, when your dreams are the longest, and when your dreams are the easiest to remember. "Simply put, (this technique) involves waking up after six hours of sleep, staying awake for twenty minutes, then going back to bed. This thrifty solution sends you back to bed right before you enter the last window of REM," which is (Rapid Eye Movement), when you are most likely to have significant dreams. Before falling asleep for the second time, say to yourself: "I am aware that I'm dreaming . . . (then behind) closed eyelids, visualize yourself inside a dream. See yourself becoming lucid and realizing that your are dreaming. Feel the excitement and emotions that come with lucid dreaming" (Tucillo, Zeizel & Peisel, 2013, pp. 101-105). Enjoy your explorations of the inner universe.

With the current waypoint in mind, sleep; if not already doing so regularly, take another stab at Wake-Back-To-Bed, dream, and tend to your dreams.

When ready, move forward to the next waypoint: "Humility." There, you will find helpful additional suggestions for what to do during your twenty minutes of awake time in your forth-coming Wake-Back-To-Bed activities.

62

Humility

DO NOTHING BUT BE SILENT

A mighty river gets its power by being lower than other bodies of water. Remember this when tempted to seek high positions in the limelight. Avoid seeking credit for your good works.

Put these ideas regarding humility and confidentiality to work for you by doing the following practice: Take the time to do nothing but be silent. Spend extended time in Nature. Take a yoga class. Make incognito contributions. And about the following statement: Humility and darkness: both unveil the radiance of Heaven.

Especially at first, describe your visions confidentially in a private journal. This will keep others from giving you doubt about your dreams. Before bringing your dreams into the realm of the seen, use prayer to make conscious contact with The Absolute Spirit in the invisible world. This will help set you on the path of righteousness. Write down your private dream(s).

To Peace…

HumaNatureConnect Activity

Start-up Protocol

If this is not a day when you prefer to spend time in nature without an agenda, do the Heartwood Path Start-up Protocol found in the Appendix. Then return here to do the remaining portion of this activity:

Staying Humble

For this activity, log your answers in your journal to the following questions, inspired by the book **The Power of Humility**, by Whitfield, Whitfield, Park, and Prevatt:

- Openness: How, if at all, am I open to learning, growth, and experience?
- Attitude Of Don't Know: How do I, if at all, admit to not knowing and thereby be open to all possibilities?
- Curiosity: How do I, if at all, express my curiosity as a way to demonstrate acceptance over prejudice and rejection?
- Innocence: How am I, if at all, innocent enough to produce peace with a person whom I am in conflict?
- Childlike Nature: How do I, if at all, alleviate sin, guilt and shame by being childlike?
- Spontaneity: How do I, if at all, live as my real self in the moment as a way to be intensely alive, dissolve unhappiness, and live with the flow of ease and joy?
- Spirituality: How do I, if at all, step away from predetermined paths and follow my own personal path, recall my integrity, surrender to the moment full of solutions, free myself from attachments, and find the fullness of inner peace?
- Tolerance: How do I, if at all, respect the beliefs, preferences, or practices of others (and myself)?

- Patience: How do I, if at all, pray for what I need without demanding it right away?
- Integrity: How am I, if at all, whole, perfect, authentic, appreciative and accepting?
- Detachment: How do I, if at all, withdraw my emotional attachment—my desire, craving, and clinging—to a person, place, thing, or outcome while remaining a caring person?
- Let Go: How do I, if at all, let go of accumulated baggage from past traumas, let go of the preeminence of the Ego, let go of attempting to fix those who do not want to be fixed, let go of the need to control, and letting go of treating others as I would not want to be treated myself? (2006, p. 15-25)

Follow-up Protocol

For best results, write down your impressions of this activity in your journal using the Heartwood Path Follow-up Protocol found in the Appendix. Afterwards, consider sharing your interpretations with others.

Heartwood Path Axioms

Key Assertions From Waypoint 2.62

2.62.1.

When tempted to seek high positions in the limelight remember that a mighty river gets its power by being lower than other bodies of water.

2.62.2.

Humility and darkness: both unveil the radiance of Heaven.

2.62.3.

Adopt Whitfield, Whitfield, Park, and Prevatt's twelve characteristics of humility: Openness, Attitude Of Don't Know, Curiosity, Innocence, Childlike Nature, Spontaneity, Spirituality, Tolerance, Patience, Integrity, Detachment, and Letting Go (Whitfield, 2006).

Nocturnal Pilgrimage 2.62

For best results, write down your impressions of each night's dreams in your journal using the Heartwood Path Dreaming Time Protocols found in the Appendix. Afterwards, consider sharing your Dream Tending with others.

Many people do not get enough sleep and, therefore, cannot imagine doing what is suggested in this section. If you are resistant to the idea of waking up in the middle of the night to process your dreams, interact with your partner, or aid in inducing vivid dreams, you may want to seriously consider what you can do to go to bed earlier. It may also be necessary to encourage your partner to go to bed earlier so he or she is, likewise, not resistant to being productively and (perhaps) enjoyably awake during the middle of the night. You are always welcome to follow your own attractions, but you are also encouraged to consider the benefits of waking up for twenty minutes or so each evening. Here are some suggestions for what to do during your twenty minutes of awake time during your Wake-Back-To-Bed activity (the early morning watch between First Sleep and Second Sleep): read your dream journal, look over your dream signs, read a book, visit the rest room, draw a picture of a dream, get up and walk around, talk or make love with your partner, write a letter to your unconscious, and continuously ask yourself "Am I dreaming?" (Tucillo, Zeizel & Peisel, 2013, p. 105).

With this in mind, sleep, enjoy your twenty minute early morning watch, return to sleep and dream. Be sure to tend to your dream.

When ready, move to the next waypoint: "The Solution In You." There, you will learn how to make repairs in your inner world.

63

The Solution In You

SEEK INNER WORLD REPARATIONS

Here we have two key fixes—important things to do to make your world better for yourself and others. The first is to seek inner world reparations for yourself. The second is to motivate others to do the same thing.

These repairs provide one with a wide range of suitable options. Humans do not have to rely solely on dogma, faith, or non-verifiable conjectures but can acquire direct experiential evidence and data to make confirmations regarding the inner world. The human brain generates a variety of electromagnetic frequencies, depending on our activities: beta waves (14-30 Hz) during awake, alert consciousness; alpha waves (9-13 Hz) during relaxation, calmness, lucidity, and absence of thinking; theta waves (4-8 Hz) during dreamful sleep, deep relaxation, meditation, and mental imagery; and delta waves (1-3 Hz) during deep, dreamless sleep.

With this variety of brain functioning, humans can summon, receive, and process empirical (or experiential) evidence. This evidence need not only come from sensory empiricism—which is how one can prove assertions in the Realm of Exteriority with one's senses. Evidence may come from either mental empiricism or spiritual empiricism—two ways to prove assertions in the Realm of Interiority.

Mental and spiritual empiricism are vital tools for eartHearts. Mental empiricism includes logic, mathematics, semiotics (the philosophical theory of signs and symbols), phenomenology (the branch of science dealing with the description and classification of phenomena, and hermaneutics (the study of methodological principles of interpretation and explanation). Spiritual empiricism includes: mysticism (the experience of mystical union or direct communion with ultimate reality); spiritual experiences; satori (sudden enlightenment and a state of consciousness obtained by intuitive illumination); and samadhi (the ultimate, ecstatic state of acute awareness through two general types of meditation).

The first type is savikalpa samadhi. This practice is a type of meditation wherein the practitioner focuses on the mental object of form. Since your chosen, attractive, natural beings are "objects of form," this is the type of meditation most often practiced along the Heartwood Path. Meditating on your being, on form, produces:

- various displays of archetypal illumination,
- expansive states of deeply felt love and compassion,
- profound motivations to be of service to others, and
- brain-hemispheric synchronization.

Savikalpa samadhi leads the practitioner to becoming a saint, a primary goal of those who follow the Heartwood Path.

The second type is nirvikalpa samadhi. This practice is a type of meditation wherein the practitioner focuses on mental objects without form, such as thoughts themselves. We won't be doing much nirvikalpa meditation since it leads to sageness rather than saintliness. It is, nevertheless, important to know the distinction between the two forms of samadhi and to be capable of practicing both forms of meditation— savikalpa the most, since we will be seeking the formation of enduring saints; but also nirvikalpa somewhat since even a brief peak into the level of a sage will be an an instructive, "ah-ha" moment.

Meditating on formlessness produces:

- a complete cessation of all mental activity,
- the experience of infinite freedom and boundless existence,
- super-alertness and wakefulness,
- the complete cessation of alpha, beta, and theta brain waves and a large increase in delta waves, and gnosis—immediate knowledge of spiritual truth.

Unfortunately, just knowing what samadhi is does not get you there. Fortunately there is a well worn path for you to follow. Getting this far on the Heartwood Path means that you have already started on your way—note in the following list how the first step towards samadhi is also the first major topic of the Heartwood Path—universal principles. Having just completed the Overture to the Heartwood Path, you may also note the similarities between the progression of this series of books and Yoga Master Patanjol's eight steps towards samadhi. With a few worthwhile departures in procedures and purpose, both the Heartwood Path and Patanjoli's steps to samadhi lead in a similar fashion to unitive consciousness (already described).

We shall identify the eight steps towards samadhi here, and then offer elaboration and related activities for the first three here and the last five at Waypoint 3.55 of the Heartwood Path: **Egos** book. The eight steps toward samadhi are:

1. guidelines for universal morality, social contracts mostly having to do with abstention;
2. personal practices, personal contracts that include including observance (respect, deference, an act done to fulfill or respect morality, or an act done for ceremonial reasons), and vows;
3. physical postures, to give focus to the body, all aimed at helping the practitioner abide and stay in the exercise;
4. breathing exercises, to give focus to the mind, aimed at controlling the Life Force;

5. sensory control, turning inward to give focus to the senses, as if one is shutting off the wi-fi on the computer-brain;
6. concentration by cultivating perceptual awareness, bringing your mind to a single focus;
7. devotion, meditation on a single concept, mediation on a single person, meditation on a single place, meditation on the Divine, and—most often in our instance—meditation on one's awareness of a single attractive natural being;
8. Samadhi, union with the Divine (bodymindgreen.com).

The topic of the attainment of samadhi is addressed in the first three books of the Heartwood Path so that the participants are given an ample chance to achieve universal consciousness—which makes them feel that environmental protection is the same thing as self protection—before proceeding on to the two Heartwood Path books about going into action—**Volitos** and **Collectivos**.

To The First Three Steps Towards Samadhi...

HumaNatureConnect Activity

Start-up Protocol

If this is not a day when you prefer to spend time in nature without an agenda, do the Heartwood Path Start-up Protocol found in the Appendix. Then return here to do the remaining portion of this activity:

Taking The First Steps Towards Universal Consciousness: Contracts And Poses

For this activity, let's work on the first three limbs, or steps, towards the attainment of samadhi—universal consciousness.

To get on the first limb, called "Yamas," assess and then write down in your journal ways that you handle the following personal contracts (describe your actions, do not simply say "Yes" or "No:"

1. do or do not consciously do no harm to others,
2. do or do not tell the truth,
3. do or do not steal,
4. do or do not appropriately satisfy your sexual needs,
5. do or do not covet,
6. and do or do not take what you do not need.

To get to the second limb, or step, towards samadhi, called "Niyamas," assess and then write down how you handle the following social contracts (again, do not simply answer "Yes" or "No:"

1. do or do not practice good nutrition;
2. do or do not practice good hygiene;
3. do or do not be mindful to the point of contentment;
4. do or do not have enough motivation to inspire others;
5. do or do not practice austerity when it comes to the consumption of calories, drinking alcohol, smoking, or other addictions;
6. do or do not know yourself, including your shadow side and your More-Than-Individual-Self;
7. do or do not treat others as you would wish to be treated; and
8. do or do not praise, respect, or surrender to the Absolute (which includes God or the Source of Everything).

To get on the third limb, called "Asanas," one has to learn how to perform certain poses. Here's how these poses are useful along the Heartwood Path: I tell Heartwood Path participants that it is acceptable to lie down, sit, or stand while attending to the attractive natural beings they use in their activities. As enjoyable as this time may be, occasionally participants will need help relieving discomforts or dispensing with the fidgetiness that can get in the way of their contemplations. For the purpose of abiding or staying with one's chosen natural being, certain yoga postures can be employed. For this part of this activity, you will need to check-off that you have tried the following poses in the presence of your chosen natural being (if unfamiliar with yoga poses, look them up online at (yogaforhealthyaging.blogspot.com) obtain a book on yoga asanas (poses), or watch related videos:

1. Supported backbend, versions 1 and 2 ____;
2. Reclined Hip Stretch Sequence ____;
3. Reclined Leg Stretch, versions and 3 ____;
4. Dynamic Bridge Pose ____;
5. Happy Baby Pose ____;
6. Easy Sitting Pose, forward version ____;
7. Sage's Twist 3, version 4 ____;
8. Upward Plank Pose, version 2 ____;
9. Downward-facing Dog Pose ____;
10. Arms Overhead Pose, classic version;
11. Crescent Moon Pose ____;
12. Dynamic Standing Forward Bend ____;
13. Extended Side Angle Pose ____;
14. Locust Pose ____;
15. Legs Up The Wall ____.

Follow-up Protocol

For best results, write down your impressions of this activity in your journal using the Heartwood Path Follow-up Protocol found in the Appendix. Afterwards, consider sharing your interpretations with others.

Heartwood Path Axioms

Key Assertions From Waypoint 2.63

2.63.1.

Awaken and motivate others to do likewise.

2.63.2

Seek inner world reparations for yourself through mental empiricism, (interpretation and explanation) and spiritual empiricism (mysticism, intuitive illumination, and samadhi).

2.63.3

Samadhi—the ultimate, ecstatic state of acute awareness— occurs through two general types of practices: meditating on form and meditating on formlessness.

2.63.4

Experience the benefits of building the circuitry between the left and right hemispheres of the brain (thereby unlocking your subconscious mind, increasing your creativity, and evoking relaxation).

Nocturnal Pilgrimage 2.63

For best results, write down your impressions of each night's dreams in your journal using the Heartwood Path Dreaming Time Protocols found in the Appendix. Afterwards, consider sharing your Dream Tending with others.

Extend the same gratitude you express in the outer world to the Dream Characters you encounter during a lucid dream. Revel for a moment about how fortunate you are to have a way to create a universe, explore it, change it, and use its Characters for your own inspiration and entertainment. Show your gratitude earnestly.

Before you prepare for sleep, thank your Dream Figures for their service. Then, go over what you learned about the first three steps towards samadhi. Sleep, dream, and tend to your dream. When ready, move to the next waypoint: "Circuity."

64

Circuity

UNLOCK YOUR SUBCONSCIOUS MIND

The following activity is a way to experience the benefits of building the circuitry between the left and right hemispheres of the brain. Doing so will show you a simple yet effective way to unlock barely noticeable memories, notions, and information in your subconscious mind. Use this activity to increase your creativity, evoke relaxation, and help you to fall asleep. It will also help you deal with low to moderate traumas and nagging feelings of depression. For serious depression, for mood swings that last longer than a month, or for any psychological malady beyond mild post-traumatic stress, seek out the assistance of a psychologist (to obtain a diagnosis and begin psychotherapy) or, if needed, a psychiatrist (if medications are needed).

The following activity involves a do-it-yourself method of EMDR-- Eye Movement Desensitization and Reprocessing. This psychotherapeutic method helps with emotional healing and lack of creativity. "When the process is complete, the brain has discarded the distorted subjective experience that had overwhelmed and remain frozen in the patient and replaced it with a positive perception of present reality" (Grand, 2001, p. 35). EMDR's hallmark is the movement of the patients' eyes from left to right repeatedly. This helps the patient because as the eyes move from left to right and right to left they simulate both sides of the brain. The "alternating bilateral stimulation enhances communication between the left and the right brains" (Grand, 2001, 24). This bilateral stimulation allows "the brain to reevaluate information frozen in a system that was overwhelmed at the time of the traumatic event" (Grand, 2001, 24).

Try it even if you are not aware that you need such healing. Doing so may reveal buried wounds that are adversely affecting your life, even if you are not presently aware that they exist.

I have tried EMDR and have found it to work amazingly well at revealing hidden sources of stress. It also was a good way for me to relieve the low-grade but persistent physical symptoms of emotional trauma.

EMDR helped me with an unnoticed trauma that I was not aware was affecting my life. After six one-hour sessions of eye movement therapy, I discovered that I had buried emotional trauma from some neglect I experienced in my early childhood and, to make up for my feelings of being neglected (and, therefore, not mattering to my parents), I have overcompensated by being a persistent nurturer in an attempt to matter, after all.

Be sure to do the following activity. EMDR will help you recover from emotional and psychological trauma (which many people have, perhaps subconsciously). Uncovering such trauma may be a critical step towards achieving success in your life. Doing the following EMDR activity repeatedly may also prepare your brain circuitry for any future samadhi meditations (like those at Waypoint 3.55 in the next Heartwood Path book).

To Repair Your Feelings...

HumaNatureConnect Activity

Start-up Protocol

If this is not a day when you prefer to spend time in nature without an agenda, do the Heartwood Path Start-up Protocol found in the Appendix. Then return here to do the remaining portion of this activity:

Healing Emotional Wounds

Do not use this activity if you are in a deep, acute, or lingering depression. Continue only if you need enhanced creativity or if your physical or psychological symptoms are moderate, low, or outside of your awareness. This activity is suggested for those who may have nagging but minor aches or pains or for someone who is only mildly out of sorts but who cannot identify the source of the problem.

To uncover traumas buried in your subconscious mind that may be blocking your success:

1. search throughout your body for what we shall call a negative target experience (a "pain" that results from a subconscious memory of a negative event, such as an unexplained pain or tightness in the chest);
2. imagine that your chosen attractive being is an emotional healer;
3. begin the series of eye-movements, moving the eyes to a natural being to the left and then to a natural being to the right, back and forth for about about ten times;
4. after each set of eye movements, tell your healer where in your body you are feeling a nagging pain, tightness other target experience;
5. each time rank the degree of the discomfort of the target experience on a scale of 1-10;
6. assign what is for you an unpleasant color to the target experience;

7. continue doing the sets of eye movements, always telling your emotional therapist where the pain is located, it's numerical degree of unpleasantness, and its color;

8. about halfway through the eye-movement sequences begin to replace the assigned unpleasant color with a preferred attractive color you associate with a discomfort-free part of your body;

9. after one of the last sequences, focus on the bridge of awareness between yourself and your chosen attractive natural being until some symbol—perhaps a mental image, a memory, or a sign— emerges that tells you what unpleasantness was buried;

10. note whether your degree of discomfort is declining or perhaps has disappeared as you continue with the eye movements and perhaps come up with a plausible source or cause of the target experience; and

11. discuss with your emotional therapist what using EMDR therapy to identify and diminish a buried trauma will likely do for your life.

Answering questions about the nature of the discomfort will activate the memory of the target in the occipital cortex, which controls sight in the brain (Grand, 2001, p. 26). Make sure your two objects (beings), one to your left and one to the right, are horizontally aligned. Keeping your head still, move your eyes slowly and gently from one object (being) to the other, repeatedly in a smooth, flowing fashion. If you are seeking relaxation, move your eyes even more slowly. After moving your eyes back and forth for a few seconds to a few minutes, re-ask the questions described earlier. Do not ask any questions during your back and forth eye movement sequences. Ask your questions before, in between, and after your eye movement sequences. Make sure your answers are honest. Give credence to all of your responses. After a few eye movement sequences, imagine replacing the unpleasant aches or feelings of tension you had in a part of your body with the positive feelings (and associated color) you feel in another part of your body.

Instigate this replacement periodically as you do your eye movements and answer the questions.

> "Once the negative has been resolved and cleared through, the positive more easily replaces it. And the force that drives this movement, the bilateral stimulation itself, came from nature" (Grand, 2001, p. 247).

In all but severe cases, you will unlock the reasons for your aches and tensions and replace these negative feelings with positive ones. If, after a few weeks of repeating this activity, you do not find emotional or physical relief, or if you do not improve your creativity, you are encouraged to seek the help of a professional EMDR therapist or a clinical psychologist.

After your last eye movement sequences, tell your chosen attractive being what you believe to be the cause of the target experience, noting the severity of the target feelings on the 1-10 scale. Give thanks for this connection experience. Either enjoy your newfound creativity and lack of distress or seek professional help.

Follow-up Protocol

For best results, write down your impressions of this activity in your journal using the Heartwood Path Follow-up Protocol found in the Appendix. Afterwards, consider sharing your interpretations with others.

Heartwood Path Axioms

Key Assertions From Waypoint 2.64

2.64.1.

Unlock your subconscious mind.

2.64.2.

Eye Movement Desensitization and Reprocessing is a psycho-therapeutic method that helps with emotional healing and lack of creativity.

2.64.3.

Uncovering trauma buried in the subconscious mind may be a critical step towards achieving success in your life.

Nocturnal Pilgrimage 2.64

For best results, write down your impressions of each night's dreams in your journal using the Heartwood Path Dreaming Time Protocols found in the Appendix. Afterwards, consider sharing your Dream Tending with others.

Having progressed this far, you are to be congratulated for your perseverance. You have only a few more waypoints to go in this book. Soon it will be time to start the next book which is all about the important task of setting your individuality before you learn in the third Heartwood Path book about the equally important task of integrating into the whole.

Keep going. What you have received so far is an orientation. You now have background information intended to give you a good start. More wondrous benefits and more time-honored but little-known methods lie ahead.

We have been talking about the importance of setting an intension in your nocturnal endeavors along the Heartwood Path. In the next book, we will expand on the important topic of incubating a dream.

In addition to important day time activities unrelated to dreaming, the first four waypoints of the next book will break the topic down in a way that will enable you to convert what used to be random and often forgotten dreams into purposeful and delightful nocturnal pilgrimages that lead you toward abiding, authentic, and abundant happiness plus an increasingly sustainable environment. To have such purposeful nocturnal pilgrimages you will need to learn how to focus your desire, you will have to learn how to use your feelings to make lucid dreaming more pronounced, you will have to experience being productively lost in the moment during your lucid dreams, you will have to know what it takes to wake up in your dreams, and you will need to learn how to induce lucid dreaming. In doing so, you will be learning to make your intentions effective.

Think about that. There are specific things you can do to . . .

make your dreams come true!

These topics are presented in just the first four waypoints of the next Heartwood Path book. Imagine what valuable information awaits you in the remaining ninety-four learning stations!

As tantalizing as it may be to jump ahead to the next book, given the treasures found there, do not miss what lies immediately in front of you. Tonight, go over what you learned about Eye Movement Desensitization and Reprocessing. Sleep. Tend to your dreams. When ready, move to the next waypoint: "The Solution Beyond Yourself."

65

The Solution Beyond Yourself

MOTIVATE OTHERS

There is no time for complacency. Everyone needs to be a part of the solution. People need information but without motivation, the facts are of little use to the cause of preserving humaNature. EartHearts use facts to inform and develop a sense of personal connection to motivate. Let us now look at what motivates, using theories of motivation summarized by Steven P. Robbins in the following activity (Undated Website). This topic is especially important for anyone involved in getting others to accompany them at work, in civic organizations, or in social activities.

To Inspire...

HumaNatureConnect Activity

Start-up Protocol

If this is not a day when you prefer to spend time in nature without an agenda, do the Heartwood Path Start-up Protocol found in the Appendix. Then return here to do the remaining portion of this activity:

Getting Others Motivated

For this activity, determine the best way to motivate yourself in your group. Ask others in your group to do the same and you will be able to see whether Theory X, Theory W, or Theory Z will, once applied, be most helpful to your group. Re-create a semblance of the following chart and fill out your re-created table in your journal or on handouts given to others in your group.

Motivational Statement Based On Motivation Theory	Your Impressions About How Each Technique Has Or Could Give You Motivation

I fit into Motivation Theory X because:

I inherently dislike work and, whenever possible, will attempt to avoid it.

I have to be coerced, controlled, or threatened with punishment.

I avoid responsibilities and seek formal direction whenever possible.

I place security above all other factors and will display little ambition.

Douglas McGregor's Theory X

I fit into Motivation Theory Y because:

I can view work as being as natural as rest or play.

I will exercise self-direction and self-control if they are committed to the objectives.

I can learn to accept, even seek, responsibility.

Douglas McGregor's Theory Y

I fit into Motivation Theory Z because:

I am provided a job for life.

My superiors have a strong focus on my well-being, both on and off the job.

Rather than being fired for poor performance, I am given re-training or other help to improve my morale and productivity.

According to Ouchi, Theory Z management, popular mainly in Japan, tends to promote stable employment, high productivity, and high employee morale and satisfaction. (Wikipedia/Theory Z.)

Dr. William Ouchi and Dr. W. Edward Deming

After determining what is needed, use what motivates best. Use punishments such as less popular assignments, suspensions, or negative write-ups if need be; but know that incentives and rewards work best to bring more productivity to those who are already willing to work.

Follow-up Protocol

For best results, write down your impressions of this activity in your journal using the Heartwood Path Follow-up Protocol found in the Appendix. Afterwards, consider sharing your interpretations with others.

Heartwood Path Axioms

Key Assertions From Waypoint 2.65

2.65.1.

Motivate others.

2.65.2.

Expect poor results when you punish those who need it so that they comply.

2.65.3.

Expect good results when you reward those who are already inspired to participate well.

2.65.4.

Do not expect anyone will take care of all participants as if they were family because in the United States the culture favors rugged individualism.

Nocturnal Pilgrimage 2.65

For best results, write down your impressions of each night's dreams in your journal using the Heartwood Path Dreaming Time Protocols found in the Appendix. Afterwards, consider sharing your Dream Tending with others.

This activity requires that you go to bed early and to wake up early enough to allow ample time before your routine daily activities. As you do your Dream Tending, build in enough time to sit in silence for about an hour. During this time, wait for the emergence of insight. Write down all tidbits of insight, looking for patterns. Be sure to be thankful to your Dream Characters, paying them tribute for sharing their insights with you.

Move to the next waypoint, entitled "Help & Insight," when you are done with your Dream Tending session. Doing so will be an important step on your pathway to saintliness.

66

Help & Insight

BECOME A SECULAR SAINT

As we will see, savikalpa samadhi is about the giving of help and nirvikalpa samadhi is about the attainment of profound and indescribable insight. Remember that the purpose of the Heartwood Path is not to seek ultimate enlightenment. The goal of the Heartwood Path is to create the eco-centric life elders need to give guidance to those who would work to help people become psychologically mature enough to work effortlessly and tireless to foster human happiness and protect the planet.

Given this purpose, we will focus more on savikalpa samadhi than on nirvikalpa samadhi for a variety of reasons—all having to do with the difference between a sage and a saint. Remember this distinction: for our purposes here: a sage (the result of nirvikalpa samadhi) is an enlightened person who may not get involved in doing much for others and a saint (the result of savikapa samadhi) is a person, enlightened or not, who works easily and effortless to eradicate injustice for the good of all sentient beings. The world needs more enlightened or nearly enlightened saints than it does un-saintly or uninvolved sages. More people are capable and willing to seek the level of a saint than are willing and able to achieve the level of the sage. The Heartwood

Path is for the masses—it is not for a few, super-committed zealots or the aged.

Despite its emphasis on saintliness rather than "sageness," enlightenment is within the reach of those who traverse the Heartwood Path. Enlightenment does not only occur as a final step of attainment by sages. People, especially those seeking the perfection of saintliness, can achieve the realization of enlightenment—recognized when everything appears to have changed when no change has taken place. Enlightenment is a matter of seeing, not manifesting. An enlightened one simply sees with new eyes, feels surrounded by peace always, and no longer identifies oneself by the boundaries of one's individual body.

Enlightenment helps but it is not a requirement of saintliness. Saintliness puts one on the verge of enlightenment. Saintliness is good preparation for "sageness." The Heartwood Path can help develop people into potentially enlightened saints. But it is really for those who value saintliness more than "sageness."

To Become A Saint...

HumaNatureConnect Activity

Start-up Protocol

If this is not a day when you prefer to spend time in nature without an agenda, do the Heartwood Path Start-up Protocol found in the Appendix. Then return here to do the remaining portion of this activity:

Becoming A Secular Saint

For this activity, consider what it will take for you to incorporate the building blocks of secular sainthood into your character. For ideas look over the following table and write down your answer in your journal.

Building Blocks Of A Secular Saint	Have I Incorporated These Building Blocks Into My Character; And, If Not, How, If At All, Will I?
A person who is respected.	
A person who is remembered for his or her noble cause.	
Selfhood for Secular Saints is identified primarily in relation to others.	
Secular saints have a "bond of care, concern, responsibility whose purpose is love itself" (Tebra, 2012).	
Secular saints "strive to make sure that the lives of human kind take (a) course that is guided by love and care or concern" (Tebra, 2012).	
Secular saints advocate for doing to others what is right out of love.	
Secular saints are often a martyr (not required along the Heartwood Path) but they are not recognized as a canonical saint by a religion.	

Follow-up Protocol

For best results, write down your impressions of this activity in your journal using the Heartwood Path Follow-up Protocol found in the Appendix. Afterwards, consider sharing your interpretations with others.

Heartwood Path Axioms

Key Assertions From Waypoint 2.66

2.66.1.

Savikalpa samadhi is about the giving of help and nirvikalpa samadhi is about the attainment of profound and indescribable insight.

2.66.2.

The goal of the Heartwood Path is to create the eco-centric life elders needed to give guidance to those who would work to help people become psychologically mature enough to work effortlessly and tireless to foster human happiness and protect the planet.

2.66.3.

The world needs more enlightened or nearly-enlightened saints than it does un-saintly or uninvolved sages.

2.66.4.

An enlightened one simply sees with new eyes, feels surrounded by peace always, and no longer identifies oneself by the boundaries of one's individual body.

2.66.5.

Enlightenment helps but it is not a requirement of saintliness.

Nocturnal Pilgrimage 2.66

For best results, write down your impressions of each night's dreams in your journal using the Heartwood Path Dreaming Time Protocols found in the Appendix. Afterwards, consider sharing your Dream Tending with others.

By now, you may be experiencing your Dream Characters as embodied, real, intelligent, and transitory. It is as if your chosen natural attractive beings have come to you in your dreams in one form and on other nights they come to you in other forms. You will change as your Dream Characters change, usually for the better. As the Dream Characters "open to their depth, we open to ours. As they gain substance, vitality, and significance, so do we . . . (Most importantly), as images shape-shift, we see into the possibilities of our own transformation" (Aizenstat, 2009, p. 56). Notice all the differences in the Dream Character's appearance. Pay attention to how you feel about each presentation. Use your daily journal entries as a montage of images moving through you now. In doing so, you are witnessing "portals to the source of life," you are connecting to "looking to the process of creation," and you are looking "into what is orchestrating your own becoming . . . (When) we experience images in this way, we feel a sense of love and caring" (Aizenstat, 2009, p. 57-58).

With continued practice, you will experience the highlighted presence of the Dream Character. Let it be. Let its living presence further open your own. As you feel ever more met or engaged by the Dream Character, open your heart and write down in what ways you feel that you are experiencing its care. How are you experiencing the love generated by the intimate heart-to-heart relationship between you and the Image?

After you are done with this Dream Tending exercise, continue your sojourn down the Heartwood Path by moving to the next waypoint: "Path To Sustainability." In the next Nocturnal Pilgrimage Section we will begin applying Dream Images to major challenges, from love relationships to money and the workplace.

67

Path To Sustainability

HELP BRING ABOUT THE ECOZOIC ERA

The next major event in the unfolding of the cosmos is on the horizon. As human beings extinguish thousands of species each year we are forced to make big changes in the way we relate to the planet. In doing so, we will recognize that the natural world is not only our primary provider but also the primary way divinity is revealed to us. If we can examine the terms of the human-earth relationship and then make necessary corrections, the Ecozoic will replace the Cenozoic. If we cannot make such corrections, we will enter the Technozoic era— that bleak time when technology, affluence, and human population will cause severe impacts on the natural world. If we fail to enter the Ecozoic era, it is difficult to imagine that the future will contain any semblance of the relative paradise we now inhabit.

Fortunately, we have already entered a time that is the necessary prerequisite for the dawning of the Ecozoic Era. In important ways, this time is similar to the first Axial period (800-600 B.C), which is marked by the spawning of the world's great religions. In this second Axial period, we are becoming more aware and appreciative of an integral view of religion and spirituality. This integral view leads us to adopt the "pereNNIAAL philosophy" that underlies all religion, a view that fosters a connection to our source in the Divine, a connection to our individual and collective selves, a connection to our neighbors, and a connection to the harmonious energy and intelligence that pervades and surrounds us all. In this second Axial period we will develop paths of paths and, in so doing, become inter-spiritual in ways that enable us to be deeply committed to a variety of spiritual preferences. We can see the emergence of this inter-spiritual perspective in the way some in the present generation neither knows nor cares about the differences between religious denominations. If such indifference is worrisome to you, just know that every new journey brings understandable fears.

To An Age Of Sustainability...

HumaNatureConnect Activity

Start-up Protocol

If this is not a day when you prefer to spend time in nature without an agenda, do the Heartwood Path Start-up Protocol found in the Appendix. Then return here to do the remaining portion of this activity:

Heading Towards The Ecozoic Era

For the next activity, determine what more you can do to help bring forth the Ecozoic Era. Use the following table to help spur ideas and organize your thinking. Write down your responses in your journal.

Action Items To Bring Forth The Ecozoic Era	What More I Can Do Regarding Each Action Item
Go Paperless	

Stop Using Bottled Water

Stop Smoking

Use Less Electricity

Recycle

Use Reusable Shopping Bags

Buy Fresh Local Produce

Save Water

Use Emails And eGreetings

Use Ceramic Cups

Print Less

Use Energy-efficient Bulbs

Use Cloth Rather Than Paper
Towels

Use The Microwave More To Save
Energy Or Never To Promote
Health

Leak Proof Your Home

Replace Air Filters

Consume Less

Plant Trees

Donate To Environmental Groups

Volunteer In Pro-environment
Cleanups, Etc.

Drive A Low-polluting Car, Such
As A Hybrid Or An Electric Car

Engage In Acts Of Uncommon
Kindness

Reduce, Reuse, Or Recycle Your
Waste

Ride Your Bike Or Join A Carpool

Vote Consciously

Add More Ideas

Follow-up Protocol

For best results, write down your impressions of this activity in your journal using the Heartwood Path Follow-up Protocol found in the Appendix. Afterwards, consider sharing your interpretations with others.

Heartwood Path Axioms

Key Assertions From Waypoint 2.67

2.67.1.

If we cannot make such corrections, we will enter the Techno-zoic era—that bleak time when technology, affluence, and human population will cause severe impacts on the natural world.

2.67.2.

If we fail to enter the Ecozoic era, it is difficult to imagine that the future will contain any semblance of the relative paradise we now inhabit.

2.67.3.

The five steps for addiction recovery in Dream Tending are: 1) acknowledging that you are caught in a specific addiction; 2) using dream association and dream amplification to drag out what is hidden (through association) and to determine its significance (through amplification); 3) stopping the compulsion; 4) face the image of your addition directly, develop empathy for the addictive Dream Character, and getting to know the addictive Dream Character; and 5) finding the true nature of the image.

2.67.4.

The six steps for improving love relationships through Dream Tending are: remembering the first six months of your relationship, recalling what you found fascinating about each other, recalling what it was like to have those long talks; both partners agreeing to stifle judging; witnessing your partner's dreams without judgement; finding the Archetype of Eros; looking for who Eros attracts as its partner in your dreams; and looking for the soul body of the bond between you and your partner.

2.67.5.

Explore your personal relationship with your finances by noticing how you feel when you experience the Dream Character of Money.

Nocturnal Pilgrimage 2.67

For best results, write down your impressions of each night's dreams in your journal using the Heartwood Path Dreaming Time Protocols found in the Appendix. Afterwards, consider sharing your Dream Tending with others.

It is now time to begin applying what you have learned about tending to your dreams to some of life's most pressing issues. In this nocturnal pilgrimage section we shall address controlling addictions, the challenges of loving relationships, and one's personal relationship with money.

Addiction Control

Aizenstat presents a method of working with Dream Figures that helps people break free of addiction. Here, we will present his five steps to recovery:

1. Acknowledge that you are caught in a specific addiction. Look for Dream Characters that exhibit "some kind of addictive or compulsive behavior" (Aizenstat, 2009, p. 92). Ask yourself how the addiction is operating your life. Name the Image that represents the addiction.

2. Use dream association (associating aspects of dreams with keywords) and dream amplification (turning Dream Characters into universal symbols) to drag out what is hidden (through association) and to determine its significance (through amplification). Watch the Dream Character closely. Look for ways the image is associated with your childhood. Then, using your imagination, connect the image to fairy tales, myths, legends, or stories. Look for what more the stories tell you about the addiction.

3. Stop the compulsion. Face the addictive Dream Character and do four things: 1) find an interruption such as a cold shower that will help you stop the mental activity surrounding the addiction; 2) extend your hands outward to the sides, identifying the right side as positive, the left side as negative, and you in the middle as curiosity. Use this curiosity to gain information about the Dream Image, paying note to how it is breaking out of its compulsivity; 3) get curious about the Dream Character, looking especially at its compulsivity, but also staying away from the compulsive whirlwind; and 4) take some small action to curtail your compulsion.

4. Once you have done something to control your compulsivity, face the image of your addition directly, develop empathy for the addictive Dream Character, and getting to know the addictive Dream Character. Move. Shake. Cry. Run. Do anything that releases your feelings. When ready, return your attention to the Dream Image.

5. Find the true nature of the Image. It will likely now be less menacing and intense. List the characteristics of the Dream Character. Place a natural being someplace in your home that represents the addictive Dream Character. Such objects that represent Dream Images we shall call "Dream Figures." To your Dream Figure, write a letter of commitment, detailing what you will do to control your compulsion. Revisit the Dream Figure, looking for signs of hope. Bring offerings to your Dream Figure. Revisit the Dream Figure repeatedly. Look for signs that the Dream Figure is acting like a muse. Tell it what you are inspired to do about your addiction. Do it.

Love Relationships

For this major life challenge, Aizenstat offers six steps:

1. Together with your partner, remember the first six months of your relationship, recalling what you found fascinating about each other, recall what it was like to have those long talks, and invite any remembered Dream Images to come forth again. Share some of your dreams with your partner, promising not to get too "psychological." Recall some enjoyable stories from your childhood. Discuss what activated your imagination when the two of you were young? Discuss what it would be like to tell your dreams to each other, and to make sure the listener does not interrupt or judge.

2. Both partners agree to stifle judging. Both partners share their concerns about sharing your dreams. Light a candle. Find a natural being to act as a "talking stick." Talk only when you have the stick. Both partners agree to confidentiality regarding what is revealed in the dream discussions. Agree that the process of discussing dreams in this way is important.

3. Witness your partner's dreams without judgement. Do not try to be helpful or useful. Be responsive rather than reactive. Just listen. Thank your partner for sharing. Do not comment on the content of your partner's dreams. Switch roles.

4. Finding the Archetype of Eros. Recognize Eros as an inner Dream Figure, both mischievous and elusive. Find Eros in your dreams. He may be cloaked and repugnant, at first, waiting for the kiss that will release him from exile. The Eros Dream Image will likely be complicated, contradictory, and paradoxical, like love itself. Name this figure and tend to him so that you can rekindle compassion and intimacy. As you befriend Eros, it will likely shape-shift. Follow Eros inside the shape-shifted Beast, if necessary. Stay away from idealizing Eros. Do not be seduced by notions of wish-fulfillment or lover's remorse. Tending to Eros takes time. Express yourself to Eros orally or with the presentation of your own poetry. Be willing to share in the process of discovering Eros with your partner.

5. Tend to the sacred marriage. Look for who Eros attracts as its partner in your dreams. With repeated attempts, allow the image of the imaginal couple to become more vivid and details. "Notice how one figure evokes the other . . .Let the dream enactment take on a life of its own" (Aizenstat, 2009, p. 125). Notice how, after witnessing the Dream Couple in your dreams for several days, your emotions begin to open up.

6. Look for the Third Body, also known as the Relationship Body, which will have a life of its own, beyond the two partners. This Third Body is the soul body of the bond between you and your partner. It shapes the feelings each partner has for the other. When this image is bright, there is a sense that each member of the couple belongs to something greater than themselves and their partner. The Third Body will be an image or a sensation that embodies the transcendent. It will seem timeless. Resist attaching this image to your children or any other external being. As a couple, make repeated offerings of fruit or flowers to this Third Body. Doing so feeds the Third Body of your relationship and this, in turn, will ignite moments of love between you and your partner.

Work Money

Explore your personal relationship with money. List your areas of expense and attach each the essential quality or benefit of each. Notice what connection exists between the vitality of the Dream Image and the energy you feel when receiving or spending money. Look for an image of money in your dreams. Notice how you feel when you experience this Dream Character.

Now shift your attention to the workplace. How does your money figure personify what is happening at your workplace? Look for a work place image in your dreams. Write a dialogue between the two images of work and money. If you were to act as a counselor to this relationship, what might you suggest to each party?

With controlling addictions, the challenges of loving relationships, and one's personal relationship with money in mind as you prepare for sleep, incubate a dream, dream, and then tend to your dreams when you wake up. Your skills will improve with practice.

When you are ready to continue on your way to Gladandgreen Junction, move to the next waypoint: "Imagination And World Dreams." Prepare to get creative and inspired.

68

Imagination And World
Dreams

GET CREATIVE AND INSPIRED

Remember that you become what you think about. For this reason, be wary of thoughts of doubt. Eliminate conditioned beliefs regarding the impossibility of planned actions. If you can conceive it, you can create it. Allow yourself to wander freely in your imagination. Exclude nothing in your fantasies. Imaginative meanderings form the unlimited river of life.

To facilitate these worthwhile meanderings, start thinking about how you would answer the following question: "What doubts or negative conditioned beliefs am I now eliminating?" You may want to focus here on outmoded patterns of thinking regarding so-called universal principles and unwanted notions of integrity generally (rather than just focusing on unwanted aspects of your own individual self). You will have a chance to let go of unworkable aspects of your individual self at the end of the next book. Here, before reading the Heartwood Path: **Egos** book, where you will identify and secure your own unique personality, come to understand and know how to use the Sling of the Imagination, pictured below.

THE SLING OF THE IMAGINATION:

CREATING SUBSTANTIAL IDEAS THAT AFFECT THE WHOLE

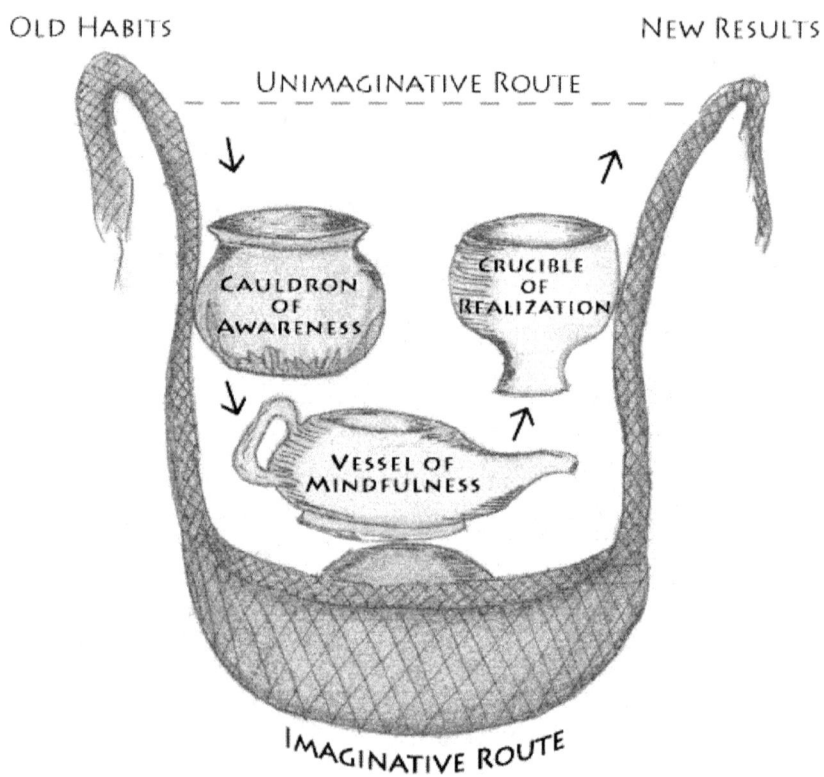

OLD HABITS   NEW RESULTS

UNIMAGINATIVE ROUTE

CAULDRON OF AWARENESS

CRUCIBLE OF REALIZATION

VESSEL OF MINDFULNESS

IMAGINATIVE ROUTE

ART WORK DONE BY THERESA GRANT

What Is The Sling

I shall present the ancient sling as a metaphorical model used to il-
lustrate what it takes for you to affect the whole—the whole household,

the whole neighborhood, the whole nation, or the whole environment. Yes, like diminutive David slaying the giant Goliath, little 'ole you can change the big 'ole world. But first you will need to do some work and grow.

There will be many new words, some lofty principles, and some metaphors in this explanation of the Sling of the Imagination. Use these literary devices to help you work your way through this section. Read it carefully, perhaps more than once, and you will come to understand a useful method for making big changes in the world. If you need more help, there are carefully trained guides available who can help you with this or any other part of this series of books.

The Sling of the Imagination is one of the most important tools for you to use to find happiness, protect the beauty of nature, secure environmental sustainability, or make any positive change in society, culture, or the world.

We will be using as a metaphor the sling David used in the Bible. Slings are ancient weapons made of many different materials, but all consist of two lengths of cord, fabric, or hide attached to a pouch.

Like David who used a sling to slay Goliath, you too are, metaphorically speaking, armed with a sling—albeit of a different sort. The sling I am talking about is not used to pitch a stone to hurt an individual. It is instead a virtual, metaphorical, symbolic one used to cast forth ideas that shift the whole for the better.

Remembering David's words that "The Lord saveth not with sword and spear" and John Lennon's lyrics "War is over, if you want it," the stone in the pouch of our virtual sling is replaced metaphorically with *personal choice*. Like a stone, choice can be used for good or for evil. To make sure your use of the sling is positive and productive, guard against picking solutions based on incomplete information, little or no self-awareness and growth, and no processes of mindfulness and realization, both explained below.

Superficial awareness (which comes from little or no use of the Imaginative Route on the Sling of the Imagination) leads to superficial reactions. We cannot truly affect the whole unless we claim our wholeness (through a deep "swoosh," so to speak, down and around the arc that represents the Imaginative Route). I call progressing from the upper left end of the Sling directly to the upper Right Sling—without "swooshing" through the whole sling—the "Unimaginative Route."

Why Use The Sling

I have personal experience going down the Unimaginative Route. My experience mentioned here has to do with the environmental movement. Despite this limited example, the Sling can be applied to any attempt to affect a change.

Not knowing a better alternative, the Unimaginative Route, which in its extreme form is but muddling through, was my blind, unintentional course during my days of lobbying and environmental organizing (full-time between 1975 and 1997). Fellow conservationists and myself used this so-called "unimaginative route" to, for example, stop the Meramec Dam nears St. Louis, Missouri, to preserve over 100,000 acres of Forest Service lands by including them in the Wilderness Preservation System (in Missouri and Illinois), to cut the funding for a nuclear power plant in central Missouri, and to lobby for what is (or was) the environmental safety net which includes the Clean Air Act, the Water Pollution Control Act, and the Endangered Species Act. Had we known to take the Imaginative route, even greater victories would have occurred; or, at least, they would have been achieved more efficiently and my cohorts would have learned more about themselves and advocacy in the process. Without the Sling, we muddled our way to accomplishment, too naive to know that there was another way that would have been faster and more far-reaching.

I was one of a couple dozen people who used the unimaginative route while lobbying daily in the weeks before the enactment of the second most significant conservation bill in the history of the United States (after the establishment of the National Park System)—the law that preserved over 80 millions acres in Alaska. I was assigned to lobby Midwest members of Congress. From these successes I can attest that the so-called Unimaginative route can be used to achieve important public policy victories. It's just not the best way because it burns up too many activists and creates less than ideal results—in this instance, not enough inner world support amongst the public that could be used to maintain the vast conservation victories in the face of perennial attempts to seize the protected resources.

I call the better approach, the one that involves deep "swooshing," the "Imaginative Route" because it affords important additions that the Unimaginative Route does not, including: 1) the Imaginative Route helps to improve the spiritual maturity of the environmentalists in the fashion outlined in this series of courses and so it affects positively not just the final outcomes but also the people making the outcomes happen and 2) it provides a way for more significant and enduring positive change. The symbolic "swoosh"—that is, following the Imaginative Route—represents what occurs from the sequence of thinking-to-experiencing-to-doing. With this three step approach, the so-called "swoosh" is personal cultivation, a systematic process of maturation.

The kinds of actions undertaken during the so-called "unimaginative route"— lobbying, grassroots organizing, holding symposia, soliciting media attention—also occur at the end of the Imaginative Route— before the Establishment stage and after the various individual development stages such as letting go, mindfulness, and letting come. In this way, the Imaginative Route, after bolstering the advocates themselves, includes everything that would happen if one was to choose only the more typical "Unimaginative Route."

I believe that had activists in the environmental, civil rights, and other progressive movements used the Imaginative Route over the last forty years, many of the policy changes adopted during the Seventies and Eighties but which are now abandoned, underfunded, or ignored could have been sustained—resulting in a much better world. The predominant use of the Unimaginative Route meant that the activists in the various progressive movements were unable to counter the setbacks in public policy that occurred during the last decade of the Twentieth Century and the first decade of the Twenty-first Century, including the weakening of the Environmental Protection Agency, the election of congressmen less willing to support the preservation of more wilderness areas, and the lack of adequate laws to ensure that all lives—including Blacks, females, school children, the disabled, and the elderly—matter, no more and no less.

To secure a magnificent future the Imaginative Route needs to be employed at all levels of organization—from amongst those who work at the United Nations to those who decide how to best think and behave in households and neighborhoods. The Imaginative Route of the Heartwood Path ought not to be used only by professional activists. It needs to also be employed in each household so that nearby improvements can be made and so that individual voters will have the inner world intentions and ethics and the outer world individual and group behaviors and physical systems needed to not only vote for the best candidates but also to monitor and, if necessary, alter government programs.

For the sake of the Earth and all its sentient beings, read on and pass the good news on to others. Much of this good news lies in the revelation that there is an Imaginative Route that encourages people to work on themselves before or while attempting to change the whole. The value of this important precursor to the establishment of better ideas lies in the following statement:

One cannot force others to change, but one can change oneself.

A better future awaits as more people undergo the kind of self improvement prescribed here and, thereby, become eartHearts.

THE SLING OF THE IMAGINATION:

CREATING SUBSTANTIAL IDEAS THAT AFFECT THE WHOLE

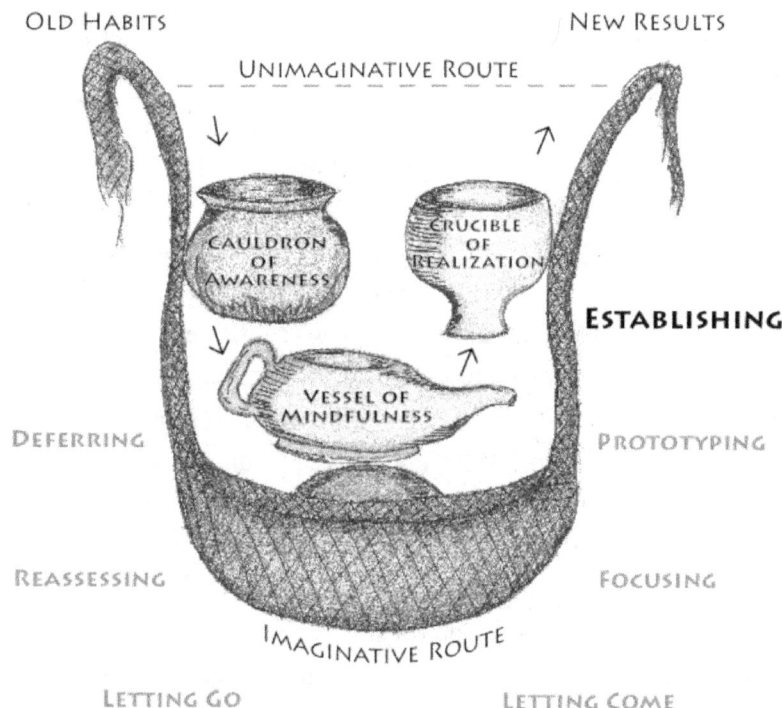

OLD HABITS

NEW RESULTS

UNIMAGINATIVE ROUTE

CAULDRON OF AWARENESS

CRUCIBLE OF REALIZATION

ESTABLISHING

VESSEL OF MINDFULNESS

DEFERRING

PROTOTYPING

REASSESSING

FOCUSING

IMAGINATIVE ROUTE

LETTING GO

LETTING COME

ART WORK DONE BY THERESA GRANT

How To Use The Sling

Thinking

1. Begin at the upper left. "Swooshing" the Sling of Imagination begins at the top left of the arc, before the cord of the sling begins to descend.

2. Enter the Cauldron of Awareness. Once the sling begins to descend (into what is labeled the Cauldron of Awareness on the accompanying graphic model), outmoded notions and strategies are deferred, new notions are tested, new identities are identified, and the need to remain static gives way to the forward momentum of the metaphorical "swoosh" of the Sling of Imagination. Control is no longer a matter of staying put.

Experiencing

3. Enter the Vessel of Mindfulness. Toward the bottom of the metaphorical arc (in what is labeled the Vessel of Mindfulness), one lets go of outmoded ways of thinking and identifying, becomes present with the moment, makes choices to serve the evolution of life towards perfect wholeness (with related but differentiated parts) and lets come a larger field of change. Midway between our old ways of thinking and better ways of acting , in the Vessel of Mindfulness, the slinger in reality laments and witnesses what amounts to her own elegy. This is the experience of one's own requiem. Without a deep" swoosh" through the Imaginative Route of the Sling of Imagination the slinger —the one using the Unimaginative Route—is likely to fail to let her old self die. If this happens, one will return to one's previous life. But if the slinger metaphorically "swooshes" through the act of suspending one's old ways of thinking, through redirecting one's thoughts to the preservation of the whole, and through letting go so one can let new approaches come, then the metaphorical forward momentum of the virtual arc of the sling in reality is the killing of one's old life and the propelling of one towards a new heaven and a new earth—a joyous and sustainable future.

Doing

4. Enter the Crucible Of Realization. As the symbolic arc of the sling moves upward before release (in what is labeled the Crucible

of Realization) one goes through various steps (described in a later Heartwood Path book, entitled "**Volitos**") toward the realization of an emerging future. Release—the result of a Personal Choice—occurs at the moment the future emerges. The course of the released "stone" of Personal Choice is determined not just by the nature (the depth) of the metaphorical "swoosh"; but, more accurately and beautifully, through the actual inner nature of the slinger.

Rather than the rock used against Goliath, the object in the metaphorical Sling of Imagination is Personal Choice. If the choice is to, metaphorically, "swoosh' deeply—(which in reality means to practice fervent mindfulness and self-examination) then after the metaphorical requiem comes a kind of actual mental focusing in the Cauldron of Realization. This metaphorical cauldron allows one to beautifully envision what one seeks to create.

After envisioning, which is called focusing in the illustration, one then creates smaller versions of the prospect one is seeking. When one builds prototypes, refinements can occur on a scale that is manageable.

Once the prototypes are enacted and revised after evaluations and feedback in the Crucible of Realization, the new becomes embodied, institutionalized, and the metaphorical projectile which is, in reality, Personal Choice continues on its new and improved course.

It takes a powerful use of the Imaginative Route in the Sling of Imagination—a deep look at Self—to battle the immune system that fights off change and rejects the unfamiliar. Don't muddle, as we did. It's too taxing. And the results are often tenuous. Take the carefully laid out Imaginative Route instead. By reading this introduction, you have already taken step one of our four steps (beginning, awareness, mindfulness, realization). Step Two comes at the end of the next Heartwood Path book—called "**Egos**"—where you learn what to do in the Cauldron Of Awareness.

To Greater Imagination And Creativity...

HumaNatureConnect Activity

Start-up Protocol

If this is not a day when you prefer to spend time in nature without an agenda, do the Heartwood Path Start-up Protocol found in the Appendix. Then return here to do the remaining portion of this activity:

Being Inspired

For this activity, which qualifies as a kind of reassessing typically done in the Cauldron of Awareness of the Sling of the Imagination, list in your journal some activities that make you feel inspired. From this list, determine who in the world is making a living doing such things. Plan how you will model their behavior, making sure you add your own individuality to the work. In making your list of what inspires you, listen mainly to the words from within. Words from without are likely to encourage you to conform rather than to contribute.

Follow-up Protocol

For best results, write down your impressions of this activity in your journal using the Heartwood Path Follow-up Protocol found in the Appendix. Afterwards, consider sharing your interpretations with others.

Heartwood Path Axioms

Key Assertions From Waypoint 2.68

2.68.1.

You become what you think about.

2.68.2.

One cannot force others to change, but one can change oneself.

2.68.3.

After focusing, one then creates smaller versions of the prospect one is seeking—building prototypes, where refinements can occur on a scale that is manageable.

2.68.4.

Some of your dreams may actually be the dreams of the world, passing through your dream-time awareness.

Nocturnal Pilgrimage 2.68

For best results, write down your impressions of each night's dreams in your journal using the Heartwood Path Dreaming Time Protocols found in the Appendix. Afterwards, consider sharing your Dream Tending with others.

You are making good progress going down the Heartwood Path, both day and night. As you dream you come across Dream Characters that live in our emotional, non-rational, intuitive, and beautiful night-time consciousness. Use your nighttime reverie and the Dream Tending that follows it as a way to find happiness and to rebalance your relationship with the world.

Sometimes the dreams are our own and sometimes the dreams come from our ensouled living world. That is why it is important to ask: "Who is dreaming?" In asking this question you will likely discover that Dream Images are informed by the subjective inner natures of the things, creatures, our chosen attractive natural beings, and the world.

Always remember that dreams do not always belong to ourselves. "They are the expression of Nature herself, effortlessly arising in our dreams" (Aizenstat, 2009, p. 151).

For this reason, look at an often forgotten aspect of your dreams —the Landscape (the Dreamscape, which feeds and enlivens Dream Characters). The Landscape/Dreamscape is the World Dream's fundamental ground, the setting in which everything in the dream happens.

To understand what I mean, pick a dream from your journal, perhaps the one you had last night. Like a naturalist, explore the setting, forgetting for a moment the drama or the characters of the dream. Resist the urge try to read the signs or to reduce the Dream to a psychological phenomenon. Just notice the location of the Dream. It is a living entity, a living place with living Characters, in your inner world.

Once your have identified the setting of the dream, explore this landscape by separating it in your mind from the drama or emotions of the dream. Open up your sense of curiosity and close down your assumptions. Follow your attractions, paying particular attention to whatever interests you in a sensual, embodied way. Pay attention to what stands out. Notice how you are not the center of its concern, yet pay attention to how you feel as you wander about. Avoid trying to find meaning at this point. Mostly just pay attention to what comes forth. In doing so, you are taking an important step in becoming an eartHeart secular saint.

Before preparing for sleep, think over what you have learned in this book—the Natural Systems Think Process, how to glean guidance from nature, important universal principles, World Dreams, and the Imaginative Route to affecting the whole. After this review, dream. Then, tend to your dreams.

After writing down your impressions in your dream journal, you are ready to move on to the next book: "**Egos**"—covering the topic of individuation. It's a whole book about you, your gifts, and how not to lose yourself before integrating into the whole.

All preparations now complete, you are ready to make some big strides towards a happier life, towards the protection of the beauty of nature, and towards a sustainable natural environment. Exactly how all of these results unfold depends on you, which happens to be the topic of the next book. Keep going.

References

Abram, David. (1987) The perceptual implications of Gaia, Revision, 9(2), 7-15).

Access to Insight Website: http://www.accesstoinsight.org/lib/authors/silananda/bl137.html

Aizenstat, Stephen, Ph.D. (2009). Dream tending. New Orleans, Louisiana: Spring Journal, Inc.

Barrett, Julie Langdon. Website: http://julielangdonbarrett.com/2011/08/11/how-to-tell-the-difference-between-intuition-and-your-imagination-or-ego/

Babauta, Leo. (2009) The power of less: the fine are of limiting yourself to the essentials . . . in business and in life. New York, New York: Hyperion.

Barasch, Marc, Ian. (2000). Healing dreams: exploring the dreams that can transform your life. New York, New York: Riverhead Books.

Beck, Larry and Cable, Ted (2002). Interpretation for the twenty-first century. Urbana, Illinois: Sagamore Publishing, Incorporated.

Beck, Martha (2012). Finding your way in a wild new world. New York, New York: Free Press

Bernard, Patrick. (2004). Music as yoga: discover the healing power of sound. San Rafael, CA: Mandala Publishing.

Borden, Richard, J. (2014). Ecology and experience: reflections from a human ecological perspective. Berkeley, California: North Atlantic Books.

Bosnak, Robert. (1986). A little course in dreams. Boston, Massachusetts: Shambala Publication, Inc.

Bosnak, Robert. (1996) Tracks in the wilderness of dreaming. New York, New York: Delacorte Press

Boston, John Website: (https://www.american.edu/spa/cep/upload/jonathan-boston-lecture-american-university.pdf).

Bowden, Jonny, Ph.d, C.N.S. (2009). The 150 most effective ways to boost your energy. Beverly, Massachusetts: Fair Winds Press.

Buddy, Cathal Br. ofm. Website: www.praying-nature.com.

Buechner, Frederick. (1993). Wishful thinking. A theological abc. San Francisco, California: Harper.

Buhner, Stephen Harrod. (2004). The secret teaching of plants. Rochester, Vermont: Bear and Company, Inner Traditions International.

Bunzl, John M. (2004). Evolutionary Biology and Simultaneous Policy: Vision-Logic for the Next Stage in our Evolutionary Future, Website: http://www.integralworld.net/bunzl.html

Byzant Kabblah Website (www.byzant.com/mystical/kaballah/Path.aspx?number=31)

Care2.com

Cairns, John Jr. (2001) Equity fairness, and the development of a sustainability ethos. Blacksburg Virginia : Ethics in Science and Environmental Politics, February 1., Blacksburg Virginia. www.mnforsustain.org/cairns_j_equity_and_a_sustainability_ethos.htm

Cameron, Julie. (2006). Finding water: the art of perseverance. New York, New York: Jeremy P. Tarcher.

Cannon, Walter B. (1963). The wisdom of the body. New York, New York: W.W. Norton & Company, Inc.

Cengagesites Website: http://www.cengagesites.com/academic/assets/sites/4713/Chapter%2015.pdf

Capra, Fritjof. (1996). The web of life. New York, New York: Anchor Books, Random House.

Castro, Dr. Anthony J. (2009). Creating space for happiness: the secret of giving room. Amherst, New York: Prometheus Books.

CGJungPage Website: http://www.cgjungpage.org/learn/articles/technology-and-environment/683-robert-romanyshyn-on-technology-as-symptom-a-dream

Chakra Tones and Notes Website: http://www.wingmakers.co.nz/Chakra_Tones_and_Notes.html

Chalquist, Craig, editor (2010). Rebearths: conversations with a world ensouled. Walnut Creek, Caliifornia: World Soul Books.

Chapman, Alan. (2003) website: http://www.businessballs.com/maslowtest.pdf

Childre, Doc and Martin, Howard. (1999). The heartmath solution. San Francisco, California: Harper Collins Publishers, Inc.

Chopra, Deepak. (2000). How to know god: the soul's journey into the mystery of mysteries. New York, New York: Harmony Books.

Chopra, Deepak. (2004). The book of secrets: unlocking the hidden dimensions of your life. New York, New York: Three Rivers Press.

Millaka Chopra Website: http://www.huffingtonpost.com/mallika-chopra/finding-serenity_b_868151.html

Cialdini, Robert B. (2009) Influence: science and practice. Boston, Massachusetts: Pearson Education, Inc.

Clark, Rawn. (2002) Journal of Wester Mystery Tradition, No. 3, Vol 1 (Website www.jwmt.org/v1n3/32 paths.)

Cohen, Michael J. Ecopsych Website: http://www.ecopsych.com/iupsm-swaiver.html.

Cohen, Michael J. Ecopsych/Ecopsychology Journal Website: http://www.ecopsych.com/ecopsychologyjournal.html.

Cohen, Green Wave, ecopsych.com

Cohen, Michael J. Ecopsych/Lifeweb Website: www.ecopsych.com/lifeweb.html.

Cohen, Michael J. Ecopsych Thesis Quote Website: www.ecopsych.com/thesisquote.html.

Cohen, Michael J. (1993) Integrated ecology: The process of counseling with nature. Humanistic Psychologist, 21(3), 277-295.

Cohen, Michael J, Ed.D. Personal email dated December 23, 2010.

Cohen, Michael J, Ed.D. Project NatureConnect Website: http://www.ecopsych.com/insight53senses.html.

Cohen, Michael J, Ed.D. Project NatureConnect Website: http://www.ecopsych.com/earthstories101.html).

Cohen, PNC Website: www.ecopshych.com/universealive.html

Cohen, Michael J, Ed.D. Green Wave Information: (Project NatureConnect Website: http://www.ecopsych.com/journalaliveness.html and personal email June 8, 2016)Comaford-Lynch, Christine. (2007). Rules for renegades. New York, New York: McGraw-Hill.

Cohen, Michael J. (2018). Principles of Organic Psychology. The Eco-Arts and Science of Unconditional Love Friday Harbor, Washington: Project Nature Connect

Cook, Charles. (2001). Awakening to nature: renewing your life by connecting with the natural world. New York, New York: Contemporary Books, MacGraw-Hill

Cope, Stephen. (1999) Yoga and the quest for the true self. New York, New York: Bantam Books.

Copenhagen Qabalah Website: www.qabalah.dk/paths.html.

Csikszentmihalyi, Mihaly. (1993) The evolving self: a psychology for the third millennium. New York, New York: HarperCollins Publishers, Inc.

Csikszentmihalyi. http://psychology.about.com/od/PositivePsychology/a/flow.htm)

Dangerfield, Dr. J. Mark Website. https://www.smashwords.com/.../how-to-love-nature-when-you-live-in-the-city.

Delaney, Gayle, Dr. (1994) Sexual dreams: why we have them, what they mean. New York, New York: Fawcett Columbine.

De Stefano, Matias, Three Earth Chakra Videos on You Tube. https://m.youtube.com/watch?v=IcfOwlVQGec.

Discovery Fit and Health Website. http://health.howstuffworks.com/wellness/stress-management/finding-serenity-in-your-life2.htm

DreamTending Website: http://dreamtending.com/naturedreaming.pdf

Dyer, Wayne, Ph.D. (2005) The power of intentions: learning to co-create your world your way. Carlsbad, California: Hay House.

Dwoskin, Hale. (2009). The Sedona Method. Sedona, Arizona: Sedona Press.

Eat, Taste, Heal: an Ayurvedic Guidebook website: http://www.eattasteheal.com/ETH_6tastes.htm

Edge Magazine Website: http://www.edgemagazine.net/1995/11/robert-sardello/

E-How. http://www.ehow.com/how_2338305_develop-character.html.

EnglishClub.com Website: http://www.englishclub.com/vocabulary/fl-making-request.htm

Evernden, Neil. (1985). The natural alien. Toronto, Canada: University of Toronto Press.

Ewolt, Dave and Weeks-Ewolt, Alison. (2001) Rational spirituality: evidence of the web of life, Attraction Retreat Website: http://www.attractionretreat.org/Writings/RationalSpirituality.html

Farley, Kent M. (2002) Developing character traits through sport/athletic participation. The Sport Digest- ISSN: 1558-6448. The United States Sports Academy Website: http://thesportdigest.com/archive/article/developing-character-through-sportathletic-participation

Ferlic, K. (2007). Tapping and sustaining the source. Website: http://ryuc.info/common/creation_process/tap_sustain_source.htm

Ferlic, K (2009) A bottom line about sex and our creativity. Website: http://ryuc.info/creativesexuality/bottom_line_about_sex.htm

Fitness Health Zone Website: http://www.fitnesshealthzone.com/meditation/walking-meditation-and-its-benefits/

Fiorenza, Nick Anthony (2010). Planetary harmonics & Neurobiological resonances, Website: http://www.lunarplanner.com/Harmonics/planetary-harmonics.

Flickstein, Matthew. Online Website: Swallowing the River Ganges: http://inner-self.com/Meditation/mindfulness.htm?phpMyAdmin=1IAC4WZXEVp9XvKg-Nokyjpr3el1.

Franden, Nathaniel. (1996). Taking responsibility, New York, New York: Simon and Schuster.

Franklin Institute Website: http://www.fi.edu/learn/brain/exercise.html.

Gallup, Inc: (http://www.gallup.com/poll/190916/americans-identification-environmentalists-down.aspx)

Gardner, Howard. (1999) "Intelligence reframed: multiple intelligences for the 21st century." New York: Basic Books.

Garon, Henry A. (2006). The cosmic mystique. Maryknoll, New York: Orbis Books.

GDRC Website: https://www.gdrc/uem/ee/Tbilissi.html.

George, James. (1995) Asking the Earth. Saftsbury, Dorset; Element Books Limited.

Goldman, Jonathan. (2002) Healing sounds: the power of harmonics. Rochester, Vermont: Healing Arts Press.

Goodreads Website: www.goodreads.com. Alan_Wilson_Watts

Grand, David, (2001) Emotional healing at warp speed. New York, New York: Harmony Books.

Gunther, Folke, and Folke, Carl, "Characteristics of Nested Living Systems," Journal of Biological Systems, 1:3, Stockholm: Sweden. Website: http://library.uniteddiversity.coop/Systems_and_Networks/Nested%20Living%20Systems%20(Holons)%20.pdf

Hargrove, Eugene C. (1988) Foundations of environmental ethics, Englewood Cliffs, New Jersey: Prentice Hall.

Hawkes, Joyce Whiteley, Ph.D. (2012) Resonance, nine practices for harmonious health and vitality, Carlsbad, California: Hay House, Inc.

Henning, Sequoia. Website: http://www.feelingsoulgood.com/index.php?id=2

Howerton, Mari and Sorensen, "Maya." Website: http://www.singandhum.com/educational-development/humming-for-health.html

Inner.org. The Gal Einai Website: http://www.inner.org/Institute of HeartMath. Online Website. Global Coherence Initiative. http://www.glcoherence.org/about-us/about.html

Hauser, Marc D. (2006) Moral minds: the nature of right and wrong. New York, New York: Harper Collins.

Helm, Russell Buddy. (2001). The way of the drum. St. Paul, Minnesota: LLewellyn Publications.

Hindu Temples and Gods Website: http://hindutemplesandgods.blogspot.com/2013/03/sri-yantra.html

Hubbard, Barbara Marx. (2001). Emergence: the shift from ego to essence. Charlottesville, Virginia: Hampton Roads Publishing Company

Huning, Barb. (2-28-11) Personal email: "Re: Editorial Help with Instructions and Marketing."

InnerVision Yoga Website: http://www.innervisionyoga.com/what-is-my-sacred-work/

Institute of Human Conceptual and Mental Development. Online Website. Experiences and Feelings: http://www.ihcmdonline.com/mentalproblems/experiences.htm.

Institute for Social Ecology Website: www.social-ecology.org/199.

Jackson, Brooks and Jamieson, Kathleen Hall. (2007). Unspun: Finding Facts In A World Of Disinformation. New York, New York: Random House Trade Paperbacks

Jensen, Derrick. (2000) A language older than words. White River Junction, Vermont: Chelsea Green Publishing Company

Jensen, Derrick. (2006) Endgame volume I: the problem of civilization. New York, New York: Seven Stories Press.

Jensen, Derrick. (2006). Endgame volume II: resistance. New York, New York: Seven Stories Press.

Jung Atlanta: http://www.jungatlanta.com/articles/winter02-decoding-hillman.pdf

Jurado, Anthony. (2010) Cracked.com Website: http://www.cracked.com/article_18405_7-insane-ways-music-affects-body-according-to-science_p2.html

Kahn , Pete3r H Jr. and Hasbach Patricia H. (2012) Ecopsychology: science, totems, and the technological species, Cambridge, MA: MIT Press.

Kawasaki, Guy (2004). The art of the start. New York, New York: the Penguin Group.

Kawasaki, Guy. (2012). Enchantment. New York, New York: Penguin Group.

Kaza, Stephanie. (1993) The attentive heart: conversations with trees. New York, New York: Fawcett Columbine.

Kittleswon, Mary Lynn. (1996). Sounding the soul: the art of listening. Einsiedeln, Switzerland: Daimon.

Kohn, Alfie (1990). The brighter side of human nature. New York, New York: Basic Books, Inc.

Kroeber, Theodora. (1961) Ishi: in two worlds. Berkeley, California: University of California Press.

Krutch, joseph Wood. (2009) The voice of the desert. New York, New York, General Books.

Kundalini Yoga Info Website: http://www.kundalini-yoga-info.com/humming.html.

Lachance, Albert (1997). "The Architecture of the Soul: Sacred Process Ecopsychology," from the book The Greening of religion: god, the environment, and the good life, edited by Carrol, John E., Broclelman, Paul, and Westfal, Mary. Hanover, New Hampshire: University Press of New England

Lama Dalai. (2011) How to be compassionate. New York, Neew York: Atria Books..

Lame Deer and Erdoes, John. (2009). Lame deer: seeker of visions. New York: New York: Simon and Schuster.

Leopold, Aldo. (1949) . A sand county almanac. London, England: Oxford University Press.

Leopold, Aldo and Flader, Susan L. (editor). (1991) The river of the mother of god and other essays by aldo leopold. Madison, Wisconsin: University of Wisconsin Press.

Lesser, Elizabeth. (2009). The seeker's guide. Website: www.oprah.com/spirit/10-Signs-of-Progress-on-Your-Spiritual-Path/10 - God is Optimistic - Oprah.com.

Lessmann, Kevin. (2004) Emotions of the Musical Keys Website: http://www.gradfree.com/kevin/some_theory_on_musical_keys.htm

Lewis, Dennis. Website: http://www.authentic-breathing.com/breathing_tips.htm

Levey, Joel and Michelle. (2003). The fine arts of relaxation, concentration & meditation: ancient skills for modern minds. Somerville, Massachutsetts: Wisdom Publications.

Levi, Renee. (2003). Group magic; an inquiry into experiences of collective resonance, doctoral dissertation executive summary: http://resonanceproject.org/execsum.cfm

Lovelock, James. (2010) The vanishing face of gaia. New York, New york: Basic Books.

Luks, Allen and Payne, Peggy. (1991). The healing power of doing good.   New York, New York: Fawcett Columbine.

Luskin, Fred and Pelletier, Kenneth R. (2005) Stress free for good. San Francisco, California: Harper Collins Publishers.

Maathai, Wangari. (2010). Replenishing the earth. New York, New York: Random House.

MacGregor, Catriona. (2010). Partnering with nature: the wild path to reconnecting to the earth. New York, New York: Atria Paperback.

Macy, Joanna and Johnstone, Chris. (2012) Active home: how to face the mess we're in without going crazy. Novato, California: New World Library.

Mander, Jerry (1979) as quoted in the website: http://www.eco-action.org/dt/elimtv.html

Marc and Angel Website Practical Tips for Productive Living: http://www.marcandangel.com/2013/04/21/8-effective-ways-to-let-go-and-move-on/

Mayo Clinic/Ranges of Self-Esteem. www.mayoclinic.org

McCraty, Rollin Ph.D., Atkinson, Mike, Tomasino, Dana and Bradley, Trevor Raymond, Ph.D. (2006). The coherent heart: heart-brain interaction, psychophysiological coherence, and system-wide order. Boulder Creek, California: Institute of Heartmath.

McCraty, Rollin Ph.D. and Tomasino, Dana. (2006). Emotional Stress, Positive Emotions and Psychophysiological Coherence, Institute of HeartMath Website: alternativeworldwidehealth.com, Heartmath_Stress_chapter.pdf

McKay, Kim and Bonnin, Jenny. (2007) True green. Washington D.C: National Geographic Society.

McKay, Pip. (2009). Website: http://www.evolvenow.com.au.

McIntosh, Steve (2007) Excerpt from Integral consciousness and the future of evolution. Website: http://www.stevemcintosh.com/books/integral-consciousness/chapter-five-integral-politics/

McTaggart, Lynne. (2002). The field: the quest for the secret force of the universe. New York, New York: HarperCollins Publishers, Inc.

Mellick, Jill. (1996). The art of dreaming. Berkeley, California: Conari Press.

Michigan Online Website. http://web1.msue.msu.edu/4h/charcoun.html

Mindbodygreen Website: mindbodygreen.com

Montgomery, Pam. (2008) Plant spirit healing. Rochester, Vermont: Bear and Company.

Morris, Jill. (1985). The dream workbook: discover; the knowledge and power hidden in your dreams. Boston, Massachusetts: Little, Brown, and Company.

Murray, William H. From the website: http://innerself.com/content/social-a-political/environment/3934-for-those-who-would-save-the-earth.html

Myersbriggs.org

Myth-Dream-Symbols Website: http://www.mythsdreamssymbols.com/432.html

Nahko Bear (Medicine for the People). Song lyrics to "Aloha Ke Akua," (Onecommunityglobal.org).

Naiman, Rubin R. Ph.D. (2006). Healing night: the science and spirit of sleeping, dreaming, and awakening. Minneapolis, Minnesota: Syren Book Company.

National Catholic Reporter Website: http://ncronline.org/blogs/eco-catholic/fr-thedreamoftheearth.

Neubauer, Joan, R. (1985). Dear diary: the art and craft of writing a creative journal. Nashville, Tennessee: Turner Publishing Company.

New Oxford American Dictionary. Online Edition.

Noll, Doug. Website: http://lawyertopeacemaker.com/heartmath.html

Norbu, Namkhai. (2002). Dream yoga and the practice of natural light. Ithaca, New York: Snow Lion Publishing.

Nordhaus, Ted and Shellenberger, Michael. (2010). Break through: why we can't leave saving the planet to environmentalists. New York, New York: First Mariner Books.

Oelschlaeger, Max. (1991). The idea of wilderness. New Haven, Connecticut: Yale University Press.

Oestreich Associates. www.teamtrustsurvey.com

Oktar, Adnan. website: http://www.secretbeyondmatter.com/ourbrains/the-worldinourbrains3.html

Orloff, Judith (2003) Website: Trust your hunches: 5 steps to develop your in-tuition - Intuitive Advice: http://findarticles.com/p/articles/mi_m0NAH/is_8_33/ai_108786014/

Ortiz, John M., Ph.D. (1997) The tao of music: sound psychology. York Beach, ME: Samuel Weiser, Inc.

Ortner, Nick. (2013). The tapping solution: a revolutionary system for stress-free living. Carlsbad, California: Hay House, Inc.

Ouderkirk, Wayne and Hill, Jim editors. Land, value, community: Callicott and environmental philosophy. State University of New York Press. Internet: Callicott_My_Reply_to_Land_Value_Community.pdf

Parker, Jonathan (2011). The soul solution: enlightening meditations for resolving life's problems. Tiburon, California: H J Kramer.

Partridge, Ernest, Ecological morality and nonmoral sentiments. Internet: 60477.pdf.

Partridge, Ernest and Holmes, Ralston III. (1984 ad 1996) The Online Gadfly: http://gadfly.igc.org/papers/values.htm

Peaceful Mind. (2011) Website: http://www.peacefulmind.com/music_therapy.htm

Peaceful Rivers Online Website. Eckhart Tolle Quotes: http://peacefulrivers.home-stead.com/EckhartTolle.html

Pearson, Carol S. (1991) Awakening the heroes within: twelve archetypes to help us find ourselves and transform our world. New York, NY: HarperCollins Publishers.

Peat, F. David. Nature and Ethics. http://www.paricenter.com/library/papers/peat23.php

Plotikin, Bill (2008). Soul craft: crossing into the mysteries of nature and the psyche. Novato, California: New World Books.

Plotkin, Bill. (2010). Nature and the human soul: cultivating wholeness and community in a fragmented world. Novato, California: New World Books.

Plotkin, Bill (2013). Wildmind: a field guid to the human psyche. Novato, California: New World Books.

Pratt, Vernon (Unknown) website: http://www.vernonpratt.com/211/

Reverso Online English Dictionary and Thesaurus: http://dictionary.reverso.net/english-cobuild/linear

Ricard, Matthieu. (2006) Happiness: A guide to developing life's most important skill. New York, NY: Little, Brown and Company.

Robbins, Stephen P. Organizational behavior, Chapter Six: website: http://www.go-bookee.net/organizational-behavior-stephen-p-robbins-14th-edition/

Root-Bernstein, Robert and Michele. (1999). Sparks of genius. Boston, Massachusetts: Houghton-Mifflin Company.

Rudd, Vols, Aaker Website: http://faculty-gsb.stanford.edu/aaker/pages/documents/TimeandAwe2012_workingpaper.pdf

Scull, J (n.d.) Eco-psychology: Where does it fit in psychology? Website: http://www.island.net/~jscull/ecopsych.htm

Scully, Matthew. (2002), Dominion. New York, New York: St. Martin's Press.

Second Journey Website, "Itineraries:" http://www.secondjourney.org/newsltr/NDX/Sullivan_frameset.htm

Selhub, Eva M. and Logan, Alan C. (2012). Your brain on nature: the science of nature's influence on your health, happiness, and vitality. Ontario, Canada: John Wiley and Sons Canada Ltd.

Seligman, Martin E.P. (2011). Flourish: a visionary new understanding of happiness and wellbeing. New York, New York: Free Press, Simon and Schuster.

Sewell, L. (1995). The Skill of ecological perception, In T. Roszak, M.E. Gomes, & A.D. Kanner (Eds.). Eco-psychology: Restoring the earth, healing the mind (pp. 201-215). San Francisco, California: Sierra Club.

Sewall, Laura Ph.D. (1999). Sight and sensibility: the ecology of perception. New York, New York: Jeremy P. Tarcher/Putnam.

Shannahoff-Khalsa, David S. (2006) Kundalini yoga mediation. New York, New York: W.W. Norton & Company

Sharp, Jonathan. (2002). Diving your dreams. New York: Simon & Shuster.

Silva Therapy Website: http://www.silvamindbodyhealing.com/articles/mind-body-healing/healing-colors/

SingingToThePlants Website: http://www.singingtotheplants.com/2014/01/dreaming-with-open-eyes/

Songwriting-guide.com Website: http://www.songwriting-guide.com/basic-music-theory.html

Sound Essence Website: http://www.soundessence.net/chakras.php

Sound-PHYSICS.com: http://www.sound-physics.com/Sound/Resonance-NaturalFrequency/

Spoto, Donald (2003). Reluctant saint: the life of francis of assissi. New York, New York: Penguin Books

Spurgeon, C.H. (1871) http://www.spurgeon.org/sermons/1005.htm

State of California, Department of Education, Regional Occupation Centers, and Department of Developmental Disability. (2014). Student Resource Guide: Direct Support Professional Training. http://www.dds.ca.gov/DSPT/Student/Student-Year1_FullVersion.pdf

Steep Path Online Website: http://www.steeppath.com/article.php?ID=6

Sun Bear. (1980). Medicine wheel: earth astrology. Austin, Texas: Touchstone.

Sunstein, Cass, R. and Nussbaum, Martha C. (2004) Animal rights. Oxford, England: Oxford University Press.

Székely, Edmond Bordeaux. The Essene Gospel of Peace. International Biogenic Society, 1981.

Tebra's Writer's Blog Website: http://www.thepensters.com/tebra/secular-saints-philosophy.html

Templin, Steven, D.O.M Website. http://www.innerbalanceconsulting.com/wp-content/uploads/2011/11/HeartMath-Guide.pdf

Tharp, Twyla. (2003). The creative habit. New York, New York: Simon and Schuster.

Thomashow, Mitchell. (1996). Ecological identity: becoming a reflective environmentalist. Cambridge, Massachusetts: MIT Press.

Thompkins, Peter and Bird, Christopher. (1973) The secret life of plants. New York, New York: Harper and Row, Publishers.

Thoms, Justine. (2008) Small pleasures: finding grace in a chaotic world. Charlottesville, Virginia: Hampton Roads Publishing Company.

Thornton, James. (1999). A field guide to the soul: down-to-earth handbook of spiritual practice. New York, New York: Bell Tower

Thoreau, Henry David. (1965) Walden and on civil disobedience. New York, New York: Harper and Rowe.

Thoreau, Henry David. Excerpt from Journal, quoted from online website: http://www.mothwingarts.com/waldenvisionquest/excerpts.html

Thorncraft, Sylvan. 2006. Website: http://www.emeraldspritestudio.com/articles_toning_and_sacred_sound.htm.

TotalWellnessWorldwide Website: www.totalwellnessworldwide.com/ions.html

Twenge, Jean M. and Campbell, Keith, W. (2009). The narcissism epidemic. New York, New York: Free Press, Simon and Schuster. United States Conference of Catholic Bishops, Themes from Catholic Social Teaching" Washington, D.C., 2005. Website: http://www.cchdbaltimore.org/soc-teach-color-inst.pdf

Uphanishads. Uphanishads quotes and sayings. Website: http://spiritquotes.com/quotes/upanishadsquotes/upanishads_quotes1.htm.

Van Dyke, Deborah.Mantras Sacred Sounds Website: http://www.kirtancommunity.com/html/mantras_sacred_sound.html

Vedicyagyacenter Website: http://www.vedicyagyacenter.com/mantras-chant/Devi-Khadgamala-Stotram-lyrics-with-meaning.pdf

Veracious. Wikihow.com Website: http://www.wikihow.com/Choose-the-Right-Life-Coach

W, Karen. How to overcome fear. Website: http://www.wikihow.com/Overcome-Fear.

Wallace, Alan B. (2012). Dream yourself awake. Boston, Massachusetts: Shambala Publications, Inc.

Webster's Online Dictionary. http://www.websters-online-dictionary.com/definitions/Ethos

Weissman, Darren, R. (2005). The power of infinite love and gratitude. Carlsbad, California: Hay House, Inc.

Whitfield, Charles, L., Whitfield, Barbara H., Park, Russell, and Prevatt, Jeneane. (2006). The power of humility. Deerfield Beach, Florida: Health Communications, Inc.

Whitworth, Laura, Kimsey-Shouse, Karen, Kimsey-House, Henry, and Sandeahl, Phillip. (2007). Co-active coaching: new skills for coaching people toward success. Mountain View, California: Davies-Black Publishing.

Wholistic Healthworks Website: www.wholistichealthworks.com/healing%20with%20colors.htm

Wilber, Ken. (1995). Sex, Ecology, and Spirit: the spirit of evolution. Boston, Massachusetts: Shambala Publications, Inc.

Wilber, Ken, (1998). The essential ken wilber: an introductory reader. Boston, Massachusetts: Shambhala Publications, Inc.

Wilber, Ken (2007) Chapter 14. Integral Politics, or Our of the Prison of Partiality ... KenWilber.com Website: http://www.kenwilber.com/Writings/PDF/14-integral%20politics.pdf

Wilber, Ken; Patton, Terry; Leonard, Adam; and Morelli, Marco. (2008) Integral life practice: a 21st –century blueprint for physical health, emotional balance, mental clarity and spiritual awakening. Boston, Massachusetts: Integral Books.

Williams, Ernest H. Jr. (2005). The nature handbook: a guide to observing the great outdoors. New York, New York: Oxford University Press.

Wikia Website: http://synchromystic.wikia.com/wiki/432

Wiki-How. http://www.wikihow.com/Strengthen-Character

Wikipedia. David Hume. website: http://en.wikipedia.org/wiki/David_Hume

Wikipedia. Theory Z: webssite: http://en.wikipedia.org/wiki/Theory_Z

Wilderness Survival Sills for Save Wilderness Travel Website: http://www.wilderness-survival-skills.com/how-to-predict-weather.html

Wilson, Carol. (1997) Online Website. Mindfulness: Gateway Into Experience: http://www.dharma.org/ij/archives/1998b/carol_wilson.htm

Wilson, Edward O. (2002). The future of life. New York, New York: Vintage Books.

Winter, Deborah Du Nann and Koger, Susan M. (2004) The psychology of environmental problems. New York: Psychology Press

Wohlforth, Charles. (2010). The fate of nature: rediscovering our ability to rescue the earth. New York, New York: Thomas Dunne Books: St. Martin's Press.

You Tube: Caposiena, Nicholas. (2011) You Tube Podcast: https://www.youtube.com/watch?v=o-r_sMYzW_w

Zeleski, Inessa. North Star Wellness Center Website: http://www.calmness.com/chakras.htm

Zohar, Dana and Marshal, Dr. Ian. (2000). Spiritual intelligence: the ultimate intelligence. New York, New York: Bloomsbury Publishing.

Appendix

Online Resources

Your senses and the Heartwood Path will all come alive as you use the following online resources:

Read the **Glossary** and watch your sense of reason come alive. (www.heartwoodpath.com/glossary)

Use your sense of language when you connect online with other EartHearts at a variety of locations:

- **EartHeart Networking Forum** (www.heartwoodpath.com/connect)
- each **online waypoint** (learning station)
- our **Instagram** account (@heartwoodpath)
- our **Facebook** Page (Heartwood Path)

Your sense of light and sight will be activated when you watch our informative and visually appealing podcasts on **YouTube** (www.youtube.com/user/heartwoodpath).

Inside or outside, online or offline, the Heartwood Path helps you overcome any breaches in your well-being that hinder increasing your happiness and the sustainability of the natural environment.

HumaNatureConnect Activity Protocols

The full meaning of each protocol is revealed as you progress, waypoint by waypoint.

Start-up Protocol

- Read The Text — Use your literary sense, your mind sense, and your reason sense to move towards happiness and sustainability by reading the Heartwood Path text but also go outdoors to the backyard or to the backwoods, where the higher levels of negative ions in the air will improve your mood and well-being.
- Attention Restoration — With a pen and journal in hand, go to a natural area that is attractive, has a variety of plants and animals, and is tranquil enough to leave room for reflection.
- Source — Spend time wandering without an agenda in nature or, if you don't have time to receive nature's magic in this way, follow the instructions in the text at each learning station.
- Attractive Natural Being — Once you are in a natural area (the wilder, the better), look to find a natural being that is attractive to you and remain near that being until the end of the activity.
- Appreciation And Gratitude — While communing with your chosen natural being, appreciate it as you inhale and show it gratitude as you exhale.
- Consent — Once you find an aspect of nature that is attractive to you continuously for at least ten seconds, think of your continued attraction as your consent to have a connection experience that will help you function optimally; receive information, guidance, and healing; and establish in your mind a more helpful egalitarian relationship with the natural being.
- The Natural Senses — Beyond seeing, hearing, and the three other commonly recognized senses, use as many of the fifty-four

Natural Senses as you see fit and prepare to document the ones that you use in your journal.

- Great Trustable Truth — Experience what is happening at the present moment in nature, paying particular attention to the role of both beauty and balance; remember that the impressions you form about attractive natural beings and natural areas, coming from your experiencing of them in the Now, are trustable; and recognize that the natural processes and features witnessed are a source of special, substantial, and irreplaceable truthfulness about both nature and yourself.
- Recall — Place the great trustable truth and any other insights that you discover in a mental lock-box so you can later record them in your journal.

Follow-up Protocol

- Date — Write down the date of your outdoor nature-communing experience.
- Activity — Write down the waypoint title and number each time each you do an activity.
- Location — Write down the location of your outdoor nature-communing experience.
- Natural Being Indicator — Draw a picture or write down in your journal a nameless way to remember your chosen attractive Natural Being; for example, call it your "____ ____ Connection Experience."
- The Natural Senses Used — Write down all of the Natural Senses you used for this activity.
- General Description — Write a general description of how you did the activity and what happened.
- Freeform — Write, in freeform, what you found attractive about your natural being.
- Three Qualities — Write down three qualities you found attractive about your natural being.

- Three Learnings — Write down three things you learned from this activity.
- Self-esteem & Trust — Write down how, if at all, this activity changed your self-esteem or trustfulness of NNIAAL (Nameless-ness, Now, Intelligence, Alive, Attraction, and Love).
- Changes To Self — Write down what aspects of your Self, if any, were changed by this activity.
- Honor Yourself — Praise yourself and your commitment to making another stop along the Heartwood Path good for yourself and the world.
- I'm A Person Who. . . — Write down three different so-called "G/G Statements" using the following format: "This connection experience tells me that I am a person who_____."
- Feelings If Activity Taken — Write down a sentence about how you would feel if you lost your ability to experience this connection.
- Nature Compared To Self — Create a sentence that reads: "I love this (insert words that identify the attractive natural being) because it is (insert words that refer to the qualities you like about the natural being); then, create a parallel sentence that reads: "I love (insert the word "myself") because I am (insert the same qualities as before)."
- Name Your Discomforts — Make a list of aspects of your negative emotional residue, if any, that lifted simply by being in nature.
- Two-word Summary — Write down two words that summarize your response to this activity.

Heartwood Path Exchange

- Comment — Post your impressions and photos in the Comments section of this waypoint—the place for on-going discussion regarding this waypoint.
- Join — Engage with others in a Heartwood Path course or salon.
- Create — Start your own Heartwood Path salon that meets regularly online, by phone, or in person.
- Talk — Share your impressions with trusted family members and friends.
- Network —Post your impressions and photos on our EartHeart Networking Forum.
- Post — To see what conversations you can ignite, upload on social media your photos and impressions about anything pertaining to your journey down the Heartwood Path.
- Connect — Follow our account on Instagram, Like our Page on Facebook, Subscribe to our Channel on YouTube, and use hashtags such as "#heartwoodpath", "#eartHeart", and "#waypoint(insert book)(insert waypoint number) i.e."#waypointlogos5").

Dreaming Time Protocols

The full meaning of each protocol is revealed as you progress, waypoint by waypoint.

Before Dreaming Protocol

- Dream Prep — Prepare yourself for productive dreaming by de-cluttering your mind before sleeping.
- Journal Ready — Prepare to record your dream impressions by placing your journal so that you can make initial recordings in it without changing your dreamtime sleeping position.

Dreaming Protocol

- Remember This — Look to your dreams to tell you what you need to remember.
- Open To Dream — Be receptive, fluid, interactive, and grounded as you dream.
- Wake-Back-To-Bed — Wake up after six hours of sleep, staying awake for twenty minutes, then go back to sleep.
- Shape-shifters — Watch characters that change in your dream to see into the possibilities of your own transformation.

After Dreaming Protocol

- First Off — Recall your dream by staying in your sleeping position as you make your first attempt to remember your dream.
- Book Of Dreams — Create an entry in your dream journal using the following linguistic tools: 1) talking in the present tense, 2) using verbs ending in "ing," 3) removing articles such as "an" or "the," and 4) using capital letters when naming the Dream

Characters—which can be any notable people, places, or things that show up in your dream.

- Title — Give your dream a memorable title.
- Date — Write down the date of your dream.
- Description — Write down a short, general summary of your dream.
- Mood — Write down how the dream affected your mood upon waking.
- Life Event Affecting Dream — Write down any events in your life that may have influenced your dream.
- Dream Characters — List all remembered notable "actors" in your dream, whether they are people, places, or things.
- Setting — Describe the location of your dream.
- Statement Of Problem — Write down the complication, challenge, predicament, situation, obstacle, plight, quandary, or misadventure presented in your dream.
- Culmination Or Response To The Problem — Describe what you or another Dream Character did in your dream to respond to the problem presented in the dream.
- Conclusion — Describe how your dream ended.
- Beings Revealed — Write down how your dream seemed to be, if at all, linked in some way to your chosen attractive natural beings.
- Freud's Approach — Associate the actions of your Dream Characters with latent, infantile, repressed, or sexual drives.
- Jung's Approach — Amplify your Dream Characters into Archetypes that are global in scale, symbolic, pervasive, positive, and helpful.
- Hillman's Approach — Recognize your Dream Characters as animated, living beings by honoring their presence, place, and body.
- Right Information — Ask yourself the two main questions for Dream Tending: "Who is visiting now?" And "What is happening here?"

- The Richest Treasures — Do not force narrow interpretations upon the natural being impressions that reappear in your dream by condensing them into limited signs when it is more fruitful to simply engage with them as living beings that reside in your dream, possibly with infinite symbolic value.
- Privacy — Store your dream journal in a safe place and, where appropriate, share your dream with others.

Dream Council Protocol

- Create Dream Figures — Periodically create physical representations of select Dream Characters using natural materials, give them some form of identification, and gather them together.

Natural Senses

The Radiation Senses

- Sense of light and sight, including polarized light.
- Sense of seeing without eyes such as heliotropism or the sun sense of plants.
- Sense of color.
- Sense of moods and identities attached to colors.
- Sense of awareness of one's own visibility or invisibility and consequent camouflaging.
- Sensitivity to radiation other than visible light including radio waves, X rays, etc.
- Sense of temperature and temperature change.
- Sense of season including ability to insulate, hibernate, and winter sleep.
- Electromagnetic sense and polarity which includes the ability to generate current (as in the nervous system and brain waves) or other energies.

The Feeling Senses

- Hearing including resonance, vibrations, sonar, and ultrasonic frequencies.
- Awareness of pressure, particularly underground, underwater, and to wind and air.
- Sensitivity to gravity.
- The sense of excretion for waste elimination and protection from enemies.
- Feel, particularly touch on the skin.
- Sense of weight, gravity, and balance.
- Space or proximity sense.

- Coriolis sense or awareness of effects of the rotation of the Earth.
- Sense of motion, body movement sensations, and sense of mobility.

The Chemical Senses

- Smell with and beyond the nose.
- Taste with and beyond the tongue.
- Appetite or hunger for food, water, and air.
- Hunting, killing, or food obtaining urges.
- Humidity sense including thirst, evaporation control and the acumen to find water or evade a flood.
- Hormonal sense, as to pheromones and other chemical stimuli.

The Mental Senses

- Pain, external and internal.
- Mental or spiritual distress.
- Sense of fear, dread of injury, death or attack.
- Procreative urges including sex awareness, courting, love, mating, paternity and raising young.
- Sense of play, sport, humor, pleasure, and laughter.
- Sense of physical place, navigation senses including detailed awareness of land and seascapes, of the positions of the sun, moon, and stars.
- Sense of time.
- Sense of electromagnetic fields.
- Sense of weather changes.
- Sense of emotional place, of community, belonging, support, trust, and thankfulness.
- Sense of self including friendship, companionship, and power.
- Domineering and territorial sense.

- Colonizing sense including compassion and receptive awareness of one's fellow creatures, sometimes to the degree of being absorbed into a superorganism.
- Horticultural sense and the ability to cultivate crops, as is done by ants that grow fungus, by fungus who farm algae, or birds that leave food to attract their prey.
- Language and articulation sense, used to express feelings and convey information in every medium from the bees' dance to human literature.
- Sense of humility, appreciation, and ethics.
- Senses of form and design.
- Sense of reason, including memory and the capacity for logic and science.
- Sense of mind and consciousness.
- Intuition or subconscious deduction.
- Aesthetic sense, including creativity and appreciation of beauty, music, literature, form, design, and drama.
- Psychic capacity such as foreknowledge, clairvoyance, clairaudience, psychokinesis, astral projection, possibly certain animal instincts, and plant sensitivities.
- Sense of biological and astral time, awareness of past, present, and future events.
- The capacity to hypnotize other creatures.
- Relaxation and sleep including dreaming, meditation, and brain wave awareness.
- Sense of pupation including cocoon building and metamorphosis.
- Sense of excessive stress and capitulation.
- Sense of survival by joining a more established organism.
- Spiritual sense, including conscience, capacity for sublime love, ecstasy, a sense of sin, profound sorrow, and sacrifice.
- Sense of homeostatic unity, of natural attraction aliveness as the singular essence-diversity attraction dance of all our other senses (NNIAAL). (Cohen, website: http://www.ecopsych.com/insight53senses.html).

Acknowledgments

I would like to thank everyone who helped me blaze the trail that has become the Heartwood Path. Initially, David Brower got me going, after asking me to "write a piece" to combat "burnout" in environmentalists. Roger Fritz helped me with my conversion from corporate executive to author. Paula Badger was a good listener on our frequent walks. Michael J. Cohen helped me to add nature's intelligence to the methodology. "Forest Maiden" Sylvia Shelton served as my "muse"—always with humor, tenderness, intelligence, and love. I started out thinking I was writing traditional books. My daughter Courtney Logue converted my text into an interactive website. Without her efforts—in editing, in creating the format, and in providing important encouragement—there would not be a Heartwood Path. To these people, and many more, I am forever grateful.

About The Author

Pierce has spent nearly his whole life working to protect the environment. After decades of work as a professional environmentalist, Pierce concluded that a new approach—one focused on the environmentalist and not just the environment—was needed.

When famed conservationist David Brower asked him to write "a piece" to show environmentalists how to persevere, the result was a series of books and courses that are good for both environmentalists and anyone seeking happiness and the preservation of nature. This series—the Heartwood Path—helps people to develop spiritually, helps people discover the benefits of communing with nature, and helps people find the abundant, abiding, and authentic happiness that comes from helping others, including natural beings.

Pierce formed his first environmental group—a tree planting club—when he was nine. After that, he was president of both his high school and college environmental organizations. After a few years as a professional river conservationist, he was hired by Brower to be the Midwest Representative of Friends of the Earth. Pierce has led numerous conservation groups, including the Illinois Chapter of the Sierra Club. He was a governor-appointed member of the Illinois Nature Preserves Commission.

He has a Bachelor's Degree in environmental science, a Master's Degree in political science, and Master's Degree in social work. When he was not working to protect the environment or guiding people down the Heartwood Path, Pierce—a qualified life coach and mental health practitioner—served those who needed his care—including those who are young, aged, mentally ill, or mentally disabled.

Currently working on his PH.D in eco-psychology, Pierce divides his time between Santa Barbara, California and St. Louis, Missouri. He is a professional drummer, an avid canoeist, and a photographer. He loves to walk in nature. He has two grown daughters (one, the mother of his two granddaughters, in Missouri and another one somewhere on a sailboat that is often close to Santa Barbara).

Heartwood Path One-On-One Guidance

(30 minute or 60 minute sessions)

Don Pierce will move you to an extraordinary awakening of personal happiness and ecological sustainability.

"Make a difference, happily."

To do so, go down the Heartwood Path under the skilled guidance of its creator, Don Pierce. Don's education and experience will help you turn your advocacy into a source of abiding, abundant, and authentic happiness. His years as an active environmentalist will enable him to teach you how to become both happy and effective in your own causes. His years as a social worker will help you fit better into your own environment. His experience as a life coach will help you set your own agenda towards meeting your goals. His years as a mental health practitioner will enable him to help you achieve the integrity that comes when your inner world enables you to be "glad" as you endeavor to make the outer world "green." By signing up for guidance, you will have Don at your side to answer questions, provide encouragement, and avoid wrong turns.

In productive and easy-to-afford steps, Guidance moves you to an extraordinary awakening of personal happiness and ecological sustainability. Guidance moves you beyond a common state of separation to an extraordinary awakening of oneness that is experienced as personal happiness, ecological sustainability, and spiritual maturity.

Sessions, which are purchased in thirty minute and one hour segments, occur online, on the phone, or in person with Heartwood Path creator Don Pierce. Elements of Heartwood Path guidance include:

- making checklists of topics or actionable items
- establishing guidelines
- setting and reviewing deadlines
- explaining and reviewing practices
- responding and questioning journal entries
- instructing
- providing individualized templates of models
- supporting individuals and teams in the field
- defining terminology and elaborating on Heartwood Path text
- mentoring on related subjects and
- assistance in interpreting signs and symbols.

Complementary Guidance sessions are available when you sign up for any Heartwood Path course.

Further Action

REVIEWS APPRECIATED AND OTHER HEARTWOOD PATH BOOKS

If you enjoyed reading **Logos**, please leave a review on Amazon. I would appreciate any comments you may wish to share. Positive reviews go a long way in spreading our important message.

For further reading, the next book in the Heartwood Path series is **Egos**, on connecting with the Individual Self. Another book in the series is **Ecos**, on connecting with the Ecological Self.

All Heartwood Path books are available on Amazon, including **Kosmos**, the Overture, which parents important and pertinent background information. Together, Heartwood Path books provide important personal necessary for the creation of happiness and a regenerated environment.

In recognition for all that you do along the Heartwood Path, I say "thank you" and "Great Work!"